D1025308

LAW
AND THE
MENTAL HEALTH
PROFESSIONS

LAW
AND THE
MENTAL HEALTH
PROFESSIONS

Friction at the Interface

Edited by
Walter E. Barton, M.D.
and
Charlotte J. Sanborn, B.A., A.R.T.

INTERNATIONAL UNIVERSITIES PRESS, INC.

New York   New York

Library of Congress Cataloging in Publication Data

Main entry under title:

Law and the mental health professions.

　Includes bibliographical references and index.
　1. Mental health laws — United States — Addresses, essays, lectures. 2. Mental health personnel — Legal status, laws, etc. — United States — Addresses, essays, lectures. 3. Psychiatrists — Malpractice — United States — Addresses, essays, lectures.
4. Informed consent (Medical law) — United States — Addresses, essays, lectures. I. Barton, Walter E., 1906-　　II. Sanborn, Charlotte J.
KF3828.A75L38　　　344'.73'041　　　77-90226
ISBN 0-8236-2950-3

Second Printing, 1979

Manufactured in the United States of America

Contents

Contributors

Walter E. Barton, M.D.
Professor of Psychiatry (Emeritus), Dartmouth Medical School
Senior Physician, Veterans Administration Center, White River Junction, Vermont, 1974-1977
Medical Director, American Psychiatric Association, 1963-1974

Allan Beigel, M.D.
Director, Southern Arizona Mental Health Center
Associate Professor of Psychiatry, University of Arizona College of Medicine
Coordinator, Combined Mental Health Care Program, Tucson, Arizona

Stanley L. Brodsky, Ph.D.
Associate Professor, Department of Psychology, University of Alabama
Former Chief of Psychology, U.S. Disciplinary Bureau, Ft. Leavenworth, Kansas
Former Associate Professor, Center for Study of Crime, Delinquency and Corection, Southern Illinois University

John Donnelly, M.D., Ch.B., D.P.M., F.R.C.P. (Great Britain)
Psychiatrist-in-Chief, Institute of Living, Hartford, Connecticut
Consultant, Windham, Hartford and St. Francis Hospitals
Lecturer in Psychiatry, Yale University School of Medicine
Editor, *Digest of Neurology and Psychiatry*
Past President, Group for Advancement of Psychiatry

Bruce J. Ennis, J.D.
> Legal Director, American Civil Liberties Union, New York City
>
> Author of four books, including *Prisoners of Psychiatry* and *The Rights of Mental Patients*

Henry H. Foster, Jr., J.D., L.L.M.
> Professor of Law, New York University School of Law
>
> Visiting Distinguished Professor of Law, University of Oklahoma, 1975
>
> Legal Consultant, Committee on Psychiatry and Law
>
> Honorary Fellow, American Psychiatric Association
>
> Legal Consultant, Committee on the Family Group for Advancement of Psychiatry

Maurice Grossman, M.D.
> Clinical Professor of Psychiatry, Stanford University School of Medicine
>
> Private practice in Palo Alto since 1953
>
> Chairman, American Psychiatric Association Task Force on Confidentiality, 1970-1975

Kenney Hegland, J.D.
> Professor of Law, University of California School of Law, Los Angeles

Louis E. Kopolow, M.D.
> Coordinator, Patients' Rights and Advocacy Programs, Division of Mental Health Service Program, National Institute of Mental Health
>
> Instructor in Psychiatry, Georgetown University School of Medicine
>
> Member, National Committee for Patients' Rights

Zigmond M. Lebensohn, M.D.
> Chief (Emeritus), Department of Psychiatry, Sibley Memorial Hospital
>
> Clinical Professor of Psychiatry, Georgetown University School of Medicine

Consultant, U.S. Naval Hospital, Bethesda, Maryland
since 1952
Member, Editorial Board, *American Journal of Psychiatry*

Henry E. Payson, M.D.
Associate Professor of Psychiatry, Department of Psychiatry, Dartmouth Medical School

Irwin N. Perr, M.D., J.D.
Professor of Psychiatry and Community Medicine (Legal Medicine), Rutgers Medical School
Forensic Psychiatric and Medicolegal Consultant and Lecturer in Law, Rutgers School of Law
Member, Ohio Bar Association
Member, Executive Council, American Academy of Psychiatry and the Law

Jacques M. Quen, M.D.
Clinical Associate Professor and Associate Director, Section in History of Psychiatry and the Behavioral Sciences, New York Hospital, Cornell Medical Center, New York
Associate Editor, *Bulletin for the American Academy of Psychiatry and the Law*

Robert L. Sadoff, M.D.
Associate Professor of Clinical Psychiatry and Director, Center for Studies in Social Legal Psychiatry, University of Pennsylvania
Lecturer in Law, Villanova University School of Law
Consultant in Forensic Psychiatry, Norristown State Hospital and Albert Einstein Hospital

Charlotte J. Sanborn, B.A., A.R.T.
Director of Community Services and Assistant Professor, Department of Psychiatry, Dartmouth Medical School
President, New Hampshire Medical Record Association
Member, Executive Committee, New England Medical Records Conference

Ralph Slovenko, L.L.B., Ph.D.
> Professor of Law and Psychiatry, Wayne State University Law School
> Member, Committee on Law and Medicine
> Manfred Guttmacher Award, American Psychiatric Association for scholarly contribution to forensic programs
> Author of over 70 articles and 20 books on law and psychiatry
> Chairman, Committee on Law, American Orthopsychiatric Association
> Director, American Psychology-Law Society, 1973-1976

Chester L. Trent, M.D.
> Private practice in Ocean, New Jersey
> Chairman, Committee on Insurance of American Psychiatric Association
> Attending Physician, Monmouth Medical Center

David Wexler, J.D.
> Professor of Law, University of Arizona School of Law

Acknowledgments

Hanover was delightful in late August of 1976 when the papers included here were first presented in the comfort of Cook Auditorium on the beautiful campus of Dartmouth College. We thank the controller of the weather who blessed us with pleasant days. And we are grateful to all those who attended the institute — the students and residents, those from Vermont, Maine, and New Hampshire, and those who traveled long distances (one came all the way from Hawaii).

We were singularly fortunate in securing an outstanding guest faculty. Most effective was their participation in the discussions throughout the sessions. The moderators of theme topics were most helpful, although often their principal task was to establish some priority among the questions and to cut off discussion as gracefully as possible when time ran out. The moderators were Peter Whybrow, Peter Hauri, Charles Culver, Henry E. Payson, Walter Barton, and Ruick Rolland, all faculty at Dartmouth Medical School.

The conference by the Department of Psychiatry at Dartmouth Medical School was made possible in part through a grant-in-aid from Geigy Pharmaceuticals, Roche Laboratories, Sandoz Pharmaceuticals, and Smith, Kline and French Laboratories.

The complex task of running an institute and promoting attendance would not have been possible without the help of our secretaries, Marilyn Stone, Margaret Anway, and Ilia Stacy.

Charlotte Sanborn
Walter Barton

Preface

Compare today's American with his middle-class counterpart in 1776 who was less educated, very probably illiterate, indifferent to national and world affairs, and accustomed to adversities we would now regard as rare and even shocking: home fevers and infections — the scourge of young and old; each autumn's "warning out" (to wilderness starvation of vaga-bonds); peonage of idiots and the weak-minded; exposure of the mentally ill in chains, garrets, and unheated outhouses; pesthouse quarantine of all contagious patients; piracy and ransom; military impression; execution sermons; public whipping and mutilation; and slow hanging ("dancing") at the county seat. The colonial youth expected calamity and in-equity. He accepted the authority of his elders. The colonial adult of every status accepted class-bound privilege, explained it as a sanctified part of God's unknowable design, and only sometimes, in mid-life, by direct involvement became aware of the corruptibility of power. Only a small minority of upper-class idealists were concerned about the function of government, equality, liberty, excessive personal power, and individual rights.

A physician with satisfactory appointments was perceived as a dangerous-to-question authoritarian who amputated, bled, cajoled, coerced, cupped, cauterized, decocted, purged, and, when necessary, punished. Although he catered to the privileged and gave only a small portion of his effort to the poor, he was regarded as a dedicated public servant — above criticism. His capacity to heal was prayed for, but never contractually expected. His income, like that of the clergy, was honoraria from those who recovered and were able and willing to pay. He was rarely paid fees, regardless of outcome. He was never expected to guarantee a result or warn about side effects. God was the only perfect physician; the doctor who healed was merely his good servant.

Today's middle-class adult views things differently. Educated, irreverent, apathetic, and consumer- rather than work-oriented, today's individual is well informed, through the mass media, on governmental issues, is insistent about his or her rights, and resists intrusion by *anyone* regardless of office, rank, seniority, social class, license, or academic degree. The modern physician is seen as a rich practitioner of the highest paid occupation in the land — a *non*servant who works only for fees — and as a technician capable of curing or relieving most forms of illness. Recovery is not initiated by God, but by the patient who (1) makes an appointment to see the physician and (2) has enough money or health insurance to pay the costs. The clinical appointment and agreement to pay are in themselves a tacit contractual agreement that the physician will, without negligence, render services which professional peers will consider acceptable, with the least side effect, complication, injury, property loss, and restriction possible. The physician's role has become part of the health business, the accepted objective of which is to make money, thereby generating possible conflicts with the patient's interests.

If eventual desanctification and disappearance of unearned and unrestricted individual privilege was foreseen by several of the Constitution's designers, it is doubtful that they conceived of the extent of advocacy of individual rights by the antiauthoritarian horde now graduating from over 60 law schools. These young attorneys are *already* familiar via the media with corruption and failure of governmental and individual power! The founding fathers may have thought of rights to representation, but they never imagined that the nation's affluence and the even more affluent insurance industry could support an almost endless market for tort services. Any attorney today can keep abreast of civil liberties law and be sensitive to the widespread dissatisfaction with medical services and costs. Hence, there is promise of even more extensive change brought by citizen participation in government through litigation to modify the quality and practice of medical care.

Until 1972, any two New Hampshire doctors could indeterminately deprive any citizen of freedom by merely signing a commitment paper. No due process was required or even considered. Most states have now revised such laws, and like Arizona, are continuing to improve them. Treatment without informed consent is still prevalent, but there are warning estimates of higher liability. Some prerogatives possessed and exercised by doctors in 1940 have all but vanished. Even the "right" to preserve life is now being successfully challenged. Psychologists and social workers, who are later arrivers in the mental health field, have always resented the established autocracy of medical men. We hear ominous references to heroes already fallen, such as e. e. cummings' "Buffalo Bill . . . handsome man . . . how do you like him Mister Death?"

Without sanctified privilege, psychiatrists, like all physicians, will have to find more effective as well as discreet ways of sharing valid information (power) with professional colleagues, patients, insurance companies, and attorneys if they wish to reduce liabilities that are avoidable and to accomplish nondivisive and protective support against those that are not.*

The legal profession devises and revises our more civilized

---

* Faith, which is essential for many therapeutic undertakings, when not arising from religious conviction, usually must be supported by contractual or "sueable" responsibility. Hence, some degree of a therapist's liability is therapeutic.

rituals to serve base as well as noble group needs: advocacy, maintenance of the peace, perpetuation of that which seems good, finding the most worthy scapegoat or sacrifice,* and setting limits of revenge. Physicians tend to ignore the central role of public needs which the shrewd lawyer facilitates by ritual and which might skew the trial outcome to the detriment of treatment or a client. ECT, psychopharmacology, influence, detention, and psychosurgery are awesome powers the public at times might wish to deny any individual. Prosperous doctors who benefit from patients' misfortunes sometimes seem to deserve to bear part of the burden. The psychiatrist might apply his or her trained sensitivity to recognizing the hidden and even unconscious facets of the legal process, not just the pure questions of fact and law. To practice carefully he or she should consider all available means.

The Second Annual Continuing Education Program at Dartmouth Medical School, which took place August 26-28, 1976, focused on several substantive aspects of psychiatric procedure which are often regarded as actionable: confidentiality, informed consent, malpractice, tort liability, and due process. These major current concerns are generated not by lawyers, but by transactional problems between modern psychiatrists and patients. Both participants, as well as the laws governing limits in their complex relationships, have not always kept pace with one another. Discussions in this book provide concepts with which members of the law and mental health professions can collaboratively accomplish the better individual health care and better rights protections now possible.

Henry E. Payson, M.D.

---

* Group process occasionally requires a scapegoat to extrude a disturbing sense of evil. By injuring or executing the "cause" of the catastrophe, the group regains a sense of cohesion and an illusion of control over its destiny. The law compulsively seeks a focus for blame.

Part I

Recent Court Decisions and Practice

Recent judicial actions have strengthened the right of hospital-ized mental patients to receive treatment and their right to liberty when the original indications for admission are no longer present. Court decisions have declared the least restrictive environment to be the place of residence as an alternative to hospitalization. Patients must be paid when they do the work of employees. Too frequent use of electroconvul-sive therapy (ECT) is controlled by strict regulations. Persons with diminished sexual control may not be confined indefinitely. These laudable principles articulated by the courts have been made on a case-by-case basis. They do not represent a unified approach other than in reaffirming the protection of individual liberty by due process.

Apparently, most judicial actions hold medicine to be a commercial enterprise that must be regulated in the public interest. This is a very different position from that held by the physician who sees himself as a patient advocate and who diagnoses and treats sickness, employing his knowledge, skill, and judgment in the patient's interest.

In the past two decades, quite independent of any judicial action, the most remarkable revolution has occurred in service delivery to the mentally ill. Mental hospitals which still have increasing admission rates and expanding numbers of patient encounters have decreased their bed population by more than

1

50 percent. The bulk of care has shifted to the psychiatric unit of the general hospital and to ambulatory treatment. Court decisions thus encourage the trends begun some time before. It is the implementation of court decisions, however, that poses serious problems. While the questions below may be interpreted as cynical resistance to change, they illustrate the difficulty in putting judicial decisions into practice.

Should obsolete mental hospitals be refurbished to meet court standards (as in *Wyatt v. Stickney*) or should priority be given to development of ambulatory care as the primary focus of the health delivery system? If this were the focus, could not most hospitalization of the mentally ill be in the general hospital?

Is jail more humane as a place of detention than a mental hospital?

Work has always been a pillar in the therapy of chronic patients. Must we now abandon work programs because of cost of administration and of funding?

Should ECT be restricted to a treatment of last resort because a few psychiatrists overuse it, or might it be employed when specific indications for its need are present?

We laud the principles the courts have articulated, struggle with the practical problems of implementations, and ponder at the actions recommended that are out of phase with changes already well advanced. Judicial actions have followed reforms. With limited resources, we need to shift the delivery to outpatient departments and general hospitals, and not spend what money we have to refurbish obsolete hospitals.

In this section Attorney Bruce J. Ennis and Dr. Zigmond M. Lebensohn present differing viewpoints, although both seek to improve the treatment of the mentally ill and eliminate abuse. Ennis is a well-known civil libertarian and crusader for the rights of patients. He places personal freedom ahead of treatment for mental illness. He rejects the medical model with its emphasis on diagnosis and treatment and its concern with biologic, psychologic, and social factors in the causation of what is defined as illness. Too much, he says, is left to subjective choice by less-than-neutral individuals. He challenges the purpose of mental hospitals and holds they are places of detention whose inmates are denied liberty.

Ennis notes with satisfaction the ferment that has led two-thirds of the states to revise mental health laws which expand legal rights of patients. Later in this book the theme of rights and involuntary admission is expanded by other authors. Ennis clearly emphasizes the need for regulation of medicine as a utility and procedural safeguards to protect liberty.

Dr. Lebensohn, in private psychiatric practice, has experience and interest in forensic psychiatry. He demonstrates the consequence of substituting legal process for medical judgment. The case he cites illustrates a four-month delay that barred access to essential treatment for an illness apparent to everyone, while costly procedural steps were taken. He asks if this is progress. Comments direct attention to the problems of the very sick with impaired judgment who reluctantly come to the hospital and, when admitted, refuse the proposed treatment. While there have been gains, the losses are also considerable. In his opinion, the move toward criminalization of the mentally ill is definitely wrong.

Chapter I

Judicial Involvement in the Public Practice of Psychiatry

BRUCE J. ENNIS, J.D.

In 1968, when I first began representing mental patients, a few pages would have been sufficient to discuss judicial involvement in the public practice of psychiatry. Today, I could not adequately canvass that subject in several hundred. Even half a dozen years ago, I knew most of the significant cases by heart, and had personally participated in a majority of them. Today, I know only a small portion of what there is to know. The point, of course, is that judges, particularly federal judges, are now extensively involved in regulating the public practice of psychiatry.

It is important to understand that this judicial involvement is a very recent development. A few years ago, psychiatrists did not have to worry about federal judges looking over their shoulders. For the first three-quarters of this century, most federal judges refused even to listen to complaints raised by mental patients. The federal courts adopted a "hands-off" policy which allowed psychiatrists virtually unlimited discretion to control the lives of mental patients as they thought best. And between 1955 and 1970, a period when psychiatrists were heralding the new tranquilizing medications and promising effective treatment for the mentally ill, many state legislatures passed statutes allowing psychiatrists to commit people to mental hospitals without the bothersome necessity of going through the state courts. The "medical model" was the order of the day. In 1969, for example, about 12,000 persons were *involuntarily* hospitalized at Bellevue Psychiatric Hospital in New York City under "medical" procedures. Fewer than 500 of those patients *ever* appeared before a judge, and no one thought that strange.

The past several years, however, have witnessed a complete turnabout. During that period over two-thirds of the state legislatures substantially revised their mental hygiene laws, in each case expanding the legal rights of patients and restricting the power of psychiatrists and hospital officials. Federal judges abandoned the "hands-off" policy and began to pay serious attention to complaints raised by mental patients. The rapidity and the extent of this change in judicial attitudes are astonishing and, to my knowledge, unprecedented. In no other area of the law of which I am aware has so much changed, so fast. In 1973, there were perhaps 30 test cases on the rights of patients pending in the state and federal courts. Today, the number is probably closer to 300, and is growing every day. In 1971, there were perhaps ten lawyers in the entire United States with substantial training or experience in representing mental patients in test-case litigation. Today, there are more than a thousand. The law is developing so rapidly that the American Bar Association's Commission on the Mentally Disabled now considers it necessary to publish a monthly *Mental Disability Law Reporter* which disseminates current judicial and legislative developments to mental health professionals and to the growing mental health bar.

In June 1975, the United States Supreme Court decided on *O'Connor v. Donaldson* (1). The decision in that case is important, though greatly misunderstood, and I will refer to it later. Even more important, however, is the fact that the case was decided at all. The *Donaldson* case represents the first time in this century that the Supreme Court even agreed to hear argument in a case involving the constitutional rights of a civilly committed mental patient. The Supreme Court's willingness to hear a mental patient's claim has made it respectable for the lower courts to consider such claims, and signals the end of the "hands-off" doctrine. Given *Donaldson*, it seems clear that the judicial pressures psychiatrists have felt in the past few years are insignificant compared to the judicial pressures they will feel in the years to come.

Because any attempt to summarize briefly the now substantial body of mental health case law would be more misleading than informative, I have chosen, instead, to focus on one recent case, which I think is both illustrative and typical of the current trend of court decisions. In *Suzuki v. Quisenberry* (2), after noting a "growing disillusionment with the 'medical model,'" a federal judge ruled that Hawaii's mental health law was unconstitutional on both substantive and procedural grounds. Substantively, the court held that persons could not be hospitalized simply because they were mentally ill. Without specifying the precise contours of a constitutional standard, the court made it clear that only persons who were in some substantial way dangerous to themselves or others could be hospitalized involuntarily. Procedurally, the court expressed its opinion that nonemergency commitments would require the following safeguards:

(A) Adequate prior notice.
(B) *Prior* hearing before a neutral judicial officer.
(C) The right to *effective* assistance of counsel.
(D) The right to be present at the hearing.
(E) The right to cross-examine witnesses and to offer evidence.

(F) Adherence to the rules of evidence applicable in *criminal* cases, including the prohibition against hearsay.

(G) The right to assert the privilege against self-incrimination.

(H) Proof beyond a reasonable doubt.

(I) A consideration of less restrictive alternatives.

(J) A record of the proceedings and written findings of fact.

(K) Appellate review.

(L) Periodic redeterminations of the basis for confinement.

Actually, the court was even more specific than that. For example, the court said the notice would have to "set forth with particularity the alleged conduct or condition upon which the proposed detention is based" and would have to give the "names" of examining physicians "and the substance of their proposed testimony," all well in advance of the commitment hearing.

I think it is important at this point to digress for a moment. Many people who are opposed to judicial involvement in the public practice of psychiatry seem to believe that a handful of activist lawyers are responsible for the current situation. That is a serious oversimplification. To believe that is greatly to underestimate the problems facing institutional psychiatry. Activist lawyers can file lawsuits, but they cannot, and do not, decide them. Cases are decided by judges, most of whom are exceedingly reluctant to tinker with social systems, and are naturally and professionally sympathetic to the problems of well-intentioned mental health professionals. The simple fact is that most judges are not radicals — they do not like to rock the social boat. In the *Suzuki* case, for example, the judge who struck down Hawaii's mental health law was quite sympathetic to the virtues, and there are some, of the medical model. He had personally chaired the committee that, six years earlier, had drafted the law in question. But though "fully aware of the implications of a return to the 'legal model' as opposed to the 'medical model,'" he felt compelled to declare the law unconstitutional. In concluding his opinion, he accurately summarized the *real* reasons why judges throughout the country are rejecting the medical model: "The overriding consideration behind recent cases . . . has been that personal freedom is involved. A close second consideration has been that the *diagnosis and treatment* of mental illness leave too much to subjective choices by less than neutral individuals."

In short, most judges believe that personal freedom is even more important than mental health, and they are unwilling to limit personal freedom when the basis for the limitation is a subjective opinion, rather than an objective and verifiable fact. As the judge in *Suzuki* put it: "Limiting a person's constitutional rights on the theory that it is in his best interests is questionable philosophy and bad law."

The basic point of tension between judges and psychiatrists is the growing judicial recognition that psychiatry is an art, not a science. As that point becomes clear, judges become more reluctant to defer to psychiatric expertise. Let me give an example.

The insanity defense is one area in which psychiatrists have actively sought power, and have not simply had it thrust upon them. Organized psychiatry bitterly criticized the traditional standard for the insanity defense — the right-wrong test — because it allegedly prevented the utilization of modern psychiatric knowledge. Responding to the criticism, Judge David Bazelon, an extremely distinguished judge, a past president of the American Orthopsychiatric Association, and a genuine friend of organized psychiatry, wrote an opinion in the *Durham* case (3) which abandoned the old standard and expanded the courtroom role of psychiatrists. Under the *Durham* standard, a criminal defendant is considered insane,

even if he *did* know that his act was wrong, if that act was the
"product" of a mental disease or defect. But over the years,
Judge Bazelon became increasingly disillusioned with the
ability of psychiatrists to provide relevant and useful knowledge under the new standard.

Finally, in *Washington v. United States* (4), Judge Bazelon
concluded that "there is no justification for permitting
psychiatrists to testify on the ultimate issue" in an insanity
defense proceeding, and therefore precluded psychiatrists
from "testifying whether the alleged offense was the 'product'
of mental illness." As Judge Bazelon subsequently wrote, for a
psychiatric audience, the *Washington* decision was made
necessary because "psychiatrists did not acknowledge the limits
of their expertise" (5; see also 6). That same point was made
again by Judge Bazelon in *United States v. Brawner* (7)
(concurring in part and dissenting in part): "In practice,
however, under *Durham* and its progeny psychiatrists have
continued to make moral and legal judgments beyond the
proper scope of their professional expertise." Finally, in *Smith
v. Schlesinger* (8), Judge Bazelon wrote:

> As the record in this case and others like it strongly sug-
> gest, conclusory psychiatric opinion tends to dominate the
> criterion for determination. We have criticized this expert
> dominance in other contexts and see no reason for not ex-
> tending this concern to the present circumstances: in both
> cases, psychiatric judgments may disguise, wittingly or
> unwittingly, political or social biases of the psychiatrist;
> and excessive reliance on diagnosis will preempt the pri-
> mary role of legal decision-makers [footnotes omitted].

Thus, the judge who was once considered the leading proponent of increased judicial reliance on psychiatric testimony,
has become skeptical, and even critical, of psychiatric testimony.

The same skepticism is responsible for most of the recent

decisions. Judges are beginning to learn that psychiatric diagnoses are not very reliable, and that psychiatric predictions of future dangerous behavior are wrong far more often than they are right (9). Accordingly, because diagnosis of mental disorder is so subjective, judges are requiring proof of dangerousness. And because psychiatric predictions of dangerousness are so inaccurate, they are requiring evidence of recent overt acts of a dangerous nature.

Which brings me to another digression. In the short run, I believe that judicial insistence on dangerousness, evidenced by an overt act, is a sensible method for narrowing the class of persons subject to commitment, and thereby limiting abuse of the commitment power. In the long run, however, preoccupation with dangerousness makes little sense.

If individuals really are physically dangerous to others, they should be confined, whether mentally ill or not. If they really are dangerous, they can almost certainly be confined under the authority of existing criminal laws. If dangerous conduct does not violate existing criminal laws, then we should either amend those criminal laws to prohibit such conduct, or forget about it. If dangerous conduct is not sufficiently dangerous to warrant criminal proscription, it is not sufficiently dangerous to warrant hospitalization. Actually, a strong argument can be made that a finding of dangerousness should *preclude*, rather than authorize, civil commitment. Dangerous people, as a class, may be more difficult to treat than nondangerous persons; their presence on a ward certainly restricts the freedom of others on the ward; and associating dangerousness with psychiatric treatment further stigmatizes the nondangerous mentally ill.

But for now, as I said, requiring proof of dangerousness as a condition of involuntary commitment seems sensible, and whether sensible or not, seems to be, in the opinion of most judges, constitutionally required. Although the Supreme Court has not definitively resolved this issue, it has ruled that the Constitution prohibits the custodial confinement, without treatment, of a mentally ill but nondangerous individual. In *O'Connor v. Donaldson* (10), the Court said that "a State cannot constitutionally confine without more a nondangerous individual who is capable of surviving safely in freedom by himself or with the help of willing and responsible family and friends." Similarly, said the Court, "the mere presence of mental illness does not disqualify a person from preferring his home to the comforts of an institution . . . incarceration is rarely if ever a necessary condition for raising the living standards of those capable of surviving safely in freedom, on their own or with the help of family or friends."

A fair reading of *O'Connor v. Donaldson* suggests the following. First, the Supreme Court apparently believes that involuntary confinement simply because of mental illness and need for treatment is not constitutionally justified. There must be proof of some degree of danger to self or others. Second, the Supreme Court apparently believes that an individual cannot be considered dangerous to *self* if that individual is *surviving* — a word used three times by the Court. The important point here is that the Court has clearly rejected a "welfare" standard in favor of a "survival" standard. Thus, even if hospitalization would be in a person's welfare or best interest, involuntary hospitalization is not constitutionally permissible if the individual is surviving.

The *Donaldson* case was considered a right-to-treatment case. Actually, right-to-treatment litigation has interfered very little with the practice of psychiatry. But right-to-*refuse*-treatment litigation interferes very substantially with the practice of psychiatry. For example, in a modification of the original decree in the *Wyatt* case, a federal court substantially restricted the freedom of state hospital psychiatrists to prescribe or utilize various forms of "extraordinary or potentially hazardous modes of treatment" (11). Some forms of treatments, such as psychosurgery, are absolutely prohibited.

Others, such as "aversive conditioning," are permitted only if the patient gives express and informed consent. Still others, such as ECT, are permitted only if the patient or a special Extraordinary Treatment Committee consent.

The key concept in right-to-refuse-treatment cases has been that of informed consent (this is discussed at length elsewhere in this volume). I think we can expect to see that concept applied, in the near future, to prohibit or restrict so-called voluntary hospitalizations. The gap between promise and reality — between the promise of treatment and the reality of custodial care, or worse — prompted federal judges to tighten the standards and procedures for involuntary hospitalization. A similar gap between the "voluntary" label and the functional reality may stimulate judicial restrictions on "voluntary" admissions. As several recent studies (12-18) have shown, the great majority of "voluntary" patients have little or no comprehension of their status or rights. In one study "only 8 of the 100 patients were rated as fully informed concerning the terms of their voluntary admission" (12).

Because the decision to be a voluntary patient is, in effect, a consent to a broad range of treatments, it seems to me only a matter of time before the requirement of informed consent — now applied only to specific treatments — will be applied to the decision to be a voluntary patient. If informed consent becomes a requirement for voluntary hospitalization, that will very substantially affect the public practice of psychiatry. We will have a better idea of likely developments in the law of voluntary hospitalization after the Supreme Court decides the case of *Bartley v. Kremens* (Docket No. 75-1064). In *Bartley* (19), as in other cases (20, 21), a federal court ruled that parents could not constitutionally hospitalize their minor children without judicial approval. Most legal observers believe the Supreme Court will probably permit, without court authorization, very brief periods of hospitalization for very young children, but will probably prohibit, without court authorization, even brief hospitalizations for older children, and long-term hospitalizations for all children. These "minor voluntary" cases require the Supreme Court to balance two competing interests to which it has afforded constitutional protection in the past — the right of parents to control the upbringing of their children, and the right of children to due process when their liberty is threatened by state action. Obviously, balancing those competing constitutional interests is a complex task, and the social consequences of the decision will be substantial.

Some of the issues of law and psychiatry now being raised in federal courts are even more complex, and even more fundamental. They go to the heart of what it means to be a human being, and what it means to be a civilized society. On balance, I believe that judicial involvement in resolving these complex issues is beneficial. Judges are not dumb, and they know a good deal about human behavior and social systems. Forcing judges to think about these issues contributes to intelligent analysis and ranking of the competing legal, philosophical, and social values. Judicial involvement often prods more sophisticated legislative analysis. And test cases certainly are a valuable mechanism for educating the public and creating a climate where social change is possible. There are also concrete benefits. Judges have the power to order the creation of social systems which mental health professionals want, but cannot themselves create. A federal judge in the District of Columbia, for example, has ordered the District to create a broad range of halfway houses, nursing homes, and other less restrictive facilities so that two-thirds of the patients at St. Elizabeth's Hospital can move into the community, as their doctors have recommended (22). More could be said about the benefits of judicial involvement. But there are problems, too, and they should not be minimized.

There is always the risk of ill-informed judges, or ill-informed decisions. Personally, I believe the *Tarasoff* (23) decision, which authorizes suits for money damages against mental health therapists who fail to warn persons who may be injured by their clients, is wrong, and has socially undesirable consequences. The slip opinion reads: "In our view, however, once a therapist does in fact determine, or under applicable professional standards reasonably should have determined, that a patient poses a serious danger of violence to others, he bears a duty to exercise reasonable care to protect the foreseeable victims of that danger" (24).

Judicial orders have to be precise, in order to be enforceable, but their very precision necessarily limits innovation and flexibility. A hospital director who is ordered to hire 20 more psychiatrists might prefer to hire ten, and use the remaining money to hire recreation therapists. Judicial orders, particularly in huge cases such as *Wyatt* (25) or Willowbrook (26), are very difficult to enforce. Ordering a state to develop a broad range of community facilities is one thing; bringing that about is quite another. Judicial decrees can improve the level of funding for mental health programs — the annual budget for Willowbrook went from $28 million, when the case was filed in March 1972, to about $80 million in 1976 — but often those funds are simply diverted from education budgets, or other equally important social systems.

Finally, lawsuits have defendants, who necessarily receive the blame and take the consequences, often quite unfairly, for conditions they deplored, but which were beyond their power to correct. Willowbrook, for example, has had five directors in less than five years. Each director was used as a scapegoat when investigations showed conditions to be unsatisfactory. Of course, some of the defendants, in some of these cases, deserved to lose their jobs, or worse. But a good many decent, competent, and progressive mental health professionals have become the scapegoats of a reform movement they would have been the first to endorse.

In short, litigation is, at best, a rather blunt instrument for social change. The conditions in most of our public mental hospitals have made litigation a moral necessity. But we should not forget, or minimize, the limitations and the consequences of judicial activism.

Which brings me to three modest, but important recommendations I would like to make to both mental health professionals and activist lawyers. These recommendations are prompted by my concern, to use a medical model metaphor, that the cure not be worse than the disease. I noted that conditions in most public mental hospitals are, at best, unspeakably barren and alienating, and at worst, inhumanly cruel and degrading. Those conditions must be changed. And they will be changed. But those of us intent on change must bring to that effort candor, humility, and professionalism. We will all have to be more candid about what the problems are, and what our limitations are. We will all have to be more humble about our abilities to solve these problems, and about the wisdom and social utility of our solutions. And in doing this, we will all have to act as professionals, as agents of the clients whose interests we all claim and profess to serve, rather than as agents of society, of our professions, or of any cause.

REFERENCES

1. *O'Connor v. Donaldson.* 422 U.S. 563, 45 L.Ed.2d 396 (1975).
2. *Suzuki v. Quisenberry.* 411 F.Supp. 1113 (D. Haw. 1976).
3. *Durham v. United States.* 214 F.2d 862 (D.C. Cir. 1954).
4. *Washington v. United States.* 390 F.2d 444 at 455-456 (D.C. Cir. 1967).
5. Bazelon, D. L. The perils of wizardry. *Amer. J. Psychiat.,* 131: 1317-1320, 1974.
6. Bazelon, D. L. Psychiatrists and the adversary process. *Sci. Amer.,* 320, June 1974.
7. *United States v. Brawner.* 417 F.2d 969 at 1019 (D.C. Cir. 1972).
8. *Smith v. Schlesinger.* 531 F.2d 462 at 476-477 (D.C. Cir. 1975).
9. Ennis, B. J., & Litwack, T. R. Psychiatry and the presumption of expertise: Flipping coins in the courtroom. *Cal. Law Rev.,* 62:693, 1974.
10. *O'Connor v. Donaldson.* 422 U.S. 563, 45 L.Ed.2d 396 at 407 (1975).

11. Wyatt v. Hardin. Unpublished opinion of July 1, 1975. Reprinted in: *Mental Disability Law Rep.,* 1:55-57, 1976.

12. Olin, G. B., & Olin, H. S. Informed consent in voluntary mental hospital admissions. *Amer. J. Psychiat.,* 132:938-939, 1975.

13. Palmer, A. B., & Wohl, J. Voluntary admission forms: Does the patient know what he's signing? *Hosp. Commun. Psychiat.,* 22:250-252, Aug. 1972.

14. Ellis. Volunteering children: Parental commitment of minors to mental institutions. *Cal. Law Rev.,* 62:840, 1974.

15. Gilboy & Schmidt. "Voluntary" hospitalization of the mentally ill. *Northwestern U. Law Rev.,* 66:429, 1971.

16. Wexler. Foreword: Mental health law and the movement toward voluntary treatment. *Cal. Law Rev.,* 62:671, 1974.

17. McGarry, L., & Greenblatt, M. Conditional voluntary mental hospital treatment. *New Eng. J. Med.,* 1972, p. 279.

18. Szasz, T. Voluntary mental hospitalization: An unacknowledged practice of medical fraud. *New Eng. J. Med.,* 1972, p. 277.

19. *Bartley v. Kremens.* 402 F.Supp. 1039 (E.D. Pa. 1975), *stay granted,* 96 S.Ct. 558, *probable jurisdiction noted,* 96 S.Ct. 1457 (1976).

20. *J. L. v. Parham.* _____ F.Supp. _____ (M.D. Ga. 1976; No. 75-163 M.A.C.), *stay granted,* 96 S.Ct. 1503 (1976).

21. *Saville v. Treadway.* 404 F.Supp. 430 (M.D. Tenn. 1974).

22. *Dixon v. Weinberger.* 405 F.Supp. 974 (D.D.C. 1975).

23. *Vitaly Tarasoff et al. v. The Regents of the University of California et al.* 529 P.2d 553 (Sup. Ct. Cal. 1974; In Bank, July 1, 1976; S.F. 23042, Super. Ct. 405694).

24. Ibid., slip opinion, p. 18.

25. *Wyatt v. Stickney.* 324 F.Supp. 781 (M.D. Ala. 1971), 344 F.Supp. 1341 (M.D. Ala. 1971), 344 F.Supp. 373 at 387 (M.D. Ala. 1972), *affirmed in part, modified in part sub nom., Wyatt v. Aderholt,* 503 F.2d 1305 (5th Cir. 1974).

26. *New York State Association for Retarded Children v. Carey.* 393 F.Supp. 715 (E.D. N.Y. 1975), 357 F.Supp. 752 (E.D. N.Y. 1973).

Chapter II

Defensive Psychiatry or How to Treat the Mentally Ill Without Being a Lawyer

ZIGMOND M. LEBENSOHN, M.D.

Despite the cynicism implied by the title of this chapter, I have for years strived to obtain the closest possible rapprochement between psychiatry and the law. Let me submit some evidence to support this claim. In 1952, as a much younger man, but after considerable experience in both institutional psychiatry and private practice, I turned my attention to the interface between psychiatry and the law as it then existed. My first effort was a paper with the more conciliatory title, "Psychiatry and the Law: A Plea for Closer Rapport" (1).

In that paper I referred to the Louisville, Kentucky survey conducted by Elmo Roper and his associates (2) in 1950 to investigate public attitudes toward psychiatry. In regard to the attitude of lawyers toward psychiatry, one of the project writers summing up the results said: "Throughout the survey, physicians, clergymen, and teachers showed themselves to be in far closer accord with modern psychiatric methods than did the lawyers. Only in the legal profession was there found to be a relatively large measure of distrust of psychiatry." Specific examples of the lawyers' distrust of psychiatry were then cited:

> Nearly 25% of the lawyers proposed punitive treatment for the juvenile delinquent in preference to either psychiatric attention or the change of environment he would get by joining a boys' club. More than 40% of the lawyers voted *against* the proposition that it is worthwhile to get a psychiatrist's help when someone begins to act strangely. More than two-thirds of them endorsed secrecy about family mental illness. They departed from the general pattern on such other points as the charge that mental patients were maltreated and the question about the experts' ability to agree on a psychiatric diagnosis.

In spite of these discouraging findings I still held out hope that if only psychiatrists and lawyers would communicate more openly and more honestly with each other, many of the misunderstandings and much of the mutual distrust would be dispelled and a bright new day would dawn. I bemoaned the lawyer's general lack of exposure to the principles and realities of modern psychiatry during his law school years and urged greater involvement of lawyers in improving the plight of the mentally ill.

That was in 1952 when the number of lawyers seriously concerned with mental health matters could be generously estimated as a few score. By 1976, the mental health bar had grown to such large numbers and litigation had increased so much that the American Bar Association began publishing a monthly law reporter to enable mental health lawyers to keep up with the rapid developments in their field. Little did I foresee the consequences if my urgings were heeded. Lawyers have swarmed into the mental health field, especially during the last ten years, but their ideas as to how to help the mentally ill (essentially by giving them liberty) and those of psychiatrists (namely, by giving the mentally ill an opportunity to receive treatment) have often been at odds with each other. I regret to say that the plight of the mental patient caught between his two sets of deliverers has not improved, and in many ways has worsened despite all the litigation by lawyers and major scientific advances in psychiatry.

A Brief Historical Note

It is one of the curious ironies of recent history that American psychiatry and its many psychiatric hospitals enjoyed a generally good reputation in the press and with the public during the twenties and thirties. This was the period before the advent of the highly effective psychotropic drugs and somatic treatments — a period marked by long confinements, large static hospital populations, and primary reliance on barbiturates, hydrotherapy, and custodial treatment. During this period the Washington, D.C. courts still required that each mental patient have a jury trial in a *de lunatico inquirendo* proceeding. As witness to many examples of this archaic and humiliating charade, I can testify to its perfunctory and barbarous character. Psychiatrists, led by the late Winfred Overholser, won plaudits from patients, lawyers and judges for leading the fight to abolish this practice.

In those remote days, before the period of rapidly rising expectations, the public held a rather fatalistic view of mental illness — a view that psychiatrists and the National Committee for Mental Hygiene (now the National Association for Mental Health) took great pains to dispel. I can still remember a large, framed legend distributed by the National Committee for Mental Hygiene, which hung in a prominent place in the main lobby of the Administration Building at St. Elizabeths Hospital. It stated clearly that mental illness was just like any other illness (which it isn't!), that it was treatable and was not hereditary, and that there should be no stigma attached to those who suffered from it. Even in those days this struck me as a rather heavy dose to swallow. Our present public relations approach tries to be more sophisticated, but the more our knowledge of the many factors responsible for mental illness has expanded and the more the disputes between the competing schools of psychiatry and legal thought have been aired publicly, the more confused the public has become. It is highly doubtful whether the mental patient or mental health in America has benefited from these conflicts.

Private Practice and Civil Commitment

The situation in the private practice sector of psychiatry and psychoanalysis in the thirties was relatively serene and uncomplicated. A relatively small number of patients were treated voluntarily in the private offices of their psychiatrists or on the few psychiatric units of general hospitals which then existed. If a patient became so psychotic as to require hospital treatment on an involuntary basis, civil commitment (with the help of the police if necessary) was possible by following a set procedure. Each case was, of course, subject to judicial review prior to commitment and to relief by habeas corpus proceedings following commitment. There was no such agency as the Public Defender's Office, nor were patients routinely provided with counsel.

In spite of this state of affairs I have never personally seen a case of illegal commitment, railroading, or illegal detention in all my 41 years in psychiatry. I am sure they must occur (my lawyer friends never cease telling me so), but not on the basis of some malevolent desire of psychiatrists to keep their charges indefinitely. In spite of the inexplicable decision of the doctor in the *Donaldson* case (3)*, psychiatrists in the institutions that I know, have been only too happy to discharge a patient, even though not entirely recovered, provided a family member or a responsible person was there to take over.

I propose in the remaining pages to discuss the impact of recent court decisions from the point of view of a practitioner of general psychiatry who also admits patients to the psychiatric unit of a general hospital where each patient enters on an informal, voluntary basis. I shall refer only tangentially to the impact of recent court decisions on institutional psychiatry. Since psychiatrists in private practice can afford to be selective in their case loads and all of their patients are "voluntary," one may well ask what relevance recent court decisions have to the private practice of psychiatry. Alan Stone (4) recently observed that " . . . the law casts its shadow on every significant decision made by institutional psychiatrists. That shadow is now inexorably reaching toward the private practice of psychiatry."

The inexorable intrusion of the law into every aspect of the practice of medicine was viewed with justifiable alarm by W. Allen Wallis, the distinguished economist and statistician, and Chancellor of the University of Rochester. In his commencement address to the graduating class of the School of Medicine and Dentistry in May 1974, he warned the future doctors:

> Probably few of you realize, that before your careers have run their courses those lawyers (who are now graduating from law schools all over the country in even larger numbers) may have more influence than you have over what you do, how you do it, and how you are rewarded.
>
> You may find lawyers defining the range of treat-

---

* Several attempts by kinfolk to remove Donaldson were resented by the doctor, and several times habeas-corpus actions sustained the doctor's decision to hold the patient even though his kinfolk had agreed to provide for his supervision and care.

ments that you are allowed to use in specified circumstances. Lawyers may prescribe the criteria by which you are to choose among the allowable treatments. Lawyers may specify the priorities you must assign to different patients. Lawyers may require you to keep detailed records to establish at all times that you are in full compliance. Lawyers may punish you unless you can refute beyond a reasonable doubt their presumption that your failures result from not following all of their rules, regulations, and requirements. And lawyers may decide what incomes you deserve.

Should you have the temerity to differ with the lawyers, you will be backed by the authority of your knowledge, your science, your skill, your art, your experience, your judgment, your dedication, and your conscience. Which is to say that in the eyes of the law you will have precious little backing; for knowledge, science, skill, art, experience, judgment, dedication, and conscience — whatever else their merits — do not constitute due process of law [5].

The psychiatrist in general practice who still remains unintimidated by the law's intrusions into his art uses psychotherapy, chemotherapy, and in some cases ECT. He may hospitalize patients on the psychiatric unit of a general hospital on a completely informal or voluntary basis. Occasionally he may be consulted in regard to a psychotic patient who refuses treatment, but who may require involuntary hospitalization. He is a close observer of the changes in the local state mental hospitals on which he relies for the treatment of acutely disturbed or long-term patients. The issue of the right to treatment rarely confronts the private practitioner, but the right to refuse treatment is often expressed by private patients. This will be discussed later. The least restrictive alternative to treatment has never been an issue with the private practitioner. He has always selected the least restrictive alternative almost on an intuitive basis. This, too, will be discussed later.

INVOLUNTARY HOSPITALIZATION:
CRIMINALIZATION OF THE MENTALLY ILL

Because involuntary hospitalization effectively deprives a person of his liberty, it has long been a logical target for the civil liberties lawyer. Many lawyers and quite a few psychiatrists have even argued in favor of abolishing *all* involuntary hospitalizations. Experienced psychiatrists and many lawyers, however, recognize that there will always be a small, irreducible number of patients (perhaps less than ten percent) who urgently require treatment on an involuntary basis for their own health and for the protection of society.

It was Isaac Ray, that great American pioneer in forensic psychiatry, who in 1869 set down the basic components of humanitarian laws governing the hospitalization of the mentally ill. He said:

> In the first place, the law should put no hindrance in the way to prompt use of those instrumentalities which are regarded as most effectual in promoting the comfort and restoration of the patient. Secondly, it should spare all unnecessary exposure of private trouble, and all unnecessary conflict with popular prejudices. Thirdly, it should protect individuals from wrongful imprisonment. It would be objection enough to any legal provision that it failed to secure these objects in the completest possible manner [6].

It is a sad commentary on what we call "progress" that, over 100 years later, we have still not been able to achieve Dr. Ray's laudable objectives.

Today, in many jurisdictions, commitment procedures

have been made so cumbersome, so time-consuming, and so difficult to accomplish even in cases obviously in need of treatment, that many good psychiatrists in private practice will have nothing to do with such matters. In Washington, D.C., for example, it is easier for a camel to pass through the eye of a needle than it is for a sick person to enter the gates of St. Elizabeths Hospital. Emergency rooms of general hospitals are unable to cope effectively with this type of patient because of the legal barriers. The police are now equally reluctant to take action. This situation often leaves a patient at large and untreated, with his illness continuing unchecked. It leaves his family frightened and frustrated because of inability to get proper help even after consulting the best available sources.

A recent case illustrates the difficulty in hospitalizing a very sick patient who desperately needed in-hospital treatment. It also points up some of the difficulties in defining "treatment."

A 43-year-old man, severely schizophrenic since the age of 19, had received many years of treatment in and out of the finest private psychiatric hospitals in this country. For over 14 months he was seen daily in a specialized private hospital by a psychoanalyst, even though he remained mute and catatonic. He was then transferred to another hospital where he improved somewhat as a result of tranquilizers and some electroconvulsive therapy. Eventually the family, after spending more than $200,000 over a ten-year period, transferred the patient to St. Elizabeths Hospital, where he made a marginal adjustment on moderate doses of medication. Attempts to extend the patient's privileges or to give him the "least restrictive alternative" usually ended in disaster. He made a serious suicide attempt in 1959. In spite of medication he remained grossly delusional, hallucinated, and withdrawn, often exhibiting silly and inappropriate behavior.

In 1969 he was placed on trial visit, but refused to return to the hospital when his symptoms worsened. On one occasion the police were needed to return him to the hospital. Shortly after this episode he was again permitted to go home and once again refused to return. This time the police refused to take action and ultimately he was dropped from the hospital rolls.

His parents, who by this time were in their seventies, were beside themselves with anxiety, grief, and fear. The father had had two heart attacks and the mother was greatly enfeebled. The patient refused to take his medication, sat in his room smoking up to five packs of cigarettes a day, and required constant watching lest he set fire to the house. He would frequently threaten or attack his parents if they went against his wishes in any way. The house became a house of terror.

In June 1974, the parents finally engaged a highly competent lawyer who had a number of consultations with the family and talked to some of the psychiatrists familiar with the case. After a tremendous amount of effort the patient was finally admitted to the psychiatric unit of a large general hospital on August 4, 1974. On August 7, a petition for Judicial Hospitalization was prepared and the affidavits of his two psychiatrists were obtained.

At this point the Public Defender entered the case and contended that commitment proceedings could not be brought against a person who had entered the hospital on a voluntary basis. The logic of such a ruling flies in the face of all medical experience and common sense. Occasionally a patient enters a hospital as a voluntary patient, but then his condition worsens to such an extent that long-term hospitalization is required and his condition now precludes his entering such a hospital on a voluntary basis. In such a case, it would be most sensible to file for involuntary hospitalizaiton on a temporary basis while the patient is still in the first hospital. However, the current law forbids such a sensible procedure.

As a result of the ruling, it was necessary to wait for the patient's discharge from the hospital, at which time an

Amended Petition was filed (on August 23). A hearing before the Commission on Mental Health was set for September 17, but was postponed until September 24. (The logistics of caring for an acutely psychotic patient at home who is waiting to appear as a reluctant participant in hearings before a Commission on Mental Health are staggering!)

At the hearing, the Commission concluded that the patient was "likely to injure himself or others if allowed to remain at liberty," but inexplicably recommended that he be committed as an outpatient to one of the community mental health centers. No doubt the Commission was greatly influenced by the protestations of the Public Defender who represented the patient.

Pursuant to local statute, the case was referred to the Superior Court for further hearings which did not begin until October 18, 1974. A second hearing to hear further testimony was required on October 21, at the close of which the Court ordered an indefinite commitment. There were further hearings on the subject of reimbursement which dragged on until March 21, 1975, when a final agreement was reached and the case was closed.

In this case, clearly requiring in-hospital treatment, it took over four months of effort and considerable expense to obtain a commitment order and over seven months before the case was finally settled. The patient's elderly parents, who had spent a small fortune on the finest hospitals and consultants, were by this time sick, weary, and impoverished. They lived in terror of what their psychotic son might do to them, and in the final months they had to expend much of their limited savings in substantial legal fees to obtain treatment for their son and to gain some degree of peace for themselves.

This case illustrates a number of problems confronting the psychiatrist in private practice. First, it seems clear that the civil commitment statutes are now weighted so heavily in favor of protecting the individual's civil rights that they often interfere with quick access to treatment on an involuntary basis. Second, the Public Defender Service seems to have a single-minded dedication to the proposition that no one, no matter how ill, should be committed involuntarily. With this in mind, they will interpose every possible legal barrier to commitment. Their zeal as advocates, which so often leads them to legal triumph, may result just as often in psychiatric catastrophe. Their motto—which seems to be "Civil liberties first and foremost!"—ignores the realities of severe mental illness. The psychiatrist who works daily with the mentally ill *also* fights for their freedom. He fights to free his patient from the shackles and imprisonment of mental illness. Severe mental illness, as any experienced psychiatrist knows, can be as great an impediment to full freedom as iron bars and locked doors. It is one of the tragedies of our time that countless numbers of the mentally ill remain untreated and prisoners of their mental illness all in the name of civil liberty. Prompt, appropriate treatment whenever possible, and not indiscriminate discharge, is the only intelligent approach to this problem.

Third, there appears to be a clear bias in favor of outpatient treatment as opposed to inpatient treatment. In recent years, perhaps as a result of the community mental health center movement, a sinister and misleading belief has surfaced which states, in brief, that: "Hospitals are bad; outpatient treatment is good." To any experienced clinician who has agonized over what type of treatment to recommend, this represents a gross and inaccurate oversimplification. The truth is that it takes seasoned clinical judgment (not executive orders, legislative decrees, or judicial fiat) to determine what is best in any given case. Furthermore, what is best for any given patient is constantly shifting. What is best for him in one phase of his illness may be totally inappropriate in another. No court or legal system could possibly keep up with these shifts.

Fourth, the principle of "least restrictive alternative"

clearly dominated the thinking of the Public Defender and
certainly influenced the recommendations of the Commission
on Mental Health when it found that the patient was "likely to
injure himself or others if allowed to remain at liberty" but
failed to recommend commitment to the hospital. Instead, the
Commission recommended treatment on an outpatient basis at
one of the community mental health centers. Such a decision,
flying in the face of all the patient's psychotic symptoms and
behavior, illustrates clearly how court decisions have subtly but
powerfully influenced recommendations that should be made
on clinical merits. Although the concept of the "least
restrictive alternative" may be new to the law, it is a
well-known concept in psychiatry. All the qualified and competent psychiatrists I have known, both in private practice and
institutional work, have operated on the principle of treating a
patient in the office or clinic as an outpatient if at all possible.
If hospitalization seemed to be indicated, partial hospitalization (day or night hospital) might be recommended. If such
facilities were unavailable or inappropriate, then hospitalization on the psychiatric unit of a local general hospital near
family and friends would be advised. Commitment to a highly
restrictive setting is considered only when all other measures
have failed.

Fifth, this case illustrates a phenomenon which has been
going on for some time and about which very little has been
written. I refer to the intimidation of the patient's family by
the seriously ill patient and the great time and expense
involved in obtaining legal relief. It would not be too far-
fetched to classify this situation as "cruel and unusual punishment" in violation of the Eighth Amendment. Macfie
Campbell, who held the chair of psychiatry at Harvard during
the thirties, once defined a family as "a tightly knit oligarchy
ruled by its sickest member." This was certainly true in the
case just presented, and the law, in its single-minded
preoccupation with the civil rights of a grossly disturbed

person, conveniently disregarded the rights and even the health of his family.

Sixth, in the above case all the principles of the criminal law were applied in an area where it was singularly inappropriate. Such criminalization of the mentally ill tends to occur when more emphasis is placed on due process than on giving the patient an opportunity to receive the best treatment for his condition in the promptest manner possible. More striking examples of criminalization of the mentally ill have occurred in California since the passage of the Lanterman-Petris-Short Act (LPS) of 1969, which made involuntary hospitalization of the mentally ill beyond a 17-day period extremely difficult to achieve. "Need for hospitalization" was no longer the standard for involuntary detention under the new law. In reviewing the impact of the new law on the treatment of the mentally ill, a psychiatrist working with the courts and corrections unit of San Mateo County writes:

> There is no easy way to know how many mentally disordered persons are being routinely processed by the criminal justice system into jail and prison, persons who before LPS could have been detained and treated in mental hospitals. Those diverted to hospitals by being considered incompetent to stand trial may be only a tiny fraction. A California prison psychiatrist said in a recent newspaper interview, "We are literally drowning in patients, running around trying to put our fingers in the bursting dikes, while hundreds of men continue to deteriorate psychiatrically before our eyes into serious psychoses . . . . The crisis stems from recent changes in the mental health laws allowing more mentally sick patients to be shifted away from the mental health department into the department of corrections . . . many more men are being sent to prison who have serious mental problems" [7].

Finally, this case illustrates that all the new laws and judicial activism of recent years have done precious little to help the mentally ill, many of whom would do much better with periods of treatment in an appropriate hospital. This point of view, held by most psychiatrists, is also shared by some prominent legal scholars. William J. Curran (8) has stated: "In the past hundred years mental illness has been by far the most legally regulated sickness in the United States. In spite of all this, there is little evidence that this legal attention has done mental patients much good. Law and government have played 'big brother is watching you' with the mentally ill for a century. Another approach may now be advisable. Less law rather than more law may be the answer for the future."

R. H. Joost, another gifted lawyer and (by his own public admission) a former state mental hospital patient who made a brilliant recovery from serious mental illness and who later collaborated in the drafting of one of the more enlightened state mental health codes, has also remained highly critical of the current antimedical bias so prevalent among members of the mental health bar. This lawyer's views on present trends in legal thought are worth noting. In commenting on a memorandum regarding proposed mental health legislation, he writes:

> There is in the materials . . . a barely concealed bias against the medical profession and in favor of the rigamarole of constitutional requirements . . . without sufficient attention to the suitability of such criminal law safeguards to a different field. It is not that you are wrong. You are not. But you are off balance. You are painting a picture of white hats and black hats in which the mentally ill person is the white hat and the mental health doctor and professional is the black hat (with the court as God) . . .
>
> Go back to the drawing boards and in your next memorandum see if you can't cite some materials in the

medical literature rather than exclusively legal literature materials [personal communication].

To all of which I say, "Amen!"

PSYCHIATRIC TREATMENT AND INFORMED CONSENT

The involved legal, ethical, and medical issues of informed consent are discussed at length elsewhere in this book. I shall confine myself here to informed consent as it affects the private practice of psychiatry.

In the past the private psychiatrist had never been much concerned with informed consent, except as it might possibly involve consent for ECT or some other psychiatric treatment with some degree of physical risk. Today, however, the concept of informed consent applies to the administration of psychotropic drugs, as well as to somatic treatments, and in the future it may extend to the entire gamut of psychiatric therapies.

Every good psychiatrist depends heavily on his ability to instill a feeling of confidence so that his patient will tend to accept his recommendations in regard to a treatment program. Without confidence, rapport, and respect for the doctor, all treatment, but especially psychiatric treatment, is well-nigh impossible. A recommended treatment program may involve drug therapy, hospital treatment, somatic treatment, or various types of psychotherapy, singly or in combination. The skilled psychiatrist usually has such good rapport with his patients that he looks on the process of explaining the details of the proposed treatment (including the possible side effects of psychotropic drugs) as an integral part of the treatment itself. It is worth noting that psychiatrists were the first medical specialists to ask pharmacists to label the contents of prescribed drugs, long before it became a general practice. In determining how much to tell a patient about the possible side effects (both immediate and remote) of a given psychotropic drug, the psychiatrist finds himself between Scylla and Charybdis. On the one hand, he wants to prescribe a drug in a spirit of scientific optimism, implying that it will most probably work or at least help the patient. He does not want to detail all the possible complications. If he wished to do this, he could ask the patient in each case to read the package insert — a practice guaranteed to give the patient such an attack of anxiety (in addition to whatever else he was suffering from) that he would probably run headlong from the office and never reach out for help again! On the other hand, the psychiatrist feels obliged by the threat of malpractice suits to tell the patient some of the possible complications, knowing full well that for certain highly suggestible patients the mere listing of symptoms is almost sure to bring them about.

In the case of ECT the practice of obtaining informed consent is well established in private practice. Since this procedure involves the temporary unconsciousness of the patient and a period of amnesia thereafter, it has always been treated as a surgical procedure and the consent forms have often been revisions of forms used in the operating room. In recent years it has been the practice to devise a longer form explaining in full detail, and in lay language, the purpose of ECT, its nature, and its possible complications. Furthermore, the whole matter is discussed fully with each patient, who reads the form and signs it. Whenever there is a next of kin, it is also advisable to have the other family member sign it and witness the signing. The form which has been in use at Sibley Memorial Hospital was devised after several years of study and we have found it most useful. A copy of this form will be found in the appendix.

There are, of course, problems unique to ECT by virtue of the fact that many candidates for ECT are quite mentally ill at the time they are presented with the consent form. A few may sign it immediately, almost without reading it, because they are so depressed that they may say, "I want to die and I hope that this treatment kills me!" The legal competence of such a patient could easily be questioned, yet ECT in such a case is clearly indicated and is most often dramatically successful. Needless to say, the signature of the next of kin is also obtained. Even so, I am sure that technical legal questions could be raised which might delay treatment, incur considerable expense in hospital fees, and worsen the patient's condition if, in each case, the doctor had to wait until a formal court order could be obtained.

Psychotherapy, psychoanalysis, and the other types of "talking therapies" have thus far been conspicuously absent from case law and legislation. Yet, anyone who has had any experience with these treatment forms knows that they are far from innocuous. It is safe to say that any treatment method in medicine (or legal device in the law) that has the power to do good also has the power to do harm.

If the current tendency to insist on fully informed consent continues, I can envision a scene such as the following in the reception room of a psychiatrist's office. The patient enters Stage Center and gives the receptionist his name. The receptionist takes down the identifying data and asks the patient to read carefully and sign a form which she presents to him and which reads something as follows:

> I, John Doe, being of sound mind, possessing the capacity to give consent, do so of my own free will with the full understanding that my doctor may recommend psychotherapy, drug therapy, electroshock therapy, hospitalization, or any combination of the above.
>
> If I receive psychotherapy, I fully understand that:
> 1. I may fail to improve.
> 2. I may get worse.
> 3. Anything I say may be used as basis for my commitment.

4. I may develop a great dependency on my therapist.
5. I may become emotionally involved with my therapist.
6. I may divorce my spouse.
7. I may commit suicide.

The form is to be signed by John Doe in the presence of two witnesses and notarized by the receptionist who is conveniently a notary public as well. Final instructions are given to the prospective patient: "Having properly executed the above form, you may now enter the private consulting room and feel free to tell the psychiatrist anything and everything that comes to your mind."

Although the above is obviously a caricature of what the future may hold in store for us, the seven items listed under what may happen to the patient undergoing psychotherapy are not. All of them, including some items not listed, have indeed occurred in the course of psychotherapy.

It is impossible to practice good medicine or good psychiatry without taking risks. If psychiatrists continue to be intimidated by the threat of malpractice suits and legal restrictions, weak, ineffective treatments will result, conforming to the letter of the law, but avoiding any of the risky treatment methods (such as the more powerful psychopharmaceuticals and ECT), with the result that these treatments will be underutilized and untold, needless suffering will result.

One serious issue now confronting many psychiatrists who see patients on the psychiatric unit of a general hospital is presented by the very sick patient who enters the hospital voluntarily (or informally) but refuses to take prescribed medication. The issue here is the right to refuse treatment. If the patient enters voluntarily, then there is no legal basis for forcing the patient to take psychiatric medication, for example, by hypodermic injection. The issue becomes more complicated when the patient, by refusing treatment, becomes such a behavior problem on the unit as to require discharge or transfer to another hospital. Does the psychiatrist or the hospital have the right to discharge the patient if he refuses the treatment offered? Court orders for treatment of committed patients have been obtained on occasion, especially for ECT, but they are rare. In the future, however, I can foresee situations in which manic patients who refuse lithium therapy or other psychotropic medication may require court orders for their treatment in much the same way that members of certain sects require court orders to receive a life-saving blood transfusion.

GAINS VS. LOSSES

As a result of the current ferment in psychiatry and the law, one thing is now certain: the private and institutional practice of psychiatry will never be the same again. But it is doubtful whether all these changes will result in better care for the mentally ill.

The invasion of psychiatry by the forces of the law (especially the judiciary) did not take place in a vacuum. Psychiatrists must take much of the blame for the present sorry state of affairs along with the lawyers. The state hospitals, long the stepchild of state legislatures, long undermanned, under-equipped, and underfinanced, have been having a hard time keeping up with the times, and it is not surprising that many of them have developed counterproductive defenses. They felt that they had become a dumping ground for society's rejects and it was almost impossible to recruit capable staff. More and more they became dependent on foreign medical graduates whose incomplete command of English often made it difficult for them to communicate linguistically or culturally with the patients in their charge. They worked in miserable settings. Many did, in fact, feel more comfortable treating patients who were legally committed because they could then take their time with the limited facilities available. No wonder they felt threatened and became defensive when it was made clear to them (especially in *Rouse* [9] and *Wyatt* [10]) that they could not detain a patient without giving him treatment.

The question of what constitutes "treatment" has always been a bone of contention between lawyers and psychiatrists. Part of the confusion lies in the myriads of treatments available in the field of psychiatry. Part lies in the fact that psychiatry has been guilty of promising more than it can deliver.

"What's in a name? That which we call a rose by any other name would smell as sweet." When the old insane asylums changed their name to "retreats" and then later to "hospitals," it was strongly implied that the treatment of the patients had changed along with the names. It was true that a number of remarkable therapies were discovered for the once untreatable maladies of the mentally ill: malarial fever therapy and later penicillin for general paresis, insulin treatment and then the tranquilizing drugs for schizophrenia, antidepressant drugs and ECT for depression. Even though the list is incomplete, it is still an impressive score. What remained unsaid, however, was that in spite of all the technological advances, there would always remain a significant number of treatment failures that would require long-term and sometimes indefinite hospital treatment. For these patients, the hospital became literally an "asylum" in the best sense of that word. This is a fact not readily grasped by many lawyers, nor by quite a number of psychiatrists.

Although the current increase of the law's interest in psychiatry has brought with it a heightened consciousness of patients' rights, the spate (I was going to say epidemic) of individual lawsuits and class action suits continues unabated. One must ask, not only as a psychiatrist, but also as a citizen: (a) Is this a healthy state of affairs? and (b) Hasn't this trend now reached a point of overkill where it is counterproductive and threatening to the quality of mental health care, the very thing that the mental health bar has been trying to improve? The lawsuits have rarely resulted in increased appropriations for mental hospitals, but they have tended to erode whatever public confidence remained in the large state mental hospitals. Staff morale has plummeted, and the tense adversary climate which exists between the Public Defender Services and the psychiatric clinicians often results in frustrations and resignations on the part of the psychiatric staff. Because of the number of lawsuits and the increased legal paper work, the few remaining psychiatrists have been taken from their clinical work and assigned to legal cases. Many psychiatrists in private practice now refuse to have anything to do with sick patients who may require involuntary hospitalization. One beleaguered superintendent wrote me recently in regard to a certain law suit, "We are now in our third year and have spent about 3,000 man hours on this suit and it has yet to benefit a single patient."

Psychiatrists and state hospital superintendents are not the only ones to express alarm. In a series in the *Washington Post*, entitled "Imperial Courts: Growing Power Alarms Critics," Robert Kaiser (11) asks, "Have America's Federal judges gone too far?" He quotes Nathan Glazer, a neoconservative critic as saying, "Courts, through interpretation of the Constitution and the laws now reach into the lives of the people, against the will of the people, deeper than they ever have in American history." Another conservative, Philip Kurland, is quoted as accusing "an imperial judiciary of imposing legislation without representation" with its decisions, orders, and decrees. Even the liberal Archibald Cox of Harvard is quoted as stating: "Excessive reliance upon courts instead of self government through democratic processes may deaden a people's sense of moral and political responsibility for their own future."

Regardless of what the legal scholars say, be they liberal

or conservative, judicial activism is probably here to stay, chiefly because of the inertness and unresponsiveness of the legislative branch in regard to these major social issues. The judiciary has tried to fill a vacuum created by public apathy, executive indifference, and legislative do-nothingness. The combined efforts of psychiatry and law should be directed at combating these three common enemies.

My deepest concerns are not for the plight of beleaguered state hospital superintendents or psychiatrists in private practice, but rather for the baleful effect all this activism may have on the innocent mental patient, who is presumably the beneficiary of all these frantic efforts. Both the law and psychiatry profess to do what they do because of their interest in helping the mentally ill. The poor patient, however, now finds himself in the position of the baby in the Bible story whose custody was bitterly disputed by the real and the false mother. You will remember that the quarrel was brought before King Solomon, who heard them out at great length and then ordered each of the two mothers to grasp the infant by one leg and pull it apart. The real mother, of course, let go at the first cry of pain and, quite naturally, King Solomon awarded the baby to her.

I see psychiatry as the real mother of the mentally ill, and even though we are sometimes forced by the law to let go of our patients, often against their own best interests, I have the hope that in the near future a King Solomon will arise who will return them to their real mother, the one who cares.

Although I am not as optimistic as I was in 1952, I still think that psychiatry has a tremendous and largely unfulfilled task to inform the legal profession, the public, and the judiciary, precisely what it can do and what it cannot do. In 1952, I stated: "The chief cause for the mutual distrust and suspicion (between psychiatry and law) lies in the ignorance of each other's functions, objectives and basic philosophy. The remedy lies in increased research and ever-widening dissemination of knowledge" (1). I closed on that occasion with the hope that our joint efforts would be successful and that we would finally be able to fulfill the noble vision of Claude Bernard: "Sometime, he hoped, the day would arrive when the physiologist, the philosopher and the poet [and may we add the psychiatrist and the lawyer] would talk the same language and understand each other. Then a dynamic medicine would arise" (12).

In closing, I would like to leave a brief word of advice. In my title I posed the question: "How to treat the mentally ill without being a lawyer?" In two words, the answer to that question is: "Very carefully."

APPENDIX
DETAILS OF ELECTROTHERAPY AND CONSENT FORM*

Electrotherapy, also known as electroconvulsive therapy (ECT) or electroshock therapy (EST), is an accepted form of treatment for certain types of psychiatric disorders. It has been used successfully in thousands of cases in this country and abroad since its introduction in 1938. It is one of the most effective ways of treating depression and certain other conditions in patients who might otherwise require prolonged hospitalization.

The psychiatrist himself gives the treatment in a specially equipped treatment room, using a calibrated electronic instrument. The treatment consists of passing a small, carefully controlled electric current between two electrodes applied to the patient's temples. Treatments are usually given in the morning before breakfast. Prior to each treatment the patient receives a hypodermic injection to reduce oral secretions. No special

* Department of Psychiatry, Sibley Memorial Hospital, Washington, D.C., 1975.

dress or gown is required. Once in the treatment room, the patient is given an intravenous anesthetic which induces sleep within a matter of seconds. He is then given a second intravenous medication which produces muscular relaxation. The patient experiences no discomfort or pain during the treatment; he does not feel the electric current and has no memory of the treatment. When the treatment is given, the patient, who is already asleep, has generalized muscular contractions of a convulsive nature. These contractions, which have been "softened" by the second intravenous medication, last approximately 60 seconds. Minutes later, the patient slowly awakens and may experience transitory confusion similar to that seen in patients emerging from any type of brief anesthesia. When the patient is ready he is then returned to his room. Following this, he is given breakfast and is permitted to be up and about. Headache, mild muscle soreness or nausea sometimes occur, but these are infrequent and usually respond to simple treatment.

The number of treatments in any given case will vary with the condition being treated, the individual response to treatment, and the medical judgment of the psychiatrist giving the treatments. A typical course of therapy may consist of four to ten treatments. In some cases more treatments may be required. Although the treatments are usually given every other day, or three a week, the frequency of treatment will also vary with each case. As the treatments progress (usually after the fourth or fifth treatment), a certain amount of haziness of memory develops. This memory impairment is transitory and clears up usually within one to three weeks following the last treatment.

Electrotherapy, like any other medical or surgical procedure, involves a certain amount of calculated risk. Careful medical evaluation will be carried out in each case to insure that there are no overriding medical contraindications to the treatment. Fatalities are extremely rare. Complications, although infrequent, may include fractures and/or dislocations or adverse reaction to intravenous medication. These may sometimes occur in spite of all precautions and must be looked upon as a recognized hazard of the treatment. Should such a complication occur, appropriate treatment will be instituted and the patient's family notified.

Convalescence

After the last scheduled treatment the patient begins a "convalescent period" the duration of which varies with each patient. During this period (usually one to three weeks) he must either remain in the hospital or be discharged under the supervision of a family member or some responsible person selected by the family. This precaution is necessary because of the temporary impairment of memory which is an expected side effect of the treatment. During the convalescent period, the patient should not drive an automobile, transact business or carry on his usual employment until so advised by his doctor. Alcoholic beverages are prohibited. A responsible person should remain with the patient until such time as convalescence is completed. The duration of the convalescent period is determined by the patient's progress in consultation with the psychiatrist.

Outpatient Treatments

In some instances outpatient treatment may be recommended; in other cases "maintenance therapy" may be more suitable. In neither case is hospitalization required.

Outpatient treatment generally consists of a full course of treatment over a two- to four-week period without the patient having to enter the hospital as an inpatient. "Maintenance treatment" consists of a regularly scheduled series of electro-convulsive treatments given over a period of time as a prophylactic measure to prevent recurrence of certain illnesses. In either event, a member of the family or a designated responsible person accepts the responsibility for:

1. seeing that the patient does not take any food or drink after midnight preceding each treatment,
2. escorting the patient to the hospital for the appointed treatment,
3. escorting him home after the treatment has been completed.

During the period of treatment and for at least two to four weeks following termination of treatment, the patient should be under the close supervision and constant companionship of the family.

Results

Finally, a word about the results of treatment. Although the results in most cases are gratifying, not all cases will respond equally well. As in all forms of medical treatment, some patients will recover promptly; others will recover only to relapse again and require further treatment; still others may fail to respond at all.

The above information has been prepared to answer some of the most frequently asked questions concerning electroshock therapy, and to inform the patient and his family of the benefits and risks involved in this treatment. This brochure represents the views of those members of the Sibley Hospital Department of Psychiatry who are most experienced in administering this treatment. The attending psychiatrists will be glad to answer any further questions which may occur to the patient or his family.

Consent for Electroshock Therapy

I, ..., a patient in

the Sibley Memorial Hospital, Washington, D.C., and I . . . . .

. . . ., of . . . .
                                                        Address

being the . . . ., and nearest relative
                       Relationship

of . . . ., do hereby authorize and
                    Patient

direct Dr. . . . . or his designee, to administer

electroshock treatment, having been fully informed of its
nature and purpose by reading or having had read to me the
above "Details of Electrotherapy." I also agree to hold the
Sibley Memorial Hospital, all its officers and employees, and
the attending physician, free from liability for any injury
which may result from such treatment.

. . . .
  Witness   Patient's Signature   Date

. . . .
  Witness   Relative's Signature   Date

References

1. Lebensohn, Z. M. Psychiatry and the law: A plea for closer rapport. *Amer. J. Psychiat.,* 109:96-101, 1952.
2. Roper, E. et al. People's attitudes concerning mental health: A study made in the city of Louisville for the city of Louisville and *Collier's Magazine.* Sept. 1950.
3. *O'Connor v. Donaldson.* 422 U.S. 563, 45 L.Ed.2d 396 (1975).

4. Stone, A. A. Overview: The right to treatment—comments on the law and its impact. *Amer. J. Psychiat.,* 132:1125-1134, 1975.
5. Wallis, W. A. *An Overgoverned Society.* New York: Free Press, 1976, pp. 71-72.
6. Ray, I. In: *Amer. Law Rev.,* 3:193, 1869.
7. Abramson, M. F. The criminalization of mentally disordered behavior: Possible side effect of a new mental health law. *Hosp. Commun. Psychiat.,* 23(4):101-105, 1972.
8. Curran, W. J. Community mental health—new legal concepts. *New Eng. J. Med.,* 271:512-513, 1964.
9. *Rouse v. Cameron.* 373 F.2d 451 (D.C. Cir. 1966).
10. *Wyatt v. Stickney.* 325 F.Supp. 781 (M.D. Ala. 1971).
11. Kaiser, R. Imperial courts: Growing power alarms critics. *Wash. Post,* July 18, 1976, p. 1.
12. Kraus, F. *Die allgemeine und spezielle Pathologie der Person,* Vol. I, Introduction V. Leipzig: Thieme, 1919.

Part II

Informed Consent

The concept of informed consent to a treatment or procedure is crucial to liability actions and to service delivery in many settings, but particularly those involving the mentally ill. Informed consent is given by an individual who has the legal capacity to give consent and who is free to exercise choice. The patient should be an active participant in an agreement to be admitted to a hospital or a facility program, to employ a treatment or procedure, or to be released. The objective is to impart sufficient information to decide intelligently among alternative choices. There should be not only a fair exploration of the alternative options and the consequences of selection, but an explanation of methods, discomforts, likely risks, and potential hazards. In practice the sick patient's trust in the physician's judgment is tremendous. When rapport between patient and physician is strong, dissatisfaction expressed in malpractice claims is less frequent.

There are some special problems in the mental health field. Children, the mentally retarded, and the mentally ill may lack the capacity to understand or be too preoccupied with their acute symptoms to grasp the implications of an explanation of a proposed treatment. Physicians have always obtained consent from the patient, or when competence was in question, from a responsible relative or guardian. When the courts added the word "informed," the new element proposed a vague standard that created new problems in interpretation.

Much of the confusion over informed consent centers on what details are necessary in explanations. Should all risks, however rare, be given, or just those that a reasonable physician would relate to aid a patient to make a decision? Sound clinical judgment has always been the foundation of medical practice. The new emphasis on informed consent is an expression of a more open society in which the citizen or consumer shares knowledge in order to participate in decisions that affect his or her welfare.

Two attorneys, Ralph Slovenko and Henry H. Foster, Jr., present very different approaches to this contemporary issue. Slovenko, an academician and expert in mental health law, notes that the commercialization of medicine has changed the public's perception of physicians. In addition, the loss of rapport with patients has contributed to a readiness to sue the doctor when things go wrong. He states that informed consent is a spurious issue — that the real intent is the development of a legal device to control the medical profession. Although informed consent is the prevailing method, if it is abandoned another method will be developed.

Slovenko makes two challenging suggestions: drop the fee-for-service and utilize a business contract to define doctor-patient relationships.

Foster, an academician with a long list of credentials attesting to active involvement in the mental health field, focuses on the clash between the individual's right to freedom, autonomy, and personal choice and the physician's duty to heal and cure.

The law requires consent for admission, treatment, and perhaps release of patients, but patients differ in their capacity to make rational decisions. Some are so confused that the emergency doctrine applies. A guardian or next of kin may act for the patient. There is a need for study of the problem of mental patients' ability to make informed judgments. One study, for example, showed that 92 out of 100 mental patients did not comprehend the conditions for admission or the alternatives presented. They were unable to act in an autonomous manner. A corollary is the ability to exercise intelligent choice of treatment.

Chapter III

Psychotherapy and Informed Consent: A Search in Judicial Regulation

RALPH SLOVENKO, L.L.B., PH.D.

Psychotherapists—"the talking doctors"—have now joined "the touching doctors" in expressing concern about "informed consent." Some have even manifested their concern by having their patients (clients) sign a consent-to-treatment form.

The informed-consent concept developed essentially as a judicial regulatory device to prompt physicians who did not talk or listen to their patients to develop a better rapport with them, and to provide aggrieved patients an alternative route to legal recovery for injury arising out of treatment. "Consent" is an act of reason, accompanied by deliberation, where the mind weighs the good and bad on each side. In law the concept of consent derives from the basic right of self-determination. Under the informed-consent doctrine, the physician is obliged to disclose and explain to the patient the nature of the ailment, the nature of the proposed treatment or operation, the probability of success, alternative methods of treatment, and the foreseeable risks.

51

Not too long ago the medical practitioner was regarded as a kindly family counselor. At this time a lawsuit against a physician was an event of the greatest rarity. The physician was next to God; he could do no wrong. However, the complexion of the physician-patient relationship began to change. Medical care degenerated into a hurried and depersonalized form of production-line service and began to look more and more like a commercial transaction. "Not only is there no God," says Woody Allen, "but try getting a doctor to talk to you."*

At mid-twentieth century a number of people began to wonder why the doctor had virtual immunity from suit. He enjoyed a highly profitable livelihood. With a streamlined practice, the ordinary practitioner (intern and resident excluded) might have a larger income than the salary of the President of the United States. Here is the way an ordinary citizen puts it: "Medicine is the best profession to go into if you're thinking of money. The doctors have gone very commercial, they live bloody well."

In the past the doctor received an honorarium, but now he charges a fee, and like other creditors he turns to a debt-collection agency in the event of delinquency. Under prevailing law he is entitled to payment whether or not the patient's condition improves, and if the patient dies, he is in many states a preferred creditor in the estate. (The practice of billing is so common now that failure to bill would indeed indi-

---

* Foremost among the factors that have contributed to the increase in malpractice claims are: the breakdown of physician-patient rapport, the impersonalization of health care, the negative image of medical professionals, increases in the demand for and delivery of health care, shortage of medical personnel and resources, the rising consumerism among patients, the growing litigiousness of society abetted by the contingent fee, the rising number of law graduates, increased public understanding of medical facts, unrealistic public expectations regarding medical treatment, and growing public reluctance to accept the inevitability of death and pain (1, 2).

cate consciousness of inadequate care!) In contrast, a person who sells a defective television set or repairs it poorly is not compensated. And the attorney is often paid on the contingency of a favorable judgment. The doctor, though, is allowed to discount failure as due to uncontrollable parameters.

As the practice of medicine became indistinguishable from a commercial enterprise, the courts modified the rules of evidence and broadened the theories of causes of action. During recent decades, the tort suit has served (in a lottery fashion) to provide a form of social security for disabled persons — just as the manufacturer of a product is expected to bear the cost of injury, though the nexus of product to injury may be slim, the medical practitioner likewise is now expected (through insurance) to bear part of the cost. As expressed in one casebook on torts: "In the law of torts the tail (damages) may often wag the dog (the other rules)" (3).

The courts abandoned the "locality rule," which required a complainant to present an expert from the same locality as the defendant-doctor. That rule in effect barred a successful prosecution of the case. One colleague would not testify against another. It gave rise to the expression, borrowed from George Bernard Shaw, that "medicine is not a profession but a conspiracy." It was a conspiracy of silence. With the abandonment of the locality rule, an expert could be called from any part of the country. The conspiracy of silence was broken (4-6). In addition, an exception to the hearsay rule was developed to permit the introduction of medical treatises as evidence.

Of most consequence was the new presumption that the injury speaks for itself (*res ipsa loquitur*). This was used to shift the burden to the defendant-doctor to prove that he was *not* at fault. Aided by this presumption, the plaintiff-patient was assured of getting his case before the jury.

The development of the concept of informed consent

added to the armamentarium of the complaining patient and prompted physicians to relate to their patients. In a claim based on malpractice or negligence, the patient has to produce an expert to establish that there was a departure from accepted medical practice. However, in a case where there is no informed consent, it is not necessary to have expert testimony to prove negligence, for the simple reason that such a case is based on the fact that had the plaintiff been informed of the risks and hazards he would not have agreed to the treatment. The legal action is categorized as *assault and battery*, because the patient's bodily integrity was invaded without his consent. The fact that the treatment was properly performed, or even brilliantly performed, is immaterial.

Physicians (and lawyers) must now ponder problems of efficiency and morality. Is every patient to be schooled in every aspect of his condition and apprised of every hazard known to medical science?* Is it sufficient to give some general idea of the consequences, or is it necessary to point out meticulously all the complications that may possibly arise? What is to be done in an emergency? What is to be told about hospitalization? Suppose the patient is a minor, deranged, unconscious, or in great distress? Is a proxy consent of value? Might the patient be given library references? Is the extent of a physician's duty to disclose determined by the professional standard for other similarly situated members of the profession?** Should the taciturn man, one who does not like to talk, be disqualified from the healing arts? And suppose he is unable to speak, like Othello the soldier, in clear language?

---

* It has been said that disclosure need not be a "disquisition" or a "short course in anatomy" (7, 8).

** The answer is bluntly no. As one court put it: "Nor can we ignore the fact that to bind the disclosure obligation to medical usage is to arrogate the decision on revelation to the physician alone. Respect for the patient's right of self-determination on particular therapy demands a standard set by law for physicians rather than one which physicians may or may not impose upon themselves (9).

And in applying the informed-consent concept, how is the law to deal with fluency of language, stress, intonation, and pronunciation? Suppose the patient understands only slang? (To help out in this regard, one teacher of English has published a book of terms for physicians (10). Thus, for "breast" it is suggested: boob, bosom, buffers, chestnut, paps, tits, titties, top part.) And how is the law to deal with levels of intelligence? Consider the dialogue: A physician says, "You need oxygen." "What's oxygen?" asks the patient. "It's what keeps you alive. You breathe in oxygen and breathe out carbon dioxide." "I do!" exclaims the patient, "That's a pretty good trick." The doctor was dumbfounded.

Contemporary law, having marched up the hill to formulate a rule on informed consent, then marches down to make exceptions, and the doctor is left not knowing where he stands. The physician feels that he faces a legal landscape which is in considerable disarray, and now looks (in vain) for a rule on consent that he can apply like a pharmacist making up a prescription. But the law posits a vague rule and then draws exceptions, equally vague.

There are circumstances, it is held, in which the patient need not give an informed consent to treatment. Full disclosure is not required when there is an emergency and the patient is not able to exercise judgment; when the explanation of every risk attendant upon treatment would alarm a patient who is already apprehensive, and who might as a result refuse to undertake a treatment involving minimal risk; or when such disclosure would, because of emotional consequences, result in actually increasing the risk itself. The exception often claimed in psychiatry—particularly in the use of electroshock—is that of permitting nondisclosure to avoid increasing the risk to the patient. But this is not always an effective claim. Rather than require proof of negligence, the court has ruled that in a case in which a psychiatrist applied electroshock to a patient who suffered a fractured bone as a result, there was no legally effective consent because the risk of fracture was not known to the patient (11, 12).

Quite likely, the information, if given, would have fallen on deaf ears. Illness or disease as a rule saps the will to go on, breeds self-doubt, blurs the memory, and blunts one's purpose in life. At this time it is primarily emotional support that is needed, and protection from exploitation.

A patient can, if he is really autonomous enough to give an informed consent, go to the library for the facts. In the commencement stage, at least, of a course of electroshock, a person who is able to understand the procedure and consent to it would not likely be a candidate for it. And after being given electroshock, the patient who is aware of what is happening more often than not says, "Not again, I'll never have it again." There is also considerable difficulty in squaring the informed-consent doctrine with chemotherapy. A pill may be only a placebo, and a pill has more success when it is prescribed with enthusiasm.* The despair or depression of a patient would not be alleviated as well by news that the anti-depressive effect of a drug works only in a percentage of cases; magic and sometimes deception form a necessary part of the healing arts. The patient's well-being may sometimes be better served by concealment than by disclosure. And in the case of civil commitment, one can hardly talk about consent, conveying of information, and respect of the subject's autonomy when his only discourse is one sentence — "I'm born to die, I want to die, I must die." In psychiatry, the person most drastically in need of care is the least competent to consent.

Informed consent, in my opinion, is a spurious issue as far as the law is concerned. To apply the time-honored test of consent literally is to expend energy needlessly, as in the case of

---

* In *Love v. Wolf* (13), the court held that proper warnings of dangers of a drug are counteracted by overpromotion and puffery in advertisements.

review committees that presently look over consent forms. The doctor, of course, must touch every base, but even if he does, he will not necessarily be home-free. Most often, the doctrine is used to facilitate proof of the complainant's case. At other times, as in certain psychosurgical procedures, it has been used as a vehicle to bar or express condemnation of a procedure (14). To this end, it can be expected to be used increasingly against electroshock.*

The informed-consent concept illustrates the use of language to achieve a purpose other than or in addition to the one expressed. To focus on the literal meaning of the concept, with some exceptions, is to engage in a metaphysical exercise. If this concept were not used, then another one would be developed to achieve the ends desired. The ingenuity of the law is hydra-headed—abort one plan and another springs forth to take its place.

Informed consent is not really a matter of information or voluntariness. To be sure, there is the occasional case where the risks are not explained or the practitioner goes beyond the agreement, but judging from all the discussion, one might suppose that physicians are dragging people off the street into the operating room. If there were really no consent, then it would be appropriate for the criminal law to intervene, but there have been no such proceedings.

To have any real meaning, informed consent would involve consultation with noninterested others. As the informed-consent concept has developed at law, sufficient information must be disclosed to the patient so that he can arrive at an intelligent opinion.** The rule says nothing about *who* is to give

---

* Even though a patient is considered in need of involuntary hospitalization, he is not to be considered incompetent as a consequence for the purpose of consenting to electroshock (15).

** A model instruction to the jury states: "A physician's duty to disclose is not governed by the standard practice in the community; rather it is the duty imposed by law. The physician violates his duty to the patient and sub-the information. A patient tends to go along with the physician's expressed or implied suggestion, especially where a relationship between the two has developed. The sophisticated patient, however, usually knows for example that surgeons are notoriously biased in favor of surgery, so an independent opinion is sought. The wealthy can afford to shop around, travel about, and gather several opinions (overcoming the professional ethic that discourages independent consultations when one has already engaged a physician). In the nature of things, this freedom of choice exists only to a limited degree for relatively few persons.

It has been asserted, as in the Detroit psychosurgery case (17, 18), that institutionalized persons, in the face of inherent institutional coercion, cannot make a valid consent. In fact, however, they may be able to make a more valid, more rational consent than does the ordinary ill person who calls upon a doctor. When in distress or pain, one tends to regress to a childlike state — one is not at that time acting as an autonomous person, one is then readily brain-washed, so to speak. Is it possible then to quantify stress to measure the legality or voluntariness of a consent? There is no evidence that this is possible.

Considering the magical nature, in part at least, of the healing arts and the nonautonomous position of the person in distress, the informed-consent doctrine is a singularly unsuitable doctrine for the regulation of the health profession. It may serve well as a judicial device to provide compensation in a case in which there has been some demonstrable injury, but taken literally by the profession (which does not realize that if this device were not used some other one would be), it leaves the practitioner confused about what is expected. The terms in the informed-consent rule and its exceptions are all

---

jects himself to liability if he withholds any facts which are necessary to form the basis of an intelligent consent by the patient to the proposed treatment" (quoted with approval in *Cobbs v. Grant* [16]).

accordionlike, and trying to measure up to them, the practitioner encumbers his practice with forms and information as he goes through the ritual of providing information, much of it nonessential. The consequence is a kind of "Gresham's Law of Information" — too much or trivial information drowns out the vital.

While the ostensible purpose of a tort suit is to compensate an injured person for a wrong done to him, either intentionally or negligently, it is at the same time the prevailing mode of control over medical care standards. The lawyer's wisdom is that the threat of a lawsuit brings about a better, more careful practice. One indeed might ask: Who has contributed most to the practice of medicine — Hippocrates, Pasteur, Osler, or the chap who gets sick? None of them, lawyers say. The answer they give is, "Melvin Belli," the noted plaintiff's attorney who broke through the conspiracy of silence.

The sad fact is that professional people are reluctant to police themselves strenuously. Indeed, the medical practitioner, reluctant to initiate disciplinary proceedings, often looks instead to the lawyer to keep his house in order.

And this brings us to the psychotherapist.

Thus far, there have been few suits against psychotherapists. The reasons, well known in legal circles, are the difficulty of establishing causation of harm and standard of care as well as the individual's reluctance to bring his psychiatric case to public attention. Those cases that have occurred against psychiatrists have involved the physical and drug therapies, improper certification for commitment, and faulty diagnosis.

In recent years, however, a number of articles have appeared in the law journals on malpractice in psychotherapy. While these articles have done little to advance the feasibility of proving a case of mal-psychotherapy, they evince growing attention to the field. One observer has said, "Psychiatry, no less than the rest of medicine, is being dragged like a petulant child towards a new accountability of its patients and the public" (19).

But how? Through regulation by licensure or certification? By peer review? By tort or contract suit? Speaking on the need for regulation, Judge Bazelon (20) has stated:

> Not only the principle of judicial review, but the whole scheme of American government, reflects an institutionalized mistrust of any such unchecked and unbalanced power over essential liberties. That mistrust does not depend on an assumption of inveterate venality or incompetence on the part of men in power, be they Presidents, legislators, administrators, judges, or doctors. It is not doctors' nature, but human nature, which benefits from the prospect and the fact of supervision. Indeed, the limited scope of judicial review of hospital decisions necessarily assumes the good faith and professional expertise of the hospital staff. Judicial review is only a safety catch against the fallibility of the best of men; and not the least of its services is to spur them to double-check their own performance and provide them with a checklist by which they may readily do so.

Regulation by licensure or certification has come in for much criticism. In almost every profession or occupation, disciplinary enforcement is virtually nonexistent. The little enforcement there is does not act as a deterrent and often protects the reputation or the economic interests of the profession rather than safeguards the public. In a study of licensing, Daniel B. Hogan, research fellow at the Harvard University Department of Psychology and Social Relations, concludes that the quality of services provided by licensed practitioners is no better than would be provided if there were no licensing laws (personal communication, April 1976). And licensure, as a quality control measure, has a number of detrimental side effects: it contributes substantially to the shortage or maldistribution of professional manpower and the nonutilization of paraprofessionals; and it inhibits innovation, experimentation, training, education, and organization of services.

Since licensure and certification are not working very well, increasing attention is being given to the judicial arena in bringing about regulation. The most important tool used by the courts in the regulation of medical care is tort law, as discussed, and to a much lesser extent, contract law.

In the case of psychotherapy, where there is no bodily contact, there is by definition no cause of action in battery. The form of trespass to the person known as "battery" involves some physical contact with the complainant. There being no touching in the talking therapies, there is no battery, and hence no need of a defense, be it informed consent or whatever. The question of defense arises only when the plaintiff has proved that a presumptive tort has been committed. It is only then that the defendant is called upon to defend himself by proving, if he can, that the plaintiff was willing.

And what about a tort case based on negligence, or malpractice as it is commonly called? "Negligence" is defined as the absence of such care, skill, and diligence as it was the duty of the person to bring to the performance of the task. But there is no consensus as to what constitutes standard of care or what skills or techniques are necessary in psychotherapy. Not too long ago, Freudian psychoanalysis was *the* form of psychotherapy. Now, given the same diagnosis, a person may be involved in individual or group psychotherapy, behavior therapy, hypnotherapy, drug therapy, electrotherapy, or he may be hospitalized. Can it reliably be said that one modality is more suitable than another? The courts tend not to pass judgment on the appropriate therapy or the efficacy of different forms of treatment (except sterilization, electroshock, and psychosurgery), a reflection of Justice Cardozo's (21) observation that the law treats medicine with diffidence and respect. Thus, the court has refused to consider which "of two equally reputable methods of psychiatric treatment" — psycho-analysis as against a physiological approach — would prove most efficacious in a particular case (21). In *Tribby v. Cameron* (22), for example, the U.S. Court of Appeals for the District of Columbia said: "We do not suggest that the court should or can decide what particular treatment this patient re-quires. The court's function here resembles ours when we review agency action. We do not decide whether one agency has made the best decision, but only make sure it has made permissible and reasonable decision in view of the relevant information and within a broad range of discretion."

Even assuming that negligence is established, can it be shown that it is the proximate cause of the harm complained about? There are those who swear by psychotherapy, and there are those who swear at it (23). What is the harm that may arise out of psychotherapy? Negligence in the air, so to speak, is not enough to impose liability; some damage or injury must result from the negligence.* What can be said to constitute damage? Some say that breakdown or disintegration of personality is essential to a redevelopment of personality, so "breakdown"

---

* Assuming a case in negligence is made out, the defense raised is the classicism, *volenti non fit injuria* — no wrong is done to one who is willing. Translated another way, *volenti* means, "You asked for it!" It corresponds to the plea of consent in actions for intended harm, and is an expression of the same philosophy of individualism. The theorists, however, now say that while it fairly describes the defense of consent to intentional conduct that would otherwise be a battery, such as the bodily contact involved in surgery or copulation, it would seldom if ever be applicable literally to situations of negligent injury. Who, after all, would freely consent to negligent injury? What might be said is that the duty of care imposed by the law on the defendant does not require him to obviate the risk in question. This confronts the plaintiff at the threshold of his case rather than as a de-fense, properly speaking (24).

ironically is a "breakthrough." Some say divorce is "a step forward when married life is arid." Suicide at times may even be a good idea. And so on.

So the tort-law track is not likely to produce effective regulation. What of a remedy in contract law?

A contract is an agreement to do something. If *A* takes *B*'s money, *B* has a right to expect *A* to do or convey something to *B*, and if he does not, *B* is entitled to his money back. In psychotherapy is the bargain simply for time or a nod or an interpretation, or is it for a result? Is there any warranty? Other individuals offering services, for example, the private detective agency, guarantee a result, so they say, or no fee.

Under prevailing law a medical practitioner is held vulnerable for breach of contract only if he implies that his treatment will cure the patient. No negligence need be proved; a patient need only establish that he contracted for a cure and that the contract was breached by the physician's failure to cure him (25). However, it is rare indeed that a physician promises a cure, and as a general principle of law, a physician is not a guarantor of a cure; he does not warrant a good result; he is not an insurer against mishaps or unusual consequences; and he is not liable for honest mistakes of judgment.

The conventional wisdom is that a contract for medical services is not to be relegated to the level of a commercial transaction, where assurances are construed as warranties (26-28). There are "qualitative differences," it is said, that exist between a construction contract, for example, and one for the removal of a human organ. A profession deals with individuals whereas a craft deals with providing things (food, clothing, and shelter), and any attempt to approximate their duties is considered wrong. With the professional person, it is said, the state of his own individual conscience, his professional spirit, determines the quality of his services.

What might be expected of psychotherapy? Does a patient

just take a chance? Ordinarily, the person seeking help from a psychotherapist expects him to help sort things out. What might be expected of one therapist (in London) who advertises: "Practical Instant Psychotherapy" (29). Relief in an hour, and in no more than an hour? A hypnotist advertises: "Hypnosis can help you to help yourself! Enjoy a better memory. Overcome stage fright and other fears. Improve your power of concentration. All this, and more!" (30). In general, hypnotherapists say phobias — of spiders or snakes or storms — can be successfully treated by hypnosis (31). Shall they be held to their promise, expressed or implied?

The Weight Watchers organization promises to "help you get on top of your eating habits and lose faster." Dale Carnegie advertises that its "sales course can help you increase your selling skills, your sales and income." Consider also the promise of the faith-healer: "The blind shall see, the deaf hear, and lame walk," but he does not charge, so one does not hold him to the promise.

Increasingly, psychotherapy may be viewed as an educational process in which an individual learns new habits and gains insight into his difficulties, rather than as part of any medical system. If this is so, then the legal regulation of psychotherapy becomes similar to the legal regulation of education.

How tolerant should the law be of disclaimers by which one party, submitting himself to medical care, purports to exempt the other from responsibility that would otherwise be due? In practice, the physician typically now advises the patient that he cannot assure results; and the patient signs a statement acknowledging that he understands the risks. A seller of goods may not exclude all liability by an expression such as "as is," "with all faults," "no guarantee given," or "no responsibility undertaken." For reasons of public policy, contractual limitation of liability or disclaimer of liability is subordinated where personal injury is involved. These clauses are construed by the courts with a heavy bias against the proponent.

One cannot have it both ways— to act as if one were in commerce and at the same time not be governed by the principles of the commercial world. Much, very much, of the assault on the health professionals, comes out of hostility engendered by the fee.

On the other hand, one tends not to look a gift horse in the mouth. The charitable institution such as the hospital traditionally enjoyed immunity from suit, which only disappeared when charity evolved into a big business which could be covered by insurance. Dr. Alex Munthe (32) a generation ago urged physicians not to charge fees.* Munthe argued that his profession was a holy office on the same level as that of the priest, if not higher, where money making should be forbidden by law. Those who want to charge fees, he argued, should leave the profession and go on the stock exchange or open a shop. "The doctors should walk about like sages honored and protected by all men," he said. "They should not count their visits or write any bills. . . . What [is] the proper fee for taking the fear of death out of a pair of terror-stricken eyes by a comforting word or a mere stroke of your hand? . . . Our profession [is] not a trade but an art, this trafficking in suffering [is] a humiliation to me."

The healer, were he to follow Munthe's advice, would again be esteemed in the public eye, and he would not likely be sued. Indeed, on the assumption that no one wants something for nothing, donations would probably be given out of gratitude. History confirms this. In ancient times, people

---

* Is that possible, even theoretically, in the case of psychotherapy? Agreeing on a fee and paying it is called one of "the ethics of psychoanalysis," one of its cornerstones (33). The Talmud too says, "Free cures seldom work." But that view may be more fancy (more self-serving) than fact, and has been repudiated not only by history but also by those who have looked at the issue with an empirical eye (34-36).

who came for cures in the sanctuaries dedicated to Aesculapius, the God whose name became the symbol of the perfect physician, left immense numbers of offerings in gratitude.

Actually, consent theory puts the fee into question. In Roman times healers and doctors were "permitted to receive only what those whom they have cured offer for their service, and not what they, when in danger, may have promised for restitution to health" (37). This dictum was based on the assumption that a sick man, influenced by fears related to his illness and its consequences, could not make a free and voluntary agreement as to payment. Thus it was stipulated that a promise relating to the healer's fees made in a moment of fear was not enforceable; the healer seeking payment could contract with his patient only when he had been cured and was out of danger. Cujacius, the French jurist, said a contract with a sick patient was in any case contrary to the Hippocratic oath. In the late seventeenth century the Dutch jurist Johannes Voet argued that not every doctor should be presumed to have used undue influence to induce his patient to contract with him to his detriment. He argued it was entirely a matter of proof (38, 39).

Gradually, the fee replaced the honorarium, and with it, came a different attitude toward the healer. Saddle sores were the chief occupational hazard of the frontier physician; today's healer, on the other hand, like the businessman, is exposed to the lawsuit. Why not? If the healer acts like a businessman, then he must expect to be measured by the laws of commerce.

In today's world, fee-for-services may produce the best care — that is not under discussion here — the point is that the fiduciary system, in which a patient relied on the professional's sense of ethics, is being replaced by a contractual system. And what is said in the commercial world applies as well in the health field. Chambers of Commerce advise businesses that they can revive confidence by insisting on better standards, honest and reliable information about goods and services, honest guarantees, and a worthwhile aftersales and complaints procedure. The customer is always right — "We return your money if not satisfied."

Increasingly, health care professionals will have to define their methods and results to the consuming public. In additon to the courts, labor unions and health insurers are beginning to examine the results of the psychiatric therapies with understandable concern about the return on the insurance dollar. And just as the public is entitled to full disclosure about a product, it is entitled to know about the healer — his successes, his failures, his type of work. Generally the public is able, if at all, to evaluate a professional only by the diplomas and certificates which adorn his office wall (whatever they may be worth) or by the usually uninformed recommendation of a friend. In the case of the legal profession, its Code of Professional Responsibility speaks of the "need to inform the public of the availability of competent, independent legal counsel" (40), but the public for the most part is in the dark. There is a directory (Martindale-Hubbell) that rates lawyers and lists selected clients to indicate the nature of their work; it is available in law libraries, but it is used mainly only by lawyers seeking out-of-town collaboration. In the selection of a healer, the professional knows where to go for his own care, or for that of his family, but it is inside information, which it may be noted, is frowned upon in the sale of securities. A data bank might store information concerning psychotherapists, what they do, how they do it, what they charge, how long they take, and who (by profession) consults them. Ralph Nader's group has made efforts in this direction.*

* The Public Citizens Health Research Group in Washington predicts that consumer involvement in medical services will lead to disclosure of such data as doctors' fees and qualifications (41). Following the U.S. Supreme Court's decision in *Goldfarb v. Virginia State Bar* (42), which held that the legal profession was not exempt from the antitrust laws, the Standing Committee on Ethics and Professional Responsibility of the

CONCLUSION

The law sometimes clothes policy decisions in dress that fits badly, but the doctrine of informed consent or *volenti* is a particularly bad fit. The core of the legal concept of consent is not an epistemological demand, though it may appear to be so, and thus is misleading. The law is expected to indicate to the subject, the healer in this case, what his rights and obligations are. To be sure, it cannot always do that with certainty, but it falls far short of that when the practitioner learns only in court, after litigation, where he stands. Where mystery begins, observed Burke, justice ends.

Given judicial regulation, and given a choice between tort and contract, the nod is to the latter. "Suit the action to the word, the word to the action," said Shakespeare in *Hamlet* (Act III, sc. 2). To try to achieve regulation via the tort suit, to embark on an inquiry into consent or *volenti* is devious and distorts the issue through false emphasis. And in the case of the talking therapies, the tort track is wholly inadequate as a judicial regulatory device.

Taking the informed-consent doctrine to heart, and seeking to avoid liability, the medical practitioner either avoids the irascible patient or resorts to wordy, ritualistic disclosures. These disclosures are not informative; they are self-serving; they are not designed to serve the best interests of the patient. In reality, when people are in distress, as they are when they are ill, they are not very receptive to information, they are not in an autonomous position, and they often have to be helped by magic.

The tort theory of informed consent is a form of

American Bar Association proposed a substantial liberalization of lawyer advertising. Like other advertising, it bears the danger of deceit. The Judicial Council of the American Medical Association advises that the public is entitled to know the names of physicians, the type of their practices, the location of their offices, their office hours, and "other useful information that will enable people to make a more informed choice of physician" (43).

utilitarianism which has served its day. For a judicial regulatory device, the contract theory will likely replace it, providing new focus (44). Apart from matters of venue, joinder, statute of limitations, measure of damages, and defenses, it will encourage a new way of thinking about the problem, and as best as one can speculate, it will provide a fairer (albeit imperfect) judicial technique in the regulation of the healing arts.*

REFERENCES

1. Senate Subcommittee on Executive Reorganization, 91st Congress, 1st Sess., 2-5, 447-451. *Medical Malpractice: The Patient Versus the Physician.* Washington, D.C.: U.S. Government Printing Office, 1969.
2. King, J. H. In search of a standard of care for the medical profession: The "accepted practice" formula. *Vanderbilt Law Rev.,* 28:1213, 1975.
3. Prosser, W. L., Wade, J. W., & Schwartz, V. E. *Cases and Materials on Torts.* Mineola, N.Y.: Foundation Press, 1976, p. xvii.
4. Belli, M. An ancient therapy still applied: The silent medical treatment. *Villanova Law Rev.,* 1:250, 1956.
5. Kayajanian, P. Confronting the conspiracy of silence: We have the tiger by the tail. *U. West L.A. Law Rev.,* 6:40, 1974.
6. Note. Overcoming the "conspiracy of silence": Statutory and common law innovations. *Minn. Law Rev.,* 45:1019, 1961.
7. *Canterbury v. Spence.* 464 F.2d 772, at 782 n. 27 (D.C. Cir. 1972).
8. *ZeBarth v. Swedish Hospital Medical Center.* 81 Wash. 2d 12, 499 P. 2d 1, at 9 (1972).
9. *Canterbury v. Spence.* 464 F.2d 772 (D.C. Cir. 1972).
10. *Parkinson, J. A Manual of English for the Overseas Doctor.* 1976.
11. *Rompel v. Botha.* T.P.D. (South Africa) April 15, 1953. Noted in: Colman, G. The patient's consent—its legal effects. *Med. Proceed.,* 8: 124, 1958.
12. *McDonald v. Moore.* 323 So. 2d 635 (Fla. 1975).
13. *Love v. Wolf.* 226 Cal. App. 2d 378, 38 Cal. Rptr. 183 (1964).
14. Slovenko, R. On psychosurgery. *Hastings Center Report,* Oct. 1975, p. 19.

* An even more effective approach seems to be a nonlegal, informal one such as the newspaper "action line" where people with problems in dealing with agencies contact the "action line" and the newspaper works out a negotiated solution (19, 45).

15. *New York City Health and Hospital Corporation v. Stein.* 70 Misc. 2d 944, 335 N.Y.S.2d 461 (1972).
16. *Cobbs v. Grant.* 8 Cal. 3d 229, 104 Cal. Rptr. 505, 502 P. 2d 1 (1972).
17. Psychotherapy: Legitimate therapy or laundered lobotomy? *Science,* March 16, 1973, p. 1109.
18. *Detroit News,* April 5, 1973, p. 1.
19. Slovenko, R. *Psychiatry and Law.* Boston: Little, Brown, 1973.
20. *Covington v. Harris.* 419 F.2d 617 at 621-622 (D.C. Cir. 1969).
21. *United States v. Klein.* 325 F.2d 283 (2d Cir. 1963).
22. *Tribby v. Cameron.* 379 F.2d 104 at 105 (D.C. Cir. 1967).
23. Schmideberg, M., with Shapiro, J. Does psychotherapy help or harm? *Good Housekeeping* (England), Nov. 1975, p. 72.
24. Fleming, J. G. *An Introduction to the Law of Torts.* Oxford: Clarendon Press, 1967, p. 143.
25. *Guilmet v. Campbell.* 385 Mich. 57, 188 N.W.2d 801 (1971).
26. Miller, A. J. The contractual liability of physicians and surgeons. *Wash. U. Law Quart.,* 1953:413, 1953.
27. Tierney, K. Contractual aspects of malpractice. *Wayne Law Rev.,* 19: 1457, 1973.
28. Annot. 43 A.L.R.3d 1221 (1972).
29. *Observer* (London). March 14, 1976, p. 10.
30. *Daily News* (Durban, South Africa). April 27, 1976, p. 3.
31. *Natal Mercury* (South Africa). April 21, 1976, p. 5.
32. Munthe, A. *The Story of San Michele.* London: Murray, 1929.
33. Szasz, T. *The Ethics of Psychoanalysis.* New York: Basic Books, 1965.
34. Adams, W. J. Clients, counselors, and fee-ingredients of a myth? *Family Coord.,* 17:288, 1968.
35. Hilles, L. The clinical management of the nonpaying patient. *Bull. Menninger Clinic,* 35:98, 1971.
36. Tievano, J. Observations about payment of psychotherapy fees. *Psychiat. Quart.,* 41:324, 1967.
37. Corpus Juris Civilis 10.52.9.
38. Jourbet, D. J. Contracts between doctors and patients. *South African Law J.,* 86:290, 1969.
39. Klass, A. A. What is a profession? *Prof. Engineer & Engineering Dig.,* March 1962, p. 17.
40. Revised Ethical Consideration E.C. 2-8.
41. Special report. The troubled professions. *Bus. Week,* Aug. 16, 1976, p. 126.
42. *Goldfarb v. Virginia State Bar.* 421 U.S. 773 (1975).
43. Physician advertising. *Psychiat. News,* Sept. 3, 1976, p. 31.
44. Epstein, R. A. Medical malpractice: The case for contract. *Amer. Bar Foundation Res. J.,* 1:87, 1976.
45. Slovenko, R. Regulation of the healing arts with particular reference to psychotherapy. Unpublished.

Chapter IV

Informed Consent of Mental Patients

HENRY H. FOSTER, JR., J.D., L.L.M.

"Informed consent" may become a major issue in malpractice litigation involving an alleged abridgment of the rights of mental patients. The issue may arise with regard to the admission, treatment, or release of such patients, but due to the paucity of court decisions and statutes, it is difficult, if not impossible, to state what the law is with certainty. Moreover, the law on informed consent by competent patients is undergoing such change and development that properly it must be considered to embody tentative rather than fixed principles (see 1-6).

The source of the uncertainty in this area of law is the conflict between significant public policies and the difficulty of effecting a workable and fair compromise. On the highest level of abstraction is the clash between the individual's right to freedom, autonomy, and personal choice, and the physician's professional duty to heal and cure. Some may view this as a conflict between self-determination and benevolent paternalism. On a lower level of abstraction, however, the problem may become one of reasonable professional behavior in communicating with patients.

At the outset physicians, therapists, and institutional authorities should be cautioned that the protective device of legal forms releasing the medical profession from liability or stating that the patient gives an "informed consent" to stipulated general or detailed procedures are of limited and doubtful efficacy.* The wide gulf between the professional's knowledge and experience and that of the lay person ordinarily places them in unequal bargaining positions, so that there is no "give and take," such as occurs in business contracts. Moreover, the patient may be *in extremis*, overwhelmed by medical control, and in no position to exercise independent judgment. Experienced trial lawyers are adept at overcoming the obstacle of tightly or loosely drawn releases and tend to regard them as minor irritants, if not with disdain (12).

Before considering the specific problem of the "informed consent" of mental patients, it is necessary to summarize the current state of flux with reference to informed consent generally. The following sketch merely hits the highlights and does not purport to cover all aspects of the problem.

DEVELOPMENT OF THE DOCTRINE OF INFORMED CONSENT

Anglo-American law, what we call the common law, has always been characterized by its emphasis on individual rights. It is fair to say that it is highly individualistic, at least with regard to the private rights and duties of citizens. Although there are instances where the public interest supersedes private rights (e.g., the law of eminent domain), and such has always been the case, generally there must be legal justification for a denigration of private rights.

In the case of bodily integrity, the tort law pertaining to assault and battery protects the individual from physical inter-

---

* For examples of recommended forms, see Mills (4) and Laforet (7) for humorous examples. For decisions holding releases invalid, see 8-11.

ferences deemed to be unauthorized or offensive (13). Proof of actual damage or injury to the person is not an essential ingredient of this intentional tort. For example, spitting on a person (14, 15) or "sneaking a feel" (16) is a battery unless there was consent to the contact. The "quality of the touch" may be important, as where a physician has a patient disrobe and submit to examination for personal rather than professional reasons. (In such instances, the ulterior purpose vitiates ostensible consent and the common law doctrine of *volenti non fit injuria* is inapplicable [17-19]).

The tort law pertaining to battery has been applied to the medical setting in cases not involving lust or voyeurism. Malpractice may consist of what has loosely been called "human experimentation," where a given treatment or procedure is regarded by the profession as rash and foolhardy (20, 21). In such cases, the fact that the patient did not protest, or went along with the doctor's advice, is no defense. If the patient dies, a criminal prosecution for murder or manslaughter may be warranted (22).

The modern doctrine of informed consent commenced in 1905 with the Minnesota case of *Mohr v. Williams* (23). A surgeon, who had permission to operate on the patient's right ear, instead operated on her left ear because it was in greater need of immediate attention. The patient lost her hearing because of the operation. In her suit she did not allege negligence and was granted recovery because of the lack of consent to surgery on the left ear, on the theory that since there was no consent, the operation was a battery.

Although the case of Anna Mohr involved *no* consent, rather than uninformed consent, it established the concept that the patient rather than the doctor should have the choice as to physical interference with her person.* Later Justice

---

* See also *Bang v. Charles T. Miller Hospital* (24), where liability was imposed for a battery because the surgeon did not tell the patient his

Cardozo, in oft-quoted language, expressed the principle of physical integrity and self-determination by stating that "a person has a right to determine what will be done with his own body" (29).

These early malpractice cases, however, did not directly involve the issue of informed consent. The latter problem came to the fore in two decisions rendered in 1957 and 1960. California in *Salgo v. Leland Stanford, Jr. University Board of Trustees* (30), sustained tort liability where the physician failed to inform the patient of the risks and benefits involved when he consented to aortography. As a result of the procedure, the patient became paralyzed from the waist down. The court imposed on the doctor and/or hospital the duty to inform the patient of the risks, consequences, and benefits of the proposed procedure, alternative procedures, and the probable consequences of no treatment. The duty, said the court, was not to explain to the patient every risk, but rather to recognize that each patient presents a separate problem, that *the patient's mental and emotional condition is important*, and that a certain amount of discretion must be employed in communicating the risks, consistent with the full disclosure of facts necessary to an informed consent.

Kansas in 1960 handed down its decision in *Nathanson v. Kline* (31), the case usually cited as initiating the doctrine of

---

spermatic cords would be cut during the agreed-upon transurethral prostatic resection. Compare also situations where the doctor is guilty of an affirmative misrepresentation or lies to the patient regarding collateral risks (see 25). For example, in *Corn v. French* (26), the doctor said he was going to perform a test only and instead, contrary to the patient's express directions, performed a mastectomy; in *Gray v. Grunagle* (27) the surgeon exceeded the patient's consent to an "exploratory" operation; in *Paulsen v. Gunderson* (28) the patient consented to a "simple" mastoid operation, but not to a "radical" one. Such cases are distinguishable from the failure-to-inform cases and properly may be regarded as based on assault and battery. In effect in such cases the patient was misled as to the nature and character of the intended procedure to which he was being asked to consent.

informed consent.* The plaintiff was suffering from breast cancer and underwent a radical mastectomy followed by cobalt treatments. Although the patient alleged negligence in that excessive dosages were used, that count in her action was dismissed. The court also rejected an approach in terms of the tort of battery and instead adopted the rationale of the 1957 decision of California in the *Salgo* case. In other words, negligence in failing to inform the patient of possible risks or side effects was the basis for tort liability, and the standard imposed in determining such negligence was "deviation from the standard of conduct of a reasonable and prudent medical doctor of the same school of practice as the defendant under similar circumstances."

Thus, both the California and Kansas courts predicated liability on general negligence theories plus a tailor-made standard of care which referred to a reasonable and prudent doctor rather than to a reasonable man or a reasonable patient. In large measure, the medical profession itself, more precisely, the doctors of the particular community, set the standard for communicating risks and benefits to patients. This is to be contrasted with the Minnesota position in *Mohr v. Williams*, where a technical battery was made out if the particular operation was not authorized by the patient, without regard to standard medical practice. In *Mohr* the patient's consent was indispensable; in *Salgo* and *Nathanson*, the patient's consent to undergo a collateral risk was unnecessary if local doctors would not seek to obtain it. Moreover, expert medical testimony was necessary for a

* At about the same time *Nathanson* was under consideration, Missouri decided *Mitchell v. Robinson* (32), which involved a claim against a psychiatrist for not having informed a patient of the collateral risk of injury (fractured vertebrae) during insulin shock treatment. The court held that there was a duty to warn of such hazard and that it was a jury question whether or not such warning had in fact been given. The opinion also suggested that expert testimony was not necessary to establish whether or not the doctor had complied with his duty to advise the patient of the hazard.

plaintiff to establish his case under the latter rule, but not the former — a matter of great practical importance in many jurisdictions (33).

Thus, since 1957, there have been competing theories as to the basis for malpractice liability where there is no consent or a failure to communicate to the patient sufficient information for an informed decision. In addition, several more recent decisions have rejected the medical model for standard of care adopted in *Salgo* and *Nathanson*. Instead of referring to local medical practice, the new model is the reasonably prudent patient. The argument is that the patient has a right to know the risks inherent in a specific procedure, and that right should not be based on standard medical practice. In order to give substance to the common law principle of self-determination, the law itself must set the standard for communication, and "the patient's right of self-decision shapes the boundaries of the duty to reveal" (34). Various courts (34-37) have adopted a "patient's right to know" approach.* It is likely that this view will prevail.

The important practical difference between the two views of determining the standard of care relates to requirements of

---

* In a New York case, *Fogel v. Genesee Hospital* (36), the court held that the doctor's duty to disclose known dangers of proposed treatment was governed by general standards of reasonable conduct and not those of the profession. However, New York Public Health Law sec. 2805-d states: "Lack of informed consent means the failure of the person providing professional treatment or diagnosis to disclose to the patient such alternatives thereto and the reasonably foreseeable risks and benefits involved *as a reasonable medical practitioner* under similar circumstances would have disclosed" (emphasis supplied). In effect, the legislature reversed the holding in *Fogel*.

Another case rejecting current medical practice as the standard of care, *Scaria v. St. Paul Fire & Marine Ins. Co.* (38), is discussed at length by Schneyer (3). Schneyer also cites a HEW report to the effect that "Of 72 appellate cases in the United States between 1950 and 1971 in which informed consent was the 'most significant issue,' 20.8% were won by patients at trial but 37.5% were won by patients on appeal," and that for the 1961-1971 period, "the corresponding figures were 21.1% and 47.4% respectively" (p. 142).

proof. If the standard is customary medical practice in the community or generally, expert witnesses will be needed to establish the plaintiff's case. If the standard is what a reasonable patient is entitled to know, such expert testimony is unnecessary, although it may be needed otherwise to establish proximate cause in an action claiming negligence (39).

In all probability the medical profession as a whole is unaware of the special status it has enjoyed with reference to tort liability. In a sense, historically the law has given the profession a subsidy in formulating the rules as to malpractice. Until recently, an injured patient could not prove his case without the aid of other doctors who appeared as expert witnesses. Such expert testimony was essential to establish a breach of the duty of care and causation as well as proximate cause.* Contrast the situation where a doctor or lawyer has a traffic accident. There the standard of care is that of a reasonable man; it is not tailor-made, i.e., the profession does not set its own standards. The result has been that liability is more certain where the professional man is careless in driving his car or a golf ball than where he drives the patient to an early grave. Since the professions have become more affluent, and malpractice insurance common (albeit at exorbitant cost), it is understandable that an avowed classless society would eliminate special subsidies and privileges for the professions. This does not mean, however, that the economics of malpractice liability do not call for statutory recognition or that other limitations on liability may not be needed in order to secure both the welfare of patients and professional responsibility.

Thus far we have been discussing general rules without

* The volume of malpractice cases has increased in part due to the doctrine of *res ipsa loquitur*, which may dispense with the need for expert testimony on the issue of negligence. Expert testimony may, however, be necessary to establish the standard of care in the professional community or to prove causation in fact or proximate cause. See Louisell and Williams (40).

regard to exceptions or qualifications. As Paul Freund once observed in connection with another problem, legal principles march in battalions, rather than single file (see Foster [41] for a discussion of interprofessional problems). Although it may be distressing or disconcerting to nonlawyers, law men are accustomed to rules, exceptions, and qualifications. Both the battery basis for malpractice liability and the negligence theory have relevant exceptions.

As previously mentioned, the public interest may justify an interference with an individual's physical integrity. For example, suicide and attempted suicide were crimes at common law, compulsory vaccination has been upheld as constitutional, some states have ordered blood transfusions for Jehovah's Witnesses, and the care or protection of minors and incompetents comes under the *parens patriae* power of government. This is not to say that there are no constitutional limitations on public authority, but merely that in some important circumstances private rights must give way to a legitimate public interest, even in a democratic society.

With reference to the individual's right to bodily integrity and to freedom from unpermitted touchings, the law has recognized that a certain amount of contact is inevitable in the crowded conditions of urban life. Thus, some jostling is to be expected on a crowded bus, subway, or elevator, not to mention at the bargain counter, and such is not a battery unless it exceeds reasonable bounds.* Moreover, a parent, teacher, or other who stands in loco parentis, usually has a privilege to commit what otherwise would be a battery on a

---

* See Prosser (42). There may also be "implied consent," as when a patient without objection holds up his arm to be vaccinated and a reasonable person would speak if he objected. "Proxy consent," another form of implied consent, exists where a guardian, parent, or spouse gives the consent on behalf of a person who lacks capacity to consent because of infancy or mental incompetence. Still another form of implied consent is where a court orders intervention.

minor for the sake of discipline, although there may be liability for the use of excessive force. There also is the privilege of self-defense, which again is forfeited if excessive. What these examples have in common is the backing of public policy to justify exceptions to the usual rule.

In accordance with general common law principles, the law pertaining to malpractice and tort liability of doctors recognizes two major exceptions based on public policy. In the case of a minor, the general rule is that he is incapable of giving a legally effective consent and that to be legally valid there must be consent to the medical procedure from his parent or guardian (43). Although this rule currently is being called into question, and some states now require consent by the minor as well as the parent (44), the general rule has always been subject to exceptions. Such exceptions include the emergency doctrine (45), the emancipated minor situation (43), and the "mature minor" exception (46). In the case of mental incompetents, legal consent to their treatment customarily has been obtained from guardians or relatives, or implied by law (47).

In general, in an emergency situation the law does not require a delay to obtain consent for appropriate procedure (45). An emergency ward need not wait until an unconscious traffic victim regains consciousness before undertaking emergency treatment to save his life. The law implies his consent, i.e., authorizes the emergency ward to go ahead without regard to consent. To fail to do so, probably would be negligence. The same is true for an injured minor where there is no time to contact the parents (45). As long as the procedure is for the patient's own benefit, it is privileged (43). In *Crouch v. Most* (48), the plaintiff was taken to a hospital after being bitten by a rattlesnake. He was given an "antivenom" as an antidote, but was not warned of the danger of gangrene from the drug. Gangrene developed and the patient's hand was amputated. The court held that the doctrine of implied consent did not apply to *emergency* conditions and that since the plaintiff was in no condition to determine any course of treatment and could in no way give consent, it would have been useless for the doctor to discuss alternatives in an effort to obtain his informed consent.

The legal context for discussion of informed consent by mental patients consists of the general rule of freedom from physical interference plus the exceptions above described. However, as long as it is conceded that mental patients differ from others, such differences may justify a departure from general principles.

Is the Doctrine of Informed Consent Applicable?

We may start with the premise that the law requires consent for the admission, treatment, and perhaps even the release of mental patients. However, such consent may be that of the patient, his guardian or next of kin, or it may be implied by law in emergency situations. Admittedly, "implied consent" is a fiction, and really means that there are considerations of public policy that outweigh individual choice.

It is also important to note at the outset that individual patients differ tremendously with regard to their capacity to make rational judgments. If an apparently mentally ill patient is sufficiently competent to make an informed decision, then a strong case must be made for depriving him of his freedom of choice. Common law, if not constitutional principles, at a minimum requires such autonomy.* Moreover, the mental

---

* Prosser (49) notes that in *Pratt v. Davis* (43) "the consent of the husband was held to be required for an operation on an insane wife. But where the patient is competent to consent, and does so, consent of the spouse is not required." He also says that if the patient is competent, the spouse's consent is ineffective, as in *Gravis v. Physician's & Surgeon's Hospital* (51). Compare this situation with the decision in regard to an abortion (52), where it was held that a Missouri statute was unconstitutional in requiring parental consent for a minor's abortion, and further that the husband's consent to his wife's abortion could not be required.

health profession now recognizes this freedom of choice in its emphasis on informal or voluntary admissions as distinguished from commitments.

The most obvious example of a possible exception to the usual rule of voluntary admission may be subsumed under the head of emergency situations. A patient with a severe depression who is suicidal may or may not be regarded as capable of making a rational decision. With regard to business or other matters he may be in control of his faculties. This does not mean, however, that his decision as to life or death is "rational." With medication and treatment his decision may change in a matter of days or weeks. In effect, he may happily ratify the medical decision. Although extreme civil libertarians may sincerely believe that a severely depressed person has an absolute right to commit suicide without interference by others,* including the medical profession, such a position is neither humane nor practical. Moreover, it ignores the legal basis for autonomy, namely an ability to make a rational decision. And the would-be suicide's decision, without intervention, may be irreversible. The drastic and final character of the alternative legally justifies the intervention.

At the other end of the spectrum are patients who are so confused about everything that the emergency doctrine clearly applies. In their case, consent to hospitalization or treatment may readily be implied by law, or the consent of a guardian or next of kin may suffice in lieu of the patient's consent. Under common law principles, the only problem is whether or not the patient has reached such level of incompetence that his individual consent is dispensed with.

In a sense, what is here advocated is that all patients (mental and otherwise) capable of rational decision should be treated the same and that the rule and the exceptions also

---

* See Ennis and Litwack (53) and Szasz (54). Compare also *Kennedy Memorial Hospital v. Heston* (55), where Chief Justice Weintaub said: "It seems correct to say there is no constitutional right to choose to die."

should apply equally to mental and other patients. The individual consent of the patient should normally be required except in emergency situations, but emergency should be defined as including the situation where the patient is unconscious or out of touch with reality and, further, at least in the case of the mental patient, is incapable of making a rational decision. Moreover, in such cases, if consent is deemed necessary, a "proxy consent" may suffice where it is obtained from a parent, spouse, or close relative.

Despite the above attempt to correlate rules and exceptions regarding mental patients and general patients, it must be conceded that there are considerations they do not ordinarily share in common. A particular mental illness may be such that by professional standards it is unwise to communicate the risk-benefit ratio which the law of informed consent contemplates. If such is the case, the professional standard of the community rather than that of a hypothetical reasonable patient should apply. Otherwise there would be a conflict between the legal duty to communicate the hazards and good therapy. This does not mean, however, that the patient has no right to refuse a particular course of treatment. Recent cases indicate that indeed he may have such a right (see 56-58). Rather, what is meant is that on the issue of *informed* consent, as distinguished from consent in general, the exception noted in the *Salgo* case should apply and the therapist should not be required to communicate detailed information which may be detrimental to the patient's progress and recovery.

There has been relatively little research into the problem of mental patients' capacity to make informed judgments. A study of 100 cases of "voluntary" admissions by Olin and Olin (59) reports that only eight mental patients were fully informed of the contract at the time of admission to a Massachusetts hospital. Upon admission, they were offered a choice between voluntary or involuntary patient status. The vast majority (92 out of 100) did not understand or comprehend the terms of admission or the alternatives. The report concluded that this vast majority did not or could not act on their own behalf in a fully autonomous manner. Of course, the breakdown in communication may have been due in part to the language on the forms or lack of communication skills by those at admissions, but the report stresses the inability of mental patients at admission to make rational decisions. In a state such as New York, presumably the Mental Health Information Service would compensate for such a breakdown in communication (see Rosenzweig [60]).

An earlier study, in 1942, undertook to find out whether or not mental patients knew what they were doing when they signed voluntary admission forms (61). The sample included 40 mental patients at a Toledo hospital who had signed three forms upon admission. The patients were questioned about their recall of the contents of the forms. If they had no recall, they were handed a copy of the forms to read, or the interviewer read them aloud. The interviews took place within one to ten days of admission. Twelve of the patients could not remember signing the forms; of the 28 who did recall signing them, 23 could not recall their provisions, four recalled part of the content, and only one person gave the substance of the forms from memory. Of those who had their memories refreshed at the interview, none were able immediately afterward to recall all of the three key provisions. The report concluded that patients had a minimal comprehension of the terms of admission, were disturbed, confused, and frightened, and further that the institutional procedures for explaining the terms of admission were inadequate.

The above two studies, meager as they are, indicate that special procedures must be undertaken at admission if there is to be meaningful informed consent by mental patients to "voluntary" admission. As suggested above, the Mental Health Information Service may be the most practical way of safeguarding the patient's interests upon admission, but, in addition, it seems clear that facilities for mental patients have an obligation to unclog the channels of communication so that where possible the patient receives a clear understanding of his status and alternatives. The patient's confusion and fear at admission requires special effort in this regard, rather than a cynical attitude that all attempts at communication will be futile. Ordinarily, an explanation would be reassuring rather than damaging to the patient and should reduce the apprehension of many patients that they will never get out of a mental hospital. Unless there is a responsible concern over the communication problem, "voluntary" is a misnomer when applied to the admission procedure.

In addition to a conscientious admission procedure, and a follow-up by the Mental Health Information Service or its equivalent, a further protection of the patient's rights is accorded under the law of many if not most states in that a court hearing (and often a jury trial) may be had as a matter of right if the patient demands it or his classification as a voluntary patient is changed to "involuntary" (62). Insofar as "consent" is concerned, a valid court order dispenses with any need for an informed consent to institutionalization. The constitutional issue, if any, is whether or not there was justification for the exercise of *parens patriae* or police power under the facts of the particular case, a matter outside the scope of this discussion.*

To summarize, the meager authorities extant indicate that the doctrine of informed consent has limited application to informal or voluntary admissions, and no application to involuntary admissions. The doctrine may provide a gloss for construing the legal meaning of "voluntary." Existing practice

* *O'Connor v. Donaldson* (63) left many issues up in the air, but it seems reasonably clear that involuntary commitment is constitutional if treatment is given and the patient is deemed incapable of living in the community.

is to make an effort at explaining the patient's rights and the procedure upon admission, but it seems probable that this is often done in a perfunctory manner. Although a Mental Health Information Service or the right to a hearing may atone for poor communication at admission, nonetheless measures should be taken to ensure that "voluntary" is related to the patient's volition. In the case of a patient's right to treatment, or to refuse treatment, informed consent is again legally significant.

A rule may be developing that a patient who is deemed to be competent to consent to a course of treatment also has the right to reject at least some alternatives (56-58) and is perhaps entitled to opt for the least restrictive alternative (64). If he does not have such competence, then his consent may be dispensed with and implied by law, as for example under the emergency doctrine. Informed consent in this context means that the relative risks and benefits of particular courses of treatment must be explained to him unless under an "emergency" theory such an explanation would be detrimental to his mental health. Although these parameters seem to be fairly clear, great uncertainty remains on the judgment to be made as to a particular case. Probably the emergency exception will bolster the medical decision in that regard, since ordinarily it is difficult to reject a medical opinion that full disclosure would be detrimental to the particular patient.

With reference to the release of a mental patient, informed consent has no direct bearing, but may come into issue if the patient is being held on a voluntary basis and a dispute arises as to whether or not he understood the terms of admission. The main and at times crucial issue, which I have studiously avoided out of deference to psychiatric authority, is that of when a particular patient has legal competence to make a meaningful decision or choice. Although ultimately a court may be called upon to decide that issue, hopefully it will be after hearing the medical evidence. Probably the law will narrow the issue of competence, as it has done so often in the civil law area,* by pinning competence to the particular function, and it may presume competence and place the burden of proof to the contrary on the party who disputes such competence.

In substance, the legal test of whether there was an "informed consent" at the time of admission so that such admission was "voluntary" probably would be the patient's capacity *at that time* to understand and appreciate the nature and consequences of the admission, to make a rational decision, and to communicate such decision to admission personnel.** In other words, it would be comparable to the test applied by civil law regarding capacity to enter into a contract, or to make a will, and would be closer to the test of competency to stand trial than to the criminal law test of insanity. The legal issue, however, is not reasonableness of conduct, but what was agreed to and understood by the parties, and in resolving that issue there may be a "substituted judgment" arrived at on a subjective basis in determining what the person would have decided if he were competent.***

CONCLUSION

Although the law wisely has shied away from problems regarding motivation, and it has been authoritatively stated

---

* On testamentary capacity, see Brooks (65) and Note (66). On contractual capacity, see *Faber v. Sweet Style Manufacturing Corporation* (67) and *Fingerhut v. Kralyn Enterprises* (68). On capacity to marry, see *Fischer v. Adams* (69).

** See *In re Buttonow* (70), and for a critique of the coercive character of many so-called voluntary admissions, see Brooks (71) and Gilboy and Schmidt (72).

*** See *City Bank Farmers Trust Co. v. McGowan* (73), *In re Guardianship of Brice* (74), and *In re Fagler* (75).

that "The Devil himself knoweth not the thought of man,"* there are exceptions to such forbearance. The doctrine of informed consent as applied to mental patients may imperil this ancient wisdom and cast the doctor in the role of a Devil who has been educated and no longer is unknowing. The law may also diminish its wisdom by the use of fictions and presumptions. For example, a well-known presumption is that a man intended the natural and probable consequences of his action. This presumption may hold even in the face of strong evidence that the person in question did not desire to bring about the particular consequence.

The ultimate problem is that of reconciling the patient's wishes, and his individual freedom and autonomy, with his mental health needs as professionally perceived. In the past the medical profession, at least in some instances, has acted paternalistically and automatically placed needs over wishes. Times are changing and participation in decision making is now regarded as a significant value. The divergence between the patient's and the doctor's point of view is illustrated by the situation of terminal patients: probably most doctors do not disclose such information to patients, although most patients claim they would prefer to get such information.

Participation in decision making today is part of the democratic process. Such socially important matters as abortion entail such a process. An attitude that father or doctor knows best, is no longer persuasive. It is therefore safe to assume that the doctrine of informed consent will be extended rather than diminished. In the larger sense, this is but legal reinforcement of the respect due every man as an autonomous individual. Freedom of choice is what democracy is all about and the fact that often such freedom will prove illusory does not detract from the ideal. That the choice may be

---

* Pollock and Maitland (76) attribute the remark to Chief Justice Brian, an English judge in the Middle Ages.

predetermined is another matter, which I leave to my betters in psychiatry and philosophy.*

In addition to the patient's right to participate in medical decisions affecting his welfare, there is the ubiquitous problem of poor communicaton between physician and patient. Poor communication leads to misunderstanding which frequently triggers off malpractice actions.** All too often the medical model of the "good patient" has been the obedient child who for his own good does what he is told to do. Apparently, psychiatrists have a better record in this regard than do surgeons or diagnosticians,*** but the fact remains that medical education and the customs and practices of the medical profession are conducive to an authoritarian attitude toward patients (87). Surveys of patients' complaints regarding their medical care stress the paternalistic if not authoritarian role played by the doctor.

Even if there is a two-way relationship between physician and patient and the lines of communication are open, the doctor generally is in control in the decision-making process. As an authority figure the doctor commands respect and more.

---

* One of the most provocative discussions on free will versus determinism as it relates to criminal justice is that by Roche (77).

** See Schneyer (3) who cites Waitzkin and Waterman (78) as authority for the proposition that both American and British patients are more dissatisfied with the information they receive from their physicians than any other aspect of medical care. He also cites Duff and Hollingshead (79) as reporting that 50 percent of patient complaints about treatment at a university hospital related to doctor and staff communications involved "physician-patient communication failure." See also Alfidi (80) who claims that a large percentage of patients want full information, but compare Frost (81). See also Parsons (82) and Pratt et al. (83).

*** Schneyer (84) says: "The only medical specialty in which observers have frequently noted professional initiatives for broader disclosure of treatment information and more active patient participation in treatment decisions is psychiatry. The usual explanation for these developments in psychiatry is the direct therapeutic benefits of decision making itself for psychiatric patients." Schneyer cites Rosenthal (85) and Rogers (86).

Transference often occurs, and the patient is compliant. The situation may differ only in degree from the "station house syndrome" (88) that produces confessions from the amateur criminal, or the submissiveness of cultists to the guru (see, for example, Sanders [89] on the Charles Manson gang).

Because of the trust and confidence the patient usually places in his doctor, both medical ethics and the law impose a duty of loyalty to the patient. The clearest example of this is that a doctor who abandons a patient without having arranged for a suitable alternative may be liable for damage caused by the abandonment (90). Although not technically so, the physician is in the nature of a fiduciary who owes the highest duty of care to his patient. Such responsibility is one aspect of professionalism. Hence, it may be a betrayal of trust if the physician fails to treat his patient as an individual human being who is entitled to know the relevent medical facts and to participate in the decision as to the proper alternative course of treatment. The doctrine of informed consent reflects this duty of professional loyalty that is the correlate of the patient's trust and confidence.

To date the law has not imposed an absolute duty to inform the patient of everything, despite the hyperbole of some medical commentators (91). A detailed blueprint is not what the doctrine contemplates. Remote or improbable collateral side effects need not be communicated (92). Moreover, if the situation is such that it would be antitherapeutic to communicate information, silence may be golden (93). In substance, the doctrine of informed consent merely requires common professional courtesy and respect for human dignity. Whether or not such duty has been met most often is a jury question, and as we have seen the jury will be instructed either in terms of the profession's standard of care in that regard, or in terms of what a reasonable man was entitled to know before the doctor was entitled to go ahead. Finally, it must be remembered that the issue of informed consent is but one of the links in the plaintiff's case. In addition, he has the burden of proving injury and damages, causation, and proximate cause, if his case is based on negligence principles.

APPENDIX

DECLARATION OF INTERESTS AND RIGHTS OF PATIENTS*

1. No person shall be admitted to or retained in a medical facility as a patient unless:
    a. it is upon the informed consent of the patient; or
    b. in an emergency the law implies such consent; or
    c. upon court order.

2. Informed consent of a person for admission to and retention in a medical facility exists where he is aware of the relevant circumstances surrounding his admission or retention and the purposes thereof and either assents or raises no objection thereto.

3. The law implies consent of a person to *emergency* admission or retention in a medical facility for observation, care, and treatment, where his present condition is such that:
    a. it is reasonable to assume that if he were competent and able to make a rational decision he would give consent to such emergency admission or retention; or
    b. he presently is unable to control his impulsivity to inflict serious harm upon himself or others.

4. A person shall be admitted to or retained in a medical facility upon the lawful order of a court of competent jurisdiction.

5. A person admitted to or retained in a medical facility

---

* Prepared by Professor Henry H. Foster for the consideration of the Psychiatry and Law Committee of the American Psychiatric Association. This draft attempts to place mental patients on the same basis as other patients insofar as possible and also to reduce to a minimum the current judicial concern with dangerousness. As this is a draft for the committee, its final form may be changed.

for emergency observation, care, and treatment shall have the right to a court hearing within 72 hours after request to determine whether or not there is an emergency and if the law implies his consent to admission or retention. If the court finds that there is no emergency or consent implied by law the patient shall be discharged immediately or released upon such conditions as the court may direct. If the court finds that there is an emergency and an implied consent to the admission or retention, it shall order retention of the patient pending such commitment or certification hearing as is required by law.

6. A patient admitted to or retained in a medical facility has the right to and shall receive medically approved care and treatment. The patient's informed consent to a particular plan or course of treatment shall be required unless there is a court order or there is an emergency and his consent is implied by law. Informed consent to a particular plan or course of treatment exists if the patient has an understanding of the probable risks and benefits to him of the proposed plan or course of treatment and assents or raises no objection thereto.

7. A person shall have the right to counsel and independent medical opinion for any court hearing held pursuant to these principles, and if indigent, such counsel or independent medical opinion shall be provided for him at public expense.

8. A person admitted to or retained in a medical facility for *emergency* observation, care, and treatment shall receive notice of his rights under these principles, and where the family or a representative of the patient are known, reasonable efforts shall be made to so notify them of the patient's rights under these principles.

9. A patient retained in a medical facility without his informed consent shall have the right to periodic medical review of his case which shall be made at least at the end of every six-month period or before the end of any period stipulated by court order.

10. No medical facility nor any person involved in the

admission, retention, or treatment of a patient shall be held civilly or criminally liable because of his compliance in good faith with these principles.

REFERENCES

1. Plante, M. L. An analysis of "informed consent." *Fordham Law Rev.,* 36:639, 1968.
2. Alsobrook, H. B., Jr. Informed consent: A right to know. *J. La. State Med. Soc.,* 126:189, June 1974.
3. Schneyer, T. J. Informed consent and the danger of bias in the formation of medical disclosure practices. *Wis. Law Rev.,* 1976:124, 1976.
4. Mills, D. H. Whither informed consent? *JAMA,* 229:305, 1974.
5. Joling, R. J. Informed consent, confidentiality and privilege in psychiatry: Legal implications. *Bull. AAPL,* 2:107, 1974.
6. Note. Spare parts from incompetents: A problem of consent. *J. Family Law,* 9:309, 1970.
7. Laforet, G. G. The fiction of informed consent. *JAMA,* 235:1579, 1975.
8. *Tunkl v. Regents.* 60 Cal. 2d 92, 32 Cal Reptr. 33, 383 P.2d 441 (1963).
9. *Rogers v. Lumberman's Mutual Casualty Co.* 119 So. 2d 649 (La. App. 1960).
10. *French v. Ochsner Clinic.* 200 So. 2d 371 (La. App. 1967).
11. Annot. 6 A.L.R.3d 704 (1965).
12. Prosser, W. L. *Law of Torts,* 4th ed., 1971, p. 442.
13. Ibid., pp. 34-35 et seq.
14. *Alcorn v. Mitchell.* 63 Ill. 553 (1872).
15. *Draper v. Baker.* 61 Wis. 450, 21 N.W. 527 (1884).
16. Prosser, p. 37.
17. *Bartell v. State.* 106 Wis. 342, 82 N.W. 142 (1900).
18. *Commonwealth v. Gregory.* 132 Pa. Super. 507, 1 A.2d 501 (1938).
19. *Bowman v. Home Life Insurance Co.* 243 F.2d 331 (3d Cir. 1957).
20. *Slater v. Baker.* 95 Eng. Rep. 860 (1767).
21. *Carpenter v. Blake.* 60 Barb. (New York) 488 (1871).
22. *Commonwealth v. Pierce.* 138 Mass. 165 (1884).
23. *Mohr v. Williams.* 95 Minn. 261, 104 N.W. 12 (1905).
24. *Bang v. Charles T. Miller Hospital.* 251 Minn. 427, 88 N.W. 2d 186 (1958).
25. McCoid, A. H. A reappraisal of liability for unauthorized medical treatment. *Minn. Law Rev.,* 41:381, 1957.
26. *Corn v. French.* 71 Nev. 280, 289 P.2d 173 (1955).
27. *Gray v. Grunagle.* 423 Pa. 144, 223 A.2d 663 (1966).

28. *Paulsen v. Gunderson.* 281 Wis. 578, 260 N.W. 448 (1935).
29. *Schleoendoff v. Society of New York Hospital.* 211 N.Y. 125, 104 N.E. 92 (1914).
30. *Salgo v. Leland Stanford, Jr., University Board of Trustees.* 154 Cal. App. 2d 560, 317 P.2d 170 (1957).
31. *Nathanson v. Kline.* 186 Kan. 393, 350 P.2d 1093 (1960), *affirmed on rehearing,* 187 Kan. 186, 354 P.2d 1093 (1960).
32. *Mitchell v. Robinson.* 334 S.W.2d 11 (Mo. 1960), *affirmed,* 360 S.W.2d 673 (Mo. 1962).
33. Alsobrook, pp. 198 ff.
34. *Canterbury v. Spence.* 464 F.2d 772 (D.C. Cir. 1972).
35. *Cobbs v. Grant.* 8 Cal. 3d 229, 502 P.2d 1 (1972).
36. *Fogel v. The Genesee Hospital.* 41 A.D.2d 468, 344 N.Y.S.2d 552 (1973).
37. *Wilkerson v. Vesey.* 110 R.I. 606, 295 A.2d 676 (1972).
38. *Scaria v. St. Paul Fire and Marine Insurance Company.* 68 Wis. 2d 1, 227 N.W.2d 647 (1975).
39. Alsobrook, pp. 198 ff.
40. Louisell, D. W., & Williams, H. *Medical Malpractice.* New York: Matthew Bender, 1970, sec. 11.20, 11.21.
41. Foster, H. What the psychiatrist should know about the limitations of law. *Wis. Law Rev.,* 1965:189 (1965).
42. Prosser, sec. 18.
43. *Bonner v. Moran.* 126 F.2d 121 (App. D.C. 1941).
44. *Bartley et al. v. Kremens et al.* 402 F. Supp. 1039 (E.D. Pa. 1975).
45. *Jackovach v. Yocom.* 212 Iowa 914, 237 N.W. 444 (1931).
46. *Bach v. Long Island Jewish Hospital.* 49 Misc. 2d 207, 267 N.Y.S.2d 289 (1966).
47. Prosser, p. 102.
48. *Crouch v. Most.* 78 N.M. 406, 432 P.2d 250 (1967).
49. Prosser, p. 102.
50. *Pratt v. Davis.* 224 Ill. 300, 79 N.E. 562 (1906).
51. *Gravis v. Physician's and Surgeon's Hospital.* 427 S.W.2d 310 (Tex. Civ. App. 1968).
52. *Planned Parenthood of Central Missouri v. Danforth.* ____U.S.____ (1976).
53. Ennis, B. J., & Litwack, T. R. Psychiatry and the presumption of expertise: Flipping coins in the courtroom. *Cal Law Rev.,* 62:693, 1974.
54. Szasz, T.S. *Law, Liberty and Psychiatry.* New York: Macmillan, 1963, pp. 52-53.
55. *Kennedy Memorial Hospital v. Heston.* 58 N.J. 576, 279 A.2d 670 (1971).
56. *Winters v. Miller.* 446 F.2d 65 (2d Cir. 1971), *cert. denied,* 404 U.S. 985.

57. *Stowers v. Ardmore Acres Hospital.* 19 Mich. App. 115, 172 N.W.2d 497 (1969), *affirmed,* 386 Mich. 119, 191 N.W.2d 355 (1971).
58. Brooks, A. D. *Law, Psychiatry and the Mental Health System.* Boston: Little, Brown, 1974, p. 897.
59. Olin, G. B., & Olin, H. S. Informed consent in voluntary mental hospital admissions. *Amer. J. Psychiat.,* 132:938, 1975.
60. Rosenzweig, S. Mental Health Information Service. *N.Y. Law J.,* 173 (75):1, cols. 3-6, 1975.
61. Voluntary admission forms: Does the patient know what he's signing? *Hosp. Commun. Psychiat.,* 23:250, 1942.
62. Brooks, pp. 785-795.
63. *O'Connor v. Donaldson.* 422 U.S. 563 (1975).
64. *Lessard v. Schmidt.* 349 F.Supp. 1078 (E.D. Wis. 1972).
65. Brooks, pp. 971-994.
66. Note. Testamentary capacity in a nutshell: A psychiatric reevaluation. *Stanford Law Rev.,* 18:1119 (1966).
67. *Faber v. Sweet Style Manufacturing Corporation.* 40 Misc. 2d 212, 242 N.Y.S. 2d 763 (1963).
68. *Fingerhut v. Kralyn Enterprises.* 337 N.Y.S.2d 394 (1971).
69. *Fischer v. Adams.* 151 Neb. 215, 38 N.W.2d 337 (1949).
70. *In re Buttonow.* 23 N.Y.2d 385, 297 N.Y.S.2d 97, 244 N.E.2d 667 (1968).
71. Brooks, pp. 737-738.
72. Gilboy & Schmidt. "Voluntary" hospitalization of the mentally ill. *Northwestern U. Law Rev.,* 66:429, 1971.
73. *City Bank Farmers Trust Company v. McGowan,* 323 U.S. 594 at 598-599 (1945).
74. *In re Guardianship of Brice.* 233 Iowa 183 at 186-187, 8 N.W.2d 576 at 578-579 (1943).
75. *In re Fagler.* 248 N.Y. 415 at 418-420, 162 N.E. 471 at 471-472 (1928).
76. Pollock, E., & Maitland, F. W. *The History of English Law,* Vol. II. London: Cambridge University Press, 1911, pp. 474-475.
77. Roche, P. Q. *The Criminal Mind.* Westford, Conn.: Greenwood Press, 1958.
78. Waitzkin, H., & Waterman, B. *The Exploitation of Illness in Capitalist Society.* Indianapolis: Bobbs-Merrill, 1974, p. 76.
79. Duff, R., & Hollingshead, A. *Sickness and Society.* New York: Harper & Row, 1968, p. 286.
80. Alfidi, R. J. Informed consent — a study of patient reaction. *JAMA, 216:1325, 1971.*
81. Frost, N. C. A surrogate system for informed consent. *JAMA,* 233: 800-803, 1975.
82. Parsons, T. *The Social System.* New York: Free Press, 1951, p. 442.
83. Pratt, Seligmann, & Reader. In: *Patients, Physicians and Illness,* ed. E. G. Jaco. New York: Free Press, 1957, pp. 222, 228.

84. Schneyer, p. 136.
85. Rosenthal, D. E. *Lawyer and Client: Who's in Charge?* New York: Russell Sage, 1975, p. 10.
86. Rogers, C. *Client-Centered Therapy.* Boston: Houghton Mifflin, 1951, p. 51.
87. Katz, J. The education of the physician-investigator. In: *Experimentation with Human Subjects,* ed. P. Freund. New York: Braziller, 1970, pp. 299-300.
88. Foster, H. Confessions and the station house syndrome. *DePaul Law Rev.,* 18:683, 1969.
89. Sanders, E. *The Family.* New York: Avon Books, 1975.
90. Louisell & Williams, sec. 8.08.
91. Waltz & Schenueman. Informed consent to therapy. *Northwestern U. Law Rev.,* 64:635, 1969.
92. *Fischer v. Wilmington General Hospital.* 51 Del. 554, 149 A.2d 749 (1959).
93. Plante, pp. 654 ff.

Part III

Malpractice

Malpractice is the unwarranted departure from accepted medical practice resulting in an injury to a patient. The physician has a legal duty toward his or her patient (he or she must have a valid license), must possess the skill and knowledge equivalent to other physicians, and must exercise judgment in the patient's best interest.

Negligence is the omission of something a reasonable person would do or the doing of something a reasonable and prudent person would not do. To recover damages in a malpractice suit, it must be shown that a duty was owed, that there was failure to do that duty, and that an injury took place to which the patient did not contribute. Abandonment of the patient is an example of failure to do duty. When a patient complains of back pains, is given another ECT treatment without first obtaining an X-ray of the spine, and a fracture of the spine is later proven, this illustrates the omission of something a reasonable person would do. An injury occurred to which the patient did not contribute.

The malpractice crisis was precipitated by the withdrawal of insurance companies from writing coverage and the charging of astronomical annual insurance premiums. Claims increased in number by more than 225 percent in five years. The cost of out-of-court settlements also went up significantly. The costs to hospitals and to individual physicians were passed on to the patients. As a consequence, a substantial increment was added to the already escalating cost of care.

Multimillion-dollar annual hospital premiums to protect against malpractice caused patients to pay anywhere from $6 to $16 for each day of care just for the liability insurance. Some specialists at risk in certain cities paid an annual premium for malpractice of $35,000 — all of which had to be recovered from the income of practice paid by patients.

The absurdity of such staggering costs led to an unprecedented outpouring of legislation during 1976 as ways were explored to control costs. Action taken varied from designating review boards to predetermine the legitimacy of a complaint, to a workman's compensation approach, to shortening the statute of limitations, to limiting the amount that could be claimed, to abolishing the lawyer's contingency fee.

Chester L. Trent, a psychiatrist in private practice, initiated and monitors the American Psychiatric Association's liability insurance program. Feedback on performance is essential to understanding and corrective action. He presents the nature of claims made against psychiatrists, the outcome to date, and provides a perspective of actuarial measures and necessary approaches to make the data credible. The small number of cases per 100 physician-years points to the desirability of keeping psychiatrists (a low-risk group) separate from those physicians who have a higher risk for claims.

Stanley L. Brodsky, an academic psychologist, heads a project in the correctional field. With the zest of radical youth, he attacks professional self-complacency. He alleges we have overreacted to the threat of malpractice and to lawyers as a group. The profession reacts with anger when services performed in the interest of patients are rejected, and Brodsky warns "that people are apt to become what they hate."

An experiment under the protection of the court in Alabama releases prisoners to the community after evaluation. Workers in the project are exposed to malpractice suits on the basis that staff lacks the psychological knowledge to predict future behavior and is vulnerable to claims entered by families of victims. Dr. Brodsky wisely advises that one must use one's best judgment and accept responsibility for decisions made. He tends to agree with Ralph Slovenko on the need for a contractual relationship with clients. He suggests we help clients develop additional coping behavior and share our knowledge with them.

Chapter V

Psychiatric Malpractice Insurance and Its Problems: An Overview

CHESTER L. TRENT, M.D.

Within the past several years physicians have become increasingly aware of problems in obtaining malpractice insurance and the burden of its premiums on themselves as well as the rest of the medical community. When the American Psychiatric Association began its new program in 1972, excluding extras, a million-dollar coverage in New Hampshire cost $64 and in California $744. In May 1976, the same coverages were $228 in New Hampshire and $2,907 to $4,059 in California depending on the area of the state. Hospital malpractice costs have escalated even more sharply. Malpractice insurance at Michael Reese Hospital in Chicago went from $3 per patient day in 1974 to $16.50 in 1976. Similarly at Presbyterian-St. Luke's in New York the cost per patient hospital day went from $2.33 in 1974 to $13.35 in 1976 (1). Lawyers in California are facing a 500 percent increase in their rates. In 1970, one insurance company reports lawyers incurred one claim for every 41 lawyers insured. In 1975, the ratio increased to one claim for every 29 lawyers. During the same time span the cost of the claim for lawyers increased from $622 per claim to $11,936 per claim. The highest judgment for lawyers thus far has been $26 million (2). Shocking as these developments may seem, the situation will worsen in the coming months and years. Insurance company actuaries predict a 15 percent inflation rate per year and a 10 percent trend factor, which has to do with increased numbers of claims and amounts of judgments. This will cause physicians' premiums to increase an average of 25 to 30 percent yearly if inflation and the trend factors continue. And, of course, all of this presupposes that physicians will continue to be able to find an insurance company willing to underwrite their risk. Groups operating national malpractice programs for physicians, such as the American Psychiatric Association, have special problems. Because the incidence of claims and the amounts of awards vary mercurially from state to state and because some states have experienced defense and/or plaintiff's attorneys while others do not, it is exceedingly difficult to set rates for and to service a nationwide malpractice program. Because of this at least two nationwide programs have collapsed, namely, the association program for the Emergency Room Physicians and the American College of Physicians.

Widespread publicity for professional liability problems prompts psychiatrists to write asking for details of the actual claims experience for American psychiatrists. Most say that they have never heard of anyone in their community who has been sued. In response to these inquiries, I reviewed early claims experience with the American Psychiatric Association Professional Liability Program (3).

From its beginning in 1972 until April 1976, the American Psychiatric Association program incurred 100 claims as detailed in Table 1, which shows the number of claims incurred per 100 doctor years of exposure since the beginning of the program. This is a graphic demonstration of

TABLE 1

NUMBER OF CLAIMS INCURRED PER 100 DOCTOR YEARS OF EXPOSURE

	Claims Incurred per 200 Doctor Years of Exposure	Claims Opened	Cumulative Number of Claims Opened	Claims per 100 Doctor Years
October 1972 - May 1, 1973	355	0	0	0/355
May 1973 - May 1974	2991	7	7	0.233/100
May 1974 - May 1975	5645	31	38	.67/100
May 1975 - April 1976	11,000 (Approximate)	71	102	.93/100

one of the several factors producing the so-called long tail of medical malpractice. In our case there were no claims opened during the first policy year, seven during the second, 31 during the third, and 71 during the fourth. So far the average lapse in time between the date of occurrence and the date of reporting the claim is five months. The ratio of claims per 100 doctor years is rapidly approaching the figure predicted earlier (4). The ratio of claims per 100 doctor years compared with other physicians nationwide is quite low. The average nationwide is five to seven claims per 100 doctor years.

Table 2 shows the number of claims closed during each calendar year. It will be noted that there were no claims closed during the first two calendar years of the program, with the remaining 37 being closed in the most recent three

TABLE 2

NUMBER OF CLAIMS CLOSED

1972	0
1973	0
1974	12
1975	10
1976	15

years, leaving a total of approximately 65 claims still open. The average time from occurrence to closure was over nine months.

The types of claims against psychiatrists are shown in Table 3. Category 1, Improper Commitment, is a frequent cause for claim in the American Psychiatric Association program and accounts for about one-fourth of all the closed claims. Such claims usually result from the psychiatrist's failure to certify a patient who is reluctant to be hospitalized or who is not duly informed about the hospital to which he or she consents to be admitted. Category 2, Death, includes claims for patients who have disappeared from a treatment facility and have been found dead at a later date, as well as one case of death from other medical conditions which occurred in connection with psychiatric treatment. Category 3, Pressing for Fee Collection, includes patients who are disgruntled or dissatisfied with psychiatric contact and who are also eager to avoid payment of their bill. They frequently file

TABLE 3
TYPE OF CLAIM OR CASE

1. Improper Commitment	9
2. Death	3
3. Pressing for Fee Collection	5
4. Subpoena to Testify	5
5. Sexual Behavior with Patients	1
6. Drug Reactions	3
7. Unauthorized Release of Confidential Information Causing Damage to Patient	2
8. Suicide	3
9. Improper Administrative Handling	1
10. ECT	2
11. Improper Treatment	2
12. Injury to Nonpatient during Professional Services	1

claims to threaten the psychiatrist and to attempt to influence him to give up his fee. Sometimes they are successful, sometimes they are not, depending on the circumstances. Category 4, Subpoena to Testify, encompasses the frequent subpoenaing of psychiatrists to testify about confidential patient information. In some of these cases the subpoena has no legal foundation. With the help of an attorney furnished by the insurance company, it can be vacated, thus helping to pre-serve the confidential treatment relationship and preventing a possible future claim because of improper release of information. Such releases may involve patients, colleagues, or others. When reported to the insurance company, a sub-poena to release confidential information has been handled in a manner considered very constructive by Association members. Again, actual suit is not necessary for this claims-advice service.

Although the American Psychiatric Association has had just one closed claim in Category 5, Sexual Activity with a Patient, it is alleged that there have been approximately 25 claims against psychologists for sexual misconduct. Recently a New York television station reported that psychologists lost their insurance coverage because of these claims. Although we have not been able to verify this, psychologists have a new professional liability program specifically excluding coverage for sexual activity. The exclusion reads: "This policy does not apply to licentious, immoral or sexual behavior intended to lead to, or culminating in any sexual act." The exclusion is very broad and possibly unfortunate in its scope. At this time the American Psychiatric Association still has a broad, com-prehensive policy without such an exclusion.

Category 6, Drug Reactions, involves cases relating to lithium and Haldol. I testified as an expert in a New Jersey case (5) where the internist was sued for damages allegedly relating to administration of Stelazine 2 mg. twice daily for approximately two years. Thereafter the patient developed an abnormal movement disorder to his upper extremities. Mov-ies of this man's condition taken prior to his death were shown to the jury. The treating neurologist had made a diagnosis of tardive dyskinesia. In this instance the case was decided for the doctor; however, with increasing numbers of patients taking major tranquilizers, there may be an increase in such claims.

Category 7, Unauthorized Release of Confidential Information Causing Damage to Patient, concerns those instances where a psychiatrist voluntarily released doctor-patient information which was unauthorized, thereby causing damage to the patient. The claims in Category 8, Suicide, usually arise in a hospital setting. The patient's relatives or estate claim the patient was unsatisfactorily supervised by the doctor and/or the hospital. The hospital itself usually carries the burden of the claim in these cases unless the doctor has been negligent in communicating proper details about the patient's suicidal nature to the hospital or has neglected to write proper suicidal precautions.

Category 9, Improper Administrative Handling, refers to a claim resulting from a dispute between the patient and the doctor as to the nature of forms to be filled out by the doctor. In Category 10, ECT, we have two claims resulting from fractures following ECT. Representatives from the insurance company indicate a possible trend for reduction in claims and suits directly related to ECT; however, there appears to be an increase in frequency of claims in the case of doctors who give ECT. These claims appear to result from other activities in their practices. It is interesting to speculate that physicians administering somatic treatments may, in general, see sicker and more disturbed patients who are less easily controlled and scheduled into a routine practice and who at the same time become easily discouraged, disgruntled, and ultimately unhappy about the unavailability of a cure for their chronic condition — all of which leads to increased claims. An additional speculation is that doctors administering somatic treatments may see a larger number of patients with a more medical orientation and thereby supply a less gratifying type of emotional relationship to the patient and be less attentive to his individual needs, whims, and idiosyncrasies.

Category 11 covers Improper Treatment, that is, treatment considered inappropriate, or if appropriate, not performed in the same manner another physician would use under the same conditions. Category 12 involves Injury to Nonpatient during Professional Services, that is, when someone other than a patient claims injury.

Table 4 shows the final disposition of claims closed through April 1976. The major category has involved legal

TABLE 4
FINAL DISPOSITION OF CLOSED CLAIMS

1. Legal expense only, no suit, no claim	21
2. Legal expense, indemnity paid (suit settled prior to trial)	4
3. No suit, no expense	5
4. Legal expense incurred, suit went against patient	1
5. Final expense data not yet available	6

expense only, with no suit filed and no claims made. The legal expenses involved were primarily for preliminary protection of the doctor and investigation by the insurance company. So far there has been only one trial in the program, which was of a minor nature and was decided in favor of the doctor. The data presented from the program in April 1976 show the development of one part of the long tail of medical and/or psychiatric malpractice. Approximately one-third of the claims accumulated to date have been closed for a minimal cost, with the larger and more serious claims still waiting in the wings for suit or settlement. Thus, the one- to three-year delay already noted in the development of claims in our program is only beginning. The wait on the trial calendar and the time for appeal, if indicated, must be added. Thus, for example, in large metropolitan areas like New York, Philadelphia, Boston, and Los Angeles, the waiting time before trial begins ranges from four to seven years.

It will, therefore, be several more years before a large body of closed psychiatric claims has been accumulated under the program. In addition, the difficulty of predicting inflation, the unknown increases in numbers of claims to be made, the idiosyncrasies of juries in giving awards, and the changes in the state liability laws in almost every state impair the actuary's ability to predict accurately future losses. In the meantime American psychiatrists agonizingly wait for time to pass while their loss experience develops (3). This then has been the recent loss development experienced by the American Psychiatric Association in its liability program.

When these data are presented to inquiring psychiatrists, a frequent response is: "Why are our premiums so high if we haven't had any losses of a significant nature?" Because of recent tremendous malpractice underwriting losses, insurance companies are wary of such arguments, which have been partially to blame for their recent losses. Insurance company actuaries did not properly anticipate inflation, the increased amount of judgments, and the increased frequency of claims which have spread across the United States. Because of these errors in judgment, the previous premiums for all physicians were probably too low. Suddenly insurance companies found themselves in the position of losing millions of dollars and not being able to recoup their losses in a bull market. Companies began to refuse renewals, install stiffer underwriting requirements, and most notoriously charge higher premiums.

Until 1976, losses on claims against psychiatrists were inextricably mixed in most places with claims against general practitioners or Class I physicians. For that reason, data have not been available for the American Psychiatric Association Insurance Committee or the broker to establish a pure premium for psychiatrists in each and every state. Everyone believed that psychiatrists probably had fewer claims and smaller judgments than other physicians, but no one knew the exact amount. For that reason the new program was started by subtracting 25 percent from the premium then charged by the leading medical society carrier in all states except California, New York, and Florida. Because the insurance company believed there was a much greater exposure for loss in these three states, the percentage was 10 percent less than the prevailing premium charge. The insurance company has indicated a willingness to eventually write the American Psychiatric Association's program on a self-rating basis when "credible data" are available. At that time the premiums will be adjusted to fit the actual losses and expenses with a reasonable profit for the company.

The concept of credible loss data is the crux of the premium cost part of the psychiatric malpractice crisis. The word "credible," as everyone knows, means capable of being believed, believable, entitled to confidence, trustworthy. In the insurance community the word has some very specific references. There is, for example, a whole area of study called credibility theory which is one of the cornerstones of actuarial science as applied to casualty and property insurance. The literature on this subject is extensive. Abstruse mathematical concepts and formulas are involved. In essence, the insurance company actuary demands what he considers to be credible data before he feels secure to self-rate an insurance program completely. One famous casualty actuary, Arthur L. Bailey, is credited with the following remark: "The basis for these credibility formulas has been a profound mystery to most people who have come into contact with them" (6).

When a casualty actuary is shown 100 claims, such as those that have occurred so far in the American Psychiatric Association program, a reasonable first response would be: "The loss experience is still too small to be fully credible." This implies that data in the future may very well be different from those so far collected, and it also implies that he has more confidence in his prior knowledge based on other data such as current rates for similar classes. In other cases a body of data may be too small to be fully credible, but large enough to have some credibility. A scale of credibility has been established which gives zero credibility to data too small to be of any use for rate making and a score of one to data which are fully credible. Credibility theory is concerned with establishing measures of credibility and standards of full credibility. What steps are taken to develop a rating for the credibility of data? There are several models. One uses the Poisson distribution, a mathematic distribution familiar to engineers and statisticians. Based on this distribution, actuaries accept 1,084 claims as the number required to reduce to negligible proportions the probable departure from the number observed which could be attributed to chance variation. With this number of claims, the probability for an error of +5 percent is at the 90-percent level. In different words this means that if one has 1,084 claims for a given number of doctor years of exposure, the insurance actuary can be comfortable at the 90-percent level that the frequency of claims will not vary by more than a plus or minus five percent in the future.

In practice, except for very large groups such as those insured under automobile, fire, or all of medicine, it is difficult to accumulate so many claims. For that reason other means of assessing the credibility of loss data have been developed. Premium volume may be used as an indicator. A standard of $5 million of premiums has been occasionally used in fire insurance as an indicator of the credibility of the data. The variation and extremes in the size of claims are also useful criteria.

Because of the large number of claims necessary to establish credibility, psychiatrists have been traditionally lumped with general practitioners into Class I. Psychiatrists are therefore disadvantaged for their virtue. They have a very small ratio of claims per 100 doctor years of experience, namely, one or two. This places the psychiatrist in an adverse position because he does not generate enough claims, except over a long period of time, to permit more rapid self-rating and claims evaluation. Before the American Psychiatric Association had a fully developed nationwide program, for example, an entire state may have had only a handful of psychiatric practitioners. Thus, at the current rate of one claim per 100 doctor years, there might have been only one lawsuit in a particular jurisdiction against a psychiatrist every ten years. Unless the psychiatrist was combined with other practitioners in the particular state, there would have been no way of determining a premium for his malpractice risk. With the advent of nationwide malpractice programs such as the one sponsored by the American Psychiatric Association, it is hoped that loss data will become available more rapidly and be considered "credible" by an insurance company actuary, thereby permitting the psychiatrist to pay insurance premiums based on his own losses and not those of other practitioners in high-risk classes such as surgeons, anesthesiologists, and neurosurgeons.

But it is just at this point that psychiatry has another of its many problems. Some who advocate a return to the mainstream of medicine and a fostering of closer ties with the medical community urge participation by psychiatrists in their local medical society insurance program as well as other medical activities. These societies, hungry for premium dollars to pay for losses incurred by high-risk specialists, tend to set premiums for psychiatrists very close to that of Class I practitioners, thus using psychiatrists' premiums to subsidize risks or losses of those subject to higher risks. In Massachusetts recently the American Psychiatric Association program had to stop functioning because of new insurance laws. Massachusetts psychiatrists were unable to obtain legislative help or support from the medical society there to obtain repeal of the pertinent laws. Allegedly, the medical society desired to keep the psychiatrists, if possible, as part of their low-risk insured population.

There is an insurance concept that some losses are so great they are uninsurable and others are so small as to require almost no premium at all. Because of this, high risks are frequently charged lower premiums than warranted and low risks are frequently charged higher premiums so that everyone pays a middle-of-the-road or average premium. This concept has been very attractive, especially to high-risk specialists, medical societies, and insurance companies for several reasons. The high-risk specialist can have his premium reduced, the medical society can offer insurance to all members at a cost it considers reasonable, and although the low-risk specialist pays more than is justified because of his risk, it is not so much that it forces strong complaints or other action. To this argument a currently popular concept has been added which echoes from the halls of insurance companies, actuaries, medical societies, and specialty societies, especially for the classes of practice of anesthesia, neurosurgery, and other high-risk surgical specialties. It goes something like this. These practitioners hold themselves to be the solvers of problems which have arisen because persons were ineptly cared for, were improperly referred, or their referral was delayed by nonsurgical practitioners. The practices of high-risk specialists are an integral and necessary service to low-risk practitioners. When there is an untoward result, it is alleged by anesthesiologists and by some surgeons that others in the chain of medical care should help pay for the insurance necessary to cover claims against them because of this implied responsibility.

Physicians in the higher-risk classes of practice frequently have a predominant voice in medical society board rooms because of their greater numbers and greater affluence. They have been able to hypnotize insurers and insurance commissioners into utilizing these concepts so as to permit rates to be set that do not strictly allocate premiums in relation to losses incurred by a particular class of practice, but permit one group to subsidize another to a greater or lesser extent.

Such an arrangement works out well for the high-risk specialist who pays the lower premium. It works out well for the medical society which keeps its membership up in part by offering desirable fringe benefits. And if the rates are kept more or less constant, it takes the pressure off insurance commissioners and their actuaries from having to answer too many pointed questions. Let me quote L. H. Longley-Cook (6):

> We must always remember insurance as a business and rates and premiums are more than mere statistical developments. They determine the actual sums of money payable for insurance coverage and these sums may be considerable. While it is essential that premium rates correctly follow overall trends, year to year fluctuations in rates can prove most unfortunate. Such fluctuations not only cast doubt in the minds of the public and of regulatory authorities on the correctness of the rate making procedure but may have a number of side effects such as leading to the cancellation and rewriting of a number of policies prior to expiration.

In the service of keeping the changes in the rate curves smooth, it is conjectured that practitioners in the low-risk groups have been financially disadvantaged insofar as malpractice premiums are concerned.

Because many low-risk specialist groups, such as psychiatrists and pathologists, have few claims and members, their cries are not heard in the uproar of the medical society board room where they must deal on a state-by-state basis for insurance. Two seldom-heard arguments *against* premium averaging, sharing, and subsidizing one class of practice by another are: (1) Some lower-risk specialists who subsidize higher-risk specialists are disadvantaged because of the marked discrepancy in income. Surgical specialists in some categories regularly net $100,000-$300,000 a year, an income significantly greater than that of psychiatrists. (2) Strict allocation of premiums in accord with loss permits quicker problem identification in the medical care system. Certainly the occurrence of large losses in one particular specialty over an adequate period of time might help expose inappropriate practices, dangerous procedures, and problems associated with poor doctor-patient relationships so as to ultimately cause constructive alterations in the care system. Spreading these costs among several classes of practice only hides problems until they have become monumental. It is fascinating to hear high-risk specialists complain about escalating malpractice premiums and ask for help from the medical society to subsidize their premium burden. At the same time it is equally fascinating to notice how little effort is made by practitioners among the other classes of practice to investigate, supervise, or determine the reason for these large losses by the high-risk specialists. In the business world no responsible corporate board would grant any of its subsidiaries long-term loans for operating in the red without assuring itself of the exact reasons for such losses and the adequacy of the management of the company involved to correct the problems. Nor would they rely solely on the word of the managers of the company involved to obtain such information. Objective independent accountants, financial analysts, and management specialists would study business procedures, inventories, and service arrangements, and make some binding recommendations. More modern and reality-oriented business procedures should be applied to the administration and management of medical liability programs.

In summary, I have attempted to outline the background and some of the major problems in psychiatric malpractice insurance at the present time. It can be concluded that so far the major problem for psychiatry is in the area of the cost of the premium and the availability of the coverage. Various authors have emphasized the threat of increased claims from sexual misconduct, adverse drug reactions, and civil rights violations. Although claims in such areas have occurred, they have not yet materialized in such substantial number as to constitute a crisis.

The recent action of the National Association of Insurance Commissioners (NAIC) may help in resolving the malpractice dilemma. They have required all insurers or groups of affiliated insurers who have at least $1 million of direct written premiums for medical professional liability insurance in any year beginning with 1970 to complete the NAIC medical professional liability insurance uniform claims report form for each claim closed on or after July 1, 1975. A separate report is required for each defendant. Eventually this regulation will make an additional body of data available on psychiatric malpractice. For the first time psychiatric claims will be reported separately from Class I pools (7).

Some psychiatrists, especially in states where malpractice premiums are very high, as in California, are known to be "going bare"—that is, practicing without liability insurance. Such a practice is strongly discouraged and is considered financially hazardous. Other physicians are going to work for the federal or state government where their insurance needs are completely or partially taken care of.

One federal solution to the malpractice problem would be a "Workman's Compensation" law for medical malpractice. This is a logical solution to the problem, but it is unpopular with doctors because of the concessions that would be required of them and unpopular with attorneys because of the loss in income which it would most likely engender. Tort law changes in various states directed at reducing rates may come over a period of years, but the battle is difficult and legislation enacted appears to have been unconstitutional in some instances.

Psychiatrists can and must await self-rating associated with the accumulation of their own credible data. Meanwhile, district branches may afford some help by becoming more active, attempting to educate insurance commissioners at public hearings, and becoming more vociferous in the halls of their medical societies where efforts are made to utilize their premium dollar to subsidize other medical practitioners.

REFERENCES

1. Brockmier, W. C. *Bus. Insurance,* July 26, 1976, p. 14.
2. Martin, W. L. *Bus. Insurance,* July 26, 1976.
3. Trent, C. L. Early claims experience with the APA professional liability program. Presented at the Annual Meeting of the American Psychiatric Association, Miami, May 1976.
4. Trent, C. L., & Muhl, W. P. Professional liability insurance and the American psychiatrist. *Amer J. Psychiat.,* 132:1312-1314, 1975.
5. *Travis v. Vadon* (N.J. 1976).
6. Longley-Cook, L. H. *An Introduction to Credibility Theory.* New York: Casualty Actuary Society, 1962.
7. National Association of Insurance Commissioners. *NAIC Malpractice Claims,* Vol. 1, No. 1. April 1976.

Chapter VI

Buffalo Bill's Defunct Now: Vulnerability of Mental Health Professionals to Malpractice

STANLEY L. BRODSKY, Ph.D.

Buffalo Bill's
defunct

who used to
ride a watersmooth-silver
stallion

and break onetwothreefourfive pigeonsjustlikethat
Jesus

he was a handsome man
and what i want to know is

how do you like your blueeyed boy
Mister Death

—e. e. cummings*

Mental health helpers have had a Buffalo Bill image, the hero or heroine rescuing the helpless in times of distress. In some

ways Buffalo Bill *is* defunct now. The model of psychiatrist as
hero and heroine is disappearing. In his book, *Even Cowgirls
Get the Blues,* Tom Robbins (1) writes, "Goats are always
testing you. They are like Zen masters. They can tell instantly
if you are faking your feelings so they play games with you to
keep you true. People should go to goats instead of
psychiatrists."

Unlike goats, mental health professionals are *not*
value-free; rather, their value-loading, with idiosyncratic
personal values and cultural professional values, has promoted
societal antagonism. The journal, *The Radical Therapist,* and
its brethren have been particularly active in calling to our
attention the extent to which we blame the victim rather than
looking to social causes. The social scientists who investigated
the University of Wisconsin student disturbances in the late
1960s reported that the people engaged in the disturbances
were largely minority group members, largely out-of-state residents, largely from big cities. The Board of Regents read this
and reduced the admission of out-of-state students to the
University of Wisconsin, thus blaming the "victims." Blaming
the victims happens in other ways. Zero Mostel played a
southern senator in the late 1940s investigating the beginning
of World War II and trying to find out why the Japanese were
able to bomb Pearl Harbor. At one point he sits back and
grumbles, "What I want to know is, what was Pearl Harbor
doing out there in the middle of the Pacific Ocean?" (see Ryan
[2]).

Professionally we have been provincial. As psychologists
and psychiatrists, we have done a good job of generously
accepting others' virtues and our own vices. We often speak far
too much for ourselves, and we try far too hard to convince
people that white is the color that it is. The public fear of
psychological control is increasing. It may be observed
particularly in science fiction, which is one harbinger of the
future. Science fiction stories increasingly depict psychologists

and psychiatrists as the villains — mad scientists and sorcerers in pursuit of political and social control. The fear of social scientists' control grows out of our successes and our failures. If we are good at what we do, we are dangerous, because who knows what insidious control we can exert over others. And if we're bad at what we do, then we are equally threatening, for what we do emerges fully out of our values and our beliefs instead of verifiable knowledge.

In part we may have a bad rap for our *potential* for doing harm, aside from those cases in which we have earned it. The reason is the nature of clinical work and dealing with individual clients. On the sixth day of creation, according to our best Judeo-Christian traditions, God created strict potty training, free enterprise, and unhappy clients. We can count on a few unhappy clients seeking a redress for their grievances and some suits developing logically out of their unhappiness.

THE REACTION OF MENTAL HEALTH PROFESSIONALS TO MALPRACTICE CONCERNS

Mental health professionals overreact emotionally and underreact functionally to malpractice threats and concerns. The fear of malpractice suits is part of mental health professionals' perception of lawyers and litigious clients as harmful and noxious. Lawyers are dangerous. Any client who hints at filing suit is dangerous. In this context it is useful to examine what we mean by "dangerous."

Theodore Sarbin (3) has noted that the word "dangerous" derives from *dominium*; its origin and in some ways its current use reflect an overthrowing of the status quo. Somebody is dangerous if they upset a state of affairs or being in which one has a personal investment.

Attorney David Seth Michaels, as he has filed suits against the Superintendent of the Mississippi State Hospital at

Whitfield and other psychiatrists, has found himself
repeatedly called a dangerous person. Mr. Michaels, indeed, is
dangerous to their welfare within this meaning of danger.

Once mental health professionals perceive someone as
dangerous, interesting transformations occur. We change our
behaviors. Practitioners who have been on the receiving end of
malpractice suits typically hate the lawyers and the clients. For
example, when an inmate files suit against the prison medical
practitioner and then goes to the prison hospital (the only
hospital available to him) for treatment, the prison doctor will
in many instances toss him out. The doctor says, with
incredible anger and hatred, "Get the hell out of here. You've
got a lot of nerve filing suit against me and then coming in for
medical treatment." The hatred toward the lawyers is equally
intense.

Hugh Prather (4), in his book *Notes to Myself*, made an
insightful observation about hating people. When Prather
hates somebody immediately and irrationally, he realizes that
it is because there is some element of himself in that person,
some element that he doesn't like, which he sees and reacts
against emotionally. In their emotional antagonism and
hating, perhaps the professionals are seeing something of
themselves in the attorneys, something of their own
consciences or concerns.

Tom Robbins (1) wrote: "People have a tendency to
become what they hate." Some mental health professionals
have become lawyer surrogates: excessively concerned,
overreacting, acting to protect themselves, no longer acting as
helpers. They develop the interpersonal equivalent of
physicians who order unnecessary X-rays because of their fear
of lawsuits.

The mirror image of this professional transformation
relating to legal actions is the transformation on the witness
stand. It is always astonishing to see an apparently competent
professional become a stammering, bumbling, contradictory

idiot on the witness stand. For a while when I saw it happen, I felt very bad and felt we should never have mental health experts on witness stands. Rather, we should avoid these situations or structure them against such harassment. Over a period of time, however, I have concluded that it is one of the true testing grounds, a place where we as mental health professionals are absolutely and publicly accountable. Absolutely. We don't have this type of public accountability at all except when we take our board exams after our formal training.

THE ALABAMA PRISON EXPERIENCE

"I should sue you, of course," David Seth Michaels said to me.* "I should sue you on behalf of two groups of clients." David sat back in my living room, propped his feet up on the foot stool, and described the two potential groups of clients for whom he should file suit.

"The first group are the people you evaluate who you would not release from prison. They should sue you because psychological knowledge is still so inadequate that you cannot competently predict that they would harm anyone or themselves or commit crimes." He paused, leaned forward, fixed me with an intense gaze, and went on. "The second group that should sue you are the families of the victims of the crimes committed by those you released from prison."

Over the last four years, a number of us have been deeply concerned about both mental health and corrections in Alabama. The extremes in Alabama corrections are enormous. In 1975, at the Fountain Correction Center, only a minority of the inmates had not been physically or sexually

---

* At the time of our conversation David Seth Michaels was an attorney with the Mississippi Mental Health Project and with Community Legal Services of Jackson, Mississippi.

assaulted, according to reports of physicians assigned there. Punishment is alive and well in Alabama prisons.

On January 13, 1976, in *Neuman v. Alabama* (5) and *Worley James v. George Wallace, et al.* (6), Judge Frank M. Johnson, Jr., ruled that the Alabama prison system in its entirety was unconstitutional. The state of Alabama had violated the Eighth Amendment rights of every inmate. Judge Johnson ordered a series of steps the state correctional system was to take to become constitutional. This court order essentially asserts a right not to be harmed. Most actions required in the order were based on classification of inmates. Over a period of time, when it became apparent that the state would not, or could not, develop and implement an acceptable classification plan, Judge Johnson ordered that the state contract with the University of Alabama Center for Correctional Psychology to evaluate every inmate in the Alabama Correctional System, make recommendations for custody, separate the harmful from the nonharmful, and identify those who were appropriate for community placement.

On July 6, 1976, twenty of us went to the Draper Correctional Institution in Elmore, Alabama. We arrived on the first day feeling as if drums ought to be beating in the background, tempted to march seven times around the institution and see if the walls would fall down, tempted to wear T-shirts emblazoned, "Let My People Go." We went, with the authority of the federal court behind us, to assess every one of the 700 prisoners there, as well as the other 3,500 prisoners under the control of the Alabama Board of Corrections. Part of the mandate was to identify every person who could safely be released from the Alabama Correctional System into the community.

When David Seth Michaels cited the potential for being sued, he referred to the enormous risk of making grievous errors. We were right on the line between the authority of the federal court and the autonomy of the state government. We were either loved or hated in everything we did in this project. David is not the only one who had thought of suing us. A correctional employee who just received his law degree told me that as soon as he is admitted to the bar, he intends to sue us on behalf of *any* victim of violent or nonviolent crime that results from releasing these people into the community. Other threats of suits have also been made.

The first great problem in undertaking this task is in the prediction of dangerousness. In their study of dangerousness, Piotrowski and Hammer (7) asked seven experienced clinicians to evaluate human figure drawings in terms of the aggressiveness or hostility of the person who drew them. They then received independent ratings of how much hostility and aggression were present in each of the clinicians. There was virtually a one-to-one rank order between the amount of aggression seen in the figure drawings and the amount of aggression present in the clinicians, with little relation to behavioral measures of aggression and violence in the artists. The *Baxstrom* decision (8) similarly showed how poorly mental health professionals do in predicting aggression. Of the 967 people diagnosed as dangerous and then released in the *Baxstrom* case, only 20 showed any evidence of actual behavioral aggression against others.

Because of this difficulty in predicting dangerousness, we thought we should use a weather-forecaster model to protect ourselves. Weather forecasters never predict any one day's weather incorrectly because they always deal with probabilities. There is never a 100 percent chance of rain, unless it is raining. If we want to protect ourselves from errors and from being sued, obviously we need to say, "There is a 70 percent chance of this person's being violent, based on actuarial tables; there is a 30 percent chance with this next person." There is a precedent for talking about college professors as weather forecasters. In one of his stories, O. Henry wrote that a useful

function for college professors is to become weather forecasters
because one thing that they can do absolutely reliably is read
the morning newspaper, check the weather forecast, go to the
telegraph office, and telegraph the weather forecast on to the
next town. As he observed, college professors, if nothing else,
can read.

There is a problem in being the weather-forecaster
equivalent in penal institutions: we *are* responsible without
equivocating in making these decisions. There are under 100
psychiatrists in the whole state of Alabama, and only 250
psychologists. There are few mental health professionals, and
we can't mobilize experienced teams quickly or well. Yet, we
assessed 700 convicted men between July 6 and August 27,
1976, proceeding with idealistic fervor. We mobilized
graduate students, psychologists and social workers, and other
qualified people and tried to teach them not to become totally
charmed by likeable inmates who have committed horrible
crimes. These convicted persons often are far more likeable
than the typical patients that they run into in a clinic.

We *are* responsible. We cannot make 70-percent
decisions. We must make yes-no decisions. The Alabama
Board of Corrections fought us at every early step, but after
the federal court defined more clearly the authority and procedures associated with our role, they have now become
compliant and agree with virtually all our recommendations.
The federal court and the government do indeed affirm our
authority when the U.S. Attorney, as an *amicus curiae*, files a
motion that serves to support our professional judgments and
says, "The United States of America moves that . . . " It is an
awesome thing, anybody speaking for the United States of
America, especially in connection with mental health
professionals in an action of this sort. Yet even with the
authority, we acquire some personal vulnerability in the risks
that we are taking, knowing there are going to be mistakes,
perhaps awful ones.

RISK AREAS FOR MALPRACTICE

The more general issues in malpractice concern institutional practices and the right to treatment. Professional persons are and should be personally responsible for the *institutional* decisions they make. On the other hand, one can't be responsible for everything that one's clients do (the *Tarasoff* decision [9] notwithstanding). Yet the courts more and more assume that mental health professionals have that resultant responsibility. The factors affecting homicide exceed by far those that emerge in individual psychotherapy sessions and go well beyond what is amenable to individual psychodiagnoses.

Sexual relations with clients are a new risk area. Intriguingly, Dr. Chester Trent (10) has noted that most of the sexual malpractice trouble lies with psychologists. It is much like what happened when I first started visiting in Mississippi. All the activist reformers in Mississippi said to me, "You know it is strange for us to drive into Alabama because we get the feeling that the state police are following us all the time, that we're likely to get busted for anything, and that it is very dangerous for us to drive around in Alabama." I responded, "My gracious! I have had the same feeling since I arrived in Mississippi." People in Alabama and Mississippi tend to look down on each other as being the most right-wing ultra-conservative group that exists, the seat of all the problems. We don't feel too bad about being in Alabama because we have all these folks in Mississippi who are doing things much worse.

I have had the opinion that it is not members of the American Psychological Association, to which I belong, but members of the American Psychiatric Association, who are doing all the unethical things. Kardener, Fuller, and Mensh (11) report that 5 to 13 percent of physicians including psychiatrists engage in erotic practices with patients. Directly comparable data are available for psychologists. Holyrod and

Brodsky (12) report that 5.5 percent of licensed Ph.D. male psychologists and 0.6 percent of female psychologists acknowledge sexual intercourse with patients. Indirect data are also present in malpractice suit rates. Psychologists for years had malpractice rates of about $30 a year, which has more than doubled since 1974, because of the suits filed. In the 12 years prior to 1974, there were no successful malpractice suits involving sex practices by psychologists in the country; there have been two since then, both of which concerned sexual relations between psychotherapists and clients.

There are other psychologically related issues of malpractice. The human growth movement, which utilizes touching and close personal contact, has considerable malpractice hazard. This is a high-risk, high pay-off area, and we should identify it to potential clients as such. There are practitioners who believe that it is beneficial to pursue extensive touching of clients, just as there are those who believe it is right to initiate sexual relations with their clients. Some such practitioners have little ability to look in perspective, beyond their own needs.

There are general weaknesses in mental health practice that do deserve attack. Any attorney interested in suing mental health professionals should first read Jay Ziskin's book, *Coping with Psychiatric and Psychological Testimony*, which beautifully describes the weaknesses in psychology and psychiatry relevant to any suit or legal action. One who would sue should know about the Rosenhan (14) study of "sane people in insane places." Normal individuals were admitted to psychiatric hospitals by saying nothing abnormal other than they heard the words "flat" and "thud" in their heads. Once Rosenhan's colleagues falsely alerted some admitting physicians that there might be such individuals seeking to fake psychopathology, over 40 percent of all individuals coming for admission were identified as faking. The weaknesses in our ongoing practice and work are so great that we are vulnerable to more errors than anybody suing us has ever dreamed of. We have been very lucky. We don't change very much. Shakespeare said, "Our crimes would despair if they were not cherished by our virtues." The things that we do wrong, we continue to cherish as an integral part of our professional practices.

THREE SOLUTIONS

In 1937, the French government went to Pablo Picasso, and asked him whether he could design a uniform that would give its paratroopers maximal invisibility. Picasso responded, "Yes, of course, I can. Dress them like harlequins." Such is the character of our current solutions. Instead of mental health professions moving to invisibility, and disguising the things that we do, we need to move toward making brilliantly visible a series of new procedures that legitimately and powerfully deal with issues of patients' rights. Discarding the invisible Emperor's clothes, we might garb our professional work in contractual robes, in constructionalists' robes, or in Promethean robes.

The contractual solution has been presented by Kirk Schwitzgebel (15), who suggests that any time one enters into a professional relationship in psychotherapy or diagnosis, one should have a contract prepared and signed. The contract would specify the procedures to be followed, what is likely to happen, the results that one can expect, the risks, the fees, and the responsibility that the professional and the client assume. The first contact session would include a presentation of the contract and a formal statement of transactions, actuarial information, and likely outcome of the particular problem. Schwitzgebel has prepared a model contract that is a thoughtful, humane document.

The second solution is "constructionalist," a term coined by Israel Goldiamond (16). It is assumed that service providers are particularly vulnerable and potentially inappropriate when they believe that they know what is best. After all, one of the continuing unstated postulates in professional work, and in fact, in college teaching, is that the practitioners know best. Its corollary is that in successful psychotherapy, the client is "more like me." The constructionalist model suggests that one should not seek to discard any of the client's behaviors through a psychotherapeutic relationship. One seeks to construct additional behaviors in a client's repertoire so that the client has everything he or she came in with plus what the client gets out of the psychotherapeutic relationship. Thus, the client is free to choose from a whole series of behavior response alternatives. The increase in the repertoire of responses allows the client to choose freely from a large number of behavior options. By never seeking to eliminate any particular behavior, the therapist never makes the value judgment that a behavior is wrong. With many dysfunctional behaviors (in the judgment of the therapist), the client will recognize them on his or her own and eliminate them. One does not have to promote that happening, one simply provides response alternatives. While the constructionalist solution was proposed for the dilemmas in behavior modification, it applies to every treatment modality.

The third solution is to become Promethean. Prometheus was the Greek demigod who risked the wrath of Zeus by sharing the knowledge and power of fire with mankind. He gave power to people who had no power. After Zeus discovered this action, Prometheus was chained to the side of a mountain where every day a vulture came along and ate out his liver. This continued until Hercules released Prometheus from his chains. The Promethean model is one of sharing power and information fully with the client, in any professional setting. All files, all information are shared with the client. No closed files are maintained and all the decision making is participatory. Are retardates able to participate? Are prisoners responsible enough to participate? What about the whole range of people who cannot make judgments about themselves? In each case people who "can't," almost always can. There are nonpejorative ways of assessing a client with the client as co-assessor. In one project positive and negative valences were attached to every descriptive term about clients with whom we worked; when many more negatively descriptive terms were used, diagnosticians were sent back to take another look to see if more positive descriptions could be found. To be Promethean means moving to a fully egalitarian relationship with the client with whom we are involved, and giving up power and control.

It's time perhaps for mental health professionals to discard the poisonous and sexist and non-Promethean techniques that we have used for too long.

REFERENCES

1. Robbins, T. *Even Cowgirls Get the Blues.* Boston: Houghton Mifflin, 1976.
2. Ryan, W. *Blaming the Victim.* New York: Vintage, 1971.
3. Sarbin, T. The dangerous individual: An outcome of social identity transformations. *Brit. J. Criminology,* 22:285-295, 1967.
4. Prather, H. *Notes to myself.* Moab, Utah: Real People Press, 1970.
5. *Neuman v. Alabama.* 406 F. Supp. 318 (M.D. Ala. 1976).
6. *Worley James v. George Wallace, et al.* Combined with *Neuman v. Alabama* (5).
7. Piotrowski, Z. A., & Hammer, E. F. Hostility as a factor in clinician's personality as it affects his interpretation of projective drawings (HTP). *J. Consult. Psychol.,* 24:210-215, 1952.
8. *Baxstrom v. Herold.* 383 U.S. 107 (U.S. Supreme Ct. 1966).
9. *Vitaly Tarasoff et al. v. The Regents of the University of California et al.* 118 Cal. Rptr. 129 (1974).
10. Trent, C. Psychiatric malpractice insurance and its problems: An overview. *This Volume,* pp. 101-117, 1978.
11. Kardener, S., Fuller, M., & Mensh, I. A survey of physicians' attitudes and practices regarding erotic and nonerotic contact with patients. *Amer. J. Psychiat.,* 130:1077-1081, 1973.
12. Holyroyd, J. C., & Brodsky, A. M. Psychologists' attitudes and practices regarding erotic and nonerotic contact with patients. *Amer. Psychol.,* 32:843-849, 1977.

13. Ziskin, J. *Coping with Psychiatric and Psychological Testimony,* 2nd ed. Beverly Hills, Cal.: Law & Psychology Press, 1975.
14. Rosenhan, D. L. On being sane in insane places. *Science,* 179:250-258, 1973.
15. Schwitzgebel, R. K. A contractual model for the protection of the rights of institutionalized mental patients. *Amer. Psychol.,* 30:815-820, 1975.
16. Goldiamond, I. Toward a constructional approach to social problems: Ethical and constitutional issues raised by applied behavior analysis. *Behaviorism,* 2:1-84, 1974.

Part IV

Confidentiality

We Americans have an insatiable curiosity which we gratify by a demand for information. Private lives are fair targets. Indiscretions of heroes and of congressman are described to an eager public. We squirrel away enormous amounts of data that could be useful for some purpose some day.

The public's legitimate need to know, the distrust of institutions in the post-Watergate era, the publication of secret documents in the press, and the right of an individual to privacy are all tangled in the same bundle. Storage of much information in computers and the ease of access to private material demand steps be taken toward the formulation of guidelines to protect privacy.

There is a legal duty not to release private information about a patient's illness without his or her consent except when required to do so by law (as in involuntary commitment, child custody and divorce cases, and situations where the patient alleges pain and suffering and introduces his or her mental condition in evidence).

The patient who waives confidentiality may be quite unaware of the material in his or her clinical record. Public release could embarrass or even destroy a career. Fact, fancy and unverified hearsay information exist side by side with patient secrets. The physician is bound by an ethical tradition of thousands of years to preserve the patient's confidences. In today's world demands are made for information to pay the hospital bill, to establish credit, or to satisfy a regulatory agency. Countless requests are made for information in the clinical records.

Privilege must be established by statute. Thirty-six states and D.C. have physician-patient privilege laws. Most are too loosely written to have value. Perhaps the best models are the psychotherapist privilege laws of Illinois and Connecticut (now also in Kentucky, Florida, Maryland, California, Georgia, and Massachusetts).

The goal here is to specify that confidential relations and communications between psychotherapist and patient be on the same privilege basis as that between attorney and client. There is an obligation to press for legislation in each state. To facilitate this drive, a National Commission on Confidentiality of Health Care Records has been formed to encourage adoption of model legislation.

Maurice Grossman is a national authority on confidentiality. He describes the origins of the right to privacy as a concept and the development of "the need to know." Patients need to know that what is recorded about them may require a reasoned compromise as to what is written in the psychiatrist's clinical record.

In presenting the problems raised by the *Tarasoff* case in California, Grossman provides more details than can be found elsewhere. He provides a weighted argument against the extension of the ruling and calls for rebellion by the psychiatric community to prevent its adoption as national policy.

John Donnelly, the head of a prestigious private mental hospital, has been active in the development of the Connecticut law on privilege. He reminds psychiatry that psychiatrists owe their prominence as a specialty to society. Centuries of tradition protect the disclosures of patients as holy secrets. Enormous changes in the structure of society have occurred, however, with a need to share certain essential information. Donnelly understands confidentiality as an aspect of the right to privacy and privilege as a specific variety of confidentiality. Privilege is not a constitutional right but a specific grant made to individuals at risk. Either the patient or his attorney can void it. It is unrealistic, he argues, to demand that only the medical department of an insurance carrier or employer review all insurance claims of psychiatric patients. Better to work toward elimination of the stigma of mental illness and avoid recording of patient secrets. He coolly views the *Tarasoff* case as not as great a threat as Grossman believes it to be. A reasoned choice to warn an intended victim is given when the therapist truly believes there is likelihood of serious harm. He asks psychiatrists, who are loath to complete insurance claim forms, to ponder coverage without confidentiality v. confidentiality without coverage.

Chapter VII

Confidentiality:
The Right to Privacy versus
the Right to Know

MAURICE GROSSMAN, M.D.

The Declaration of Independence weaves together the phrases "We hold these truths to be self-evident," "men are created equal," "they are endowed by their Creator with certain unalienable Rights," and "among these are Life, Liberty, and the pursuit of Happiness." The entire document was an indictment by the people against their government for intolerable interference with these rights. New Hampshire was the first state to endorse these ideals by having its state representatives sign just below John Hancock.

The right to privacy is fundamentally necessary in health care. Ill health is a threat to life and interferes with and limits liberty, thus eliminating ill health is obviously in the pursuit of happiness. Legal, as well as medical, authorities agree that fear of disclosure of certain medical confidences would lead many to avoid treatment, or, at best, they would fail to disclose information necessary for their physician to make a diagnosis and plan treatment. This assurance of confidentiality is most marked in psychiatric care only by reason of the intimacy of the disclosures and the vulnerability of most patients. It is just as necessary in all medical care because every patient will have his or her emotions involved in an illness and treatment.

The Declaration of Independence was the earliest legal base for the supreme position of confidentiality in medical care. Health and privacy are not listed as such, but as just noted ill health threatens "Life, Liberty and the pursuit of Happiness." Whatever interferes with sound medical treatment deprives one of a basic "unalienable Right."*

Actually, these pronouncements did not achieve legal codification until after the U.S. Constitution was adopted in 1789. There was an uproar that the original Constitution did not carry guarantees to protect individuals from their government — the very problem that led to the War of Independence. In order to get all the colonies to join, the supporters of the Constitution promised a Bill of Rights to guarantee such protection. These first ten amendments were drafted to protect our inalienable rights and ratified in 1791 (1, 2). Usually the Fourth and Fifth Amendments are given as the support for the right to privacy.** Note that the Ninth Amendment blankets in all rights not specifically alluded to in the preceding eight amendments: "The enumeration in the Constitution, of certain rights, shall not be construed to deny or disparage others retained by the people." Certainly that would include any rights listed in the Declaration of Independence. That would include prohibition against any legal measures that interfere with "Life, Liberty and the pursuit of Happiness" — not just the deprivations given in the First, Fourth, and Fifth Amendments. Again, not until 1828

---

* Until then, these concepts were embodied in the *moral* dicta formulated in the fourth century B.C. by the Pythagoreans in what we call the Hippocratic Oath.

** The Fourteenth Amendment in 1868 obligated state governments to acknowledge the same limits theretofore applicable only to the federal government.

was this legal base for medical privacy codified specifically when New York State created the Physician-Patient Privilege. New York's action was followed by most states—but not all.

It may seem elementary to define certain terms of common usage, generally well understood. Yet some far-reaching court decisions have failed to differentiate between such "simple" concepts. It is necessary to differentiate the following. "Privacy" refers to all that encompasses the individual's thoughts, knowledge, acts including associations, property, and person which he has an inalienable right to hold to himself against encroachment by others, including his government. "Confidentiality" arises when this individual entrusts to another that which is of his privacy—usually because of a vital need to share. It requires the explicit or implicit mutual understanding that this second individual will use it only for the first individual's vital need, and not make it available to a third party without the first party's consent.

The law takes the position there may be other constitutional rights that outweigh the individual's constitutional right to privacy. It then can legally demand the surrender of that which is private. Under certain circumstances, legislatures can determine a "pecking order" of importance and ascribe such an inviolable position to "confidentiality" that even the government (courts) cannot compel disclosure. Such communications are thereby "privileged." Classes of confidentiality so ordained might be "husband-wife privilege," "attorney-client privilege," "physician-patient privilege," "psychotherapist-patient privilege." Only the attorney-client and clergy-penitent privileges are usually free of exceptions. Do note that "privilege," as a protection, applies against demands made in judicial or quasi-judicial proceedings by bodies having this overriding power to compel disclosure. Legislatures have this power and can delegate it. The eminent legal authority's, J. H. Wigmore, discussion of privilege, including his four postulates required before legislating a privilege, tends to govern the legal profession's view (3).

The rights of the individual to the privacy of his medical course have usually had a low priority. Slovenko (4) points out how the Hippocratic concept was a minority view well into the Middle Ages. In England up through the eighteenth century confidentiality was practiced as an attribute of the professional gentleman. The government's attack on this right of privacy and privilege was standardized for Anglo-Saxon law in 1776 by Lord Chief Justice Mansfield's forcing physician Hawkins to testify in a suit against the Duchess of Kingston for bigamy (5). The history of medical privilege, which began in the United States with New York's 1828 law, is one of escalating erosions until today physician-patient privilege offers no protection (6). From the beginning, in English courts, "the King has a right to know," and even earlier, from roots in the ecclesiastical courts, when the "truth will be discovered" by ordeal or combat, the Anglo-Saxon court systems have justified the legal demand to know on the basis that the legal system could not function otherwise (7), and this right to demand disclosure must disregard what injury it does to the subject of disclosure. Wigmore (8) quotes from the Massachusetts Constitution of 1788: "This inconvenience which he may suffer, in consequence of his testimony, by way of enmity, or disgrace, or ridicule or other disfavoring action of fellow members of the community is also a contribution which he makes in payment of his duties to society in its function of executing justice." To this day this is the attitude of the legal system.

Oddly enough, in its dedication to the state's function of executing justice, the law makes special provision for the attorney. "In order to promote freedom of consultation of legal advisors by clients, the apprehension of compelled disclosures by the legal advisor must be removed; hence the law must prohibit such disclosures except on the client's consent"; and in a 1943 statement ". . . all people and all courts have looked upon that confidence between the party and attorney to be so great that it would be destructive to all business if attorneys were to disclose the business of their clients" (9). Quoting L. C. Brougham in 1833:

> The foundation of the rule is not difficult to discover. It is not (as has sometimes been said) on account of any particular importance which the law attributes to the business of legal profession . . . (though certainly it may not be very easy to discover why a like privilege has been refused to other, and especially to medical advisors). But it is our regard to the interests of justice which cannot be beholden, and to the administration of justice . . . . If the [attorney-client] privilege did not exist at all . . . a man would not venture to consult any skillful person or would only dare tell his counsellor half his case [9].

The catch in the protecting features of the Bill of Rights is that these rights can be forfeited by "due process," which consists of legislation by representatives of the people ordering the forfeiture because of overriding needs of the social community. Sometimes this "due process" stems from the common law transplanted from British law prior to the Declaration of Independence. The law has thus endowed the government with "divine rights" that seem to neutralize the intent of our separation from Britain. This argument does not overlook the phenomenon that at times in court one right of the Constituiton conflicts with another right. The way these conflicting rights are weighed might well be examined in the laws and court decisions affecting confidentiality. The background of inherent bias can best be absorbed in reading Wigmore's discussions of privilege (10). His eminent authority penetrates the legal profession, which thereupon is reluctant to see the paradoxes of argument created to bolster inconsistent positions.

Two examples may whet your appetite enough to read the many discussions and authorities cited in the unabridged text. Wigmore quotes a judicial opinion in 1836 upholding the New York 1828 law (11): "The ground on which communications to counsel are privileged is the supposed necessity of a full knowledge of the facts to advise correctly, and to prepare for the proper defence or prosecution of a suit. But surely the necessity of consulting a medical adviser, when life itself may be in jeopardy is still stronger."* Wigmore then "defeats" this argument (12). He first indicates that disclosure by an attorney might defeat his client, whereas disclosure by a physician would not impair his ability to cure his patient. In this he ignores what all authorities have repeated through the ages, that faced with the knowledge his physician might disclose his secrets at a later date, the patient will initially withhold vital information necessary for proper diagnosis and treatment. He ignores that the 1836 statement is based on "full knowledge of the facts to advise correctly, and to prepare" and, in the case of the physician, switches the argument base by assuming the physician already has all the information for diagnosis and overlooking the chilling effect of possible disclosure. Given the avowed tenet that the "truth must be exposed in court for proper justice," and Wigmore's fear that the client might lose if the attorney disclosed all, one wonders how absolute the tenet of truth really is.

The second example demonstrates that these paradoxes flourish throughout current legal thought. Wigmore continues in his "demolition" of the 1836 statement with the same argument today given for the patient-litigant exceptions to physician- or psychotherapist-patient privilege. The patient who fears disclosure has an option because "the patient has voluntarily brought the [issue requiring disclosure] into court." It is difficult to see how this does not apply to the clients of

* In the same context refer to L. C. Brougham's statement given above.

attorneys. This will be referred to again in discussing the *Lifschutz* decision (13).

If we get away from the professional treatment sphere, where as we shall see later practically absolute confidentiality is legislatively demanded, and get into the arena with lawyers, the "right to privacy" with its constitutional armor seems to vaporize into an impotent nonentity. Physician-patient privilege has been subjected to so many exceptions by legislatures and courts that the loopholes have replaced the protective fabric as noted above (6). Even the psychotherapist-patient privilege has a patient-litigant exception that nullifies its usefulness (14).

Originally there was no medical privilege in the Code of Evidence proposed by the U.S. Supreme Court in 1969. Before it was sent to Congress for approval, the psychotherapist-patient privilege (Rule 504) was added because there was a good constitutional basis for it (15). It even fitted Wigmore's postulates (3)—perhaps better than the attorney-client privilege. A joint committee of the American Medical Association (AMA) and the American Bar Association (ABA) recommended action to eliminate Rule 504 from the code. The AMA wrote Congress to defeat this protection and expressed favor for the impotent physician-patient privilege (16). Eventually in Congress *all* privilege was deleted from the code, largely in a battle of states' rights vs. federal power (17). The ABA is continuing its battle against privilege. It favors broadening of the law's dictum of "discovery" (the right to know). It still does not apply this principle of "discovery" to attorney-client privilege or to the attorney's "work papers." It might be suspected that, in contrast to the above, the legal profession would support wholeheartedly the inviolability of confidentiality should one of its members find a case where an attorney violates his client's confidence and could be sued for malpractice.

The ABA opposition to a psychotherapist-patient privilege bill passed by the New York Legislature undoubtedly influenced Governor Carey to veto that bill in 1975. The ABA again opposed the measure as it went through the New York Legislature in 1976. Again the legislature passed the bill which was then vetoed. Personal communications indicate the ABA is again studying the problem with an April 1976 report by Professor Gomberg to the Criminal Justice Section, allegedly following their traditional lines.

The private information about this report refers to another issue that suggests a paradoxical bias. Since privilege is based on privacy of the individual, the privilege is that of the *patient* or *client — not* of the physician or attorney. Courts have ruled that all of the physician-psychiatrist's records on a patient are part of the patient's privacy. However, the U.S. Supreme Court has ruled that an attorney's work file and his notes, including data about his client's case contained therein, are not affected by the client's acts nor subject to discovery demands as would be documents in the attorney's possession. The key element was "it would be unfair to have all the attorney's 'work' made available to opposing counsel" (18). (It does again raise the question of how overriding is "the need for the truth" in court.)

In contrast, it can be demonstrated that psychotherapy, even intense, in-depth, frequent treatment, can be conducted effectively without any note taking or records. Some exceedingly well-qualified psychiatrists are convinced that note taking may even interfere with treatment. Therefore notes of treatment sessions are not necessary for the effectiveness of treatment. Most often they are kept, especially if in detail, for research and teaching purposes. The "habit" is sometimes a carryover from residency days when it was required for learning and supervisory purposes. In most of these situations the notes will include the thought processes and reactions of the therapist. While the commercial, professional aspects of a rival profiting do not enter here, the "search for the truth" about the patient does. The notes are recorded for the needs of society that are served by research, teaching, and learning integral to perfecting a profession's service to society, but the patient can suffer from disclosure in court.

Even more important is the nature of the psychotherapeutic material recorded. All of it is the free flow of thought, encouraged by the therapeutic process, *uncensored* by reality, truth, or reason, in order to reach the distortions and unreason of the unconscious. Yet the law (chiefly the legal profession) would demand this be exposed as "truth." All the wild fantasy, childhood distortions, and the "protective," sometimes self-damaging, beliefs created for psychological defenses that get into such records will be exposed in public as "truth." This distorted material, labeled "truth," can be used by opposing counsel to a fare-thee-well. The highest court of the land decrees one approach for the attorney and another for the physician. The ABA could hardly do less.

The process of getting the information from confidential files into the public domain is by subpoena or search warrant. The subpoena and search warrant route are part of the protective fruits of the Fourth Amendment. The current machinery for their issuance is for the convenience of the legal profession even though it circumvents the protection of the amendment. It is surprising how frequently physicians and hospitals are intimidated by the threatening language of a subpoena. In private discussions attorneys admit that the harassing tactic of using these writs is as important in court contests as the legal "right to the truth." The reasons for, and the need to question, and at times challenge, the legality of these court orders has been discussed in another paper in greater detail (19). Instances have occurred of using search warrants in lieu of subpoenas because there is no time to challenge the legality of surrendering the confidential data. When one considers that search warrants are usually obtained

by officials dedicated to upholding the law, and issued by
courts of even greater dedication, such occurrences make it
hard not to succumb to cynicism.

But perhaps cynicism can be differentiated from realism
by the steps taken to circumvent the consequences of distrusted
practices. John Adams was not being cynical when he
observed, "Reason, justice, and equity never had weight
enough on the face of the earth to govern the councils of men.
It is interest alone which can be trusted" (20). Jefferson agreed
that the attempt to build a just society must not presuppose
just men: "In questions of power, then, let no more be said of
confidence in man, but bind him down from mischief by the
chains of the Constitution" (21).*

It was noted above that in spite of Adams's and Jefferson's
views the framers of the original Constitution ran into great
opposition because that document did not protect the people
from their government. In 1789, the experience that such a
need was paramount was still too recent to forget. Learned
Hand in the Oliver Wendell Holmes lectures on *The Bill of
Rights* notes that the Bills of Rights had been "foreshadowed
though not fully anticipated in the exordium of the
Declaration of Independence (22). He goes on to state that all
departments "were bound to accept the decision of the
Supreme Court even if there was no authority for this" even
with the understanding "that the three Departments were
separate and coequal" (23). He then quotes Hamilton:

> "It is far more rational to suppose that the courts were de-
> signed to be an intermediate body between the people and
> the legislature, in order, among other things, to keep the

---

* I am indebted to Jehane Burns for the leads to the original
Jefferson sources. The quotes were a striking part of the IBM Bi-
centennial exhibit, *Franklin and Jefferson*, at the British Museum,
London, 1975, and at the Los Angeles County Museum, 1976. Burns is on
the staff of Charles and Ray Eames, Venice, California, creators of the exhibit.

latter within the limits assigned to their authority . . . [It does not] suppose a superiority of the judicial to the legislative power. It only supposes that the power of the people is superior to both; and that where the will of the legislature, declared in its statutes, stands in opposition to that of the people declared in the Constitution, the Judges ought to be governed by the latter rather than the former" [24].

Hand continues further: ". . . it was altogether in keeping with the established practice for the Supreme Court to assume an authority to keep the States, Congress and the President within their prescribed powers. Otherwise, the government could not proceed as planned . . . However, this power is not a logical deduction from the structure of the Constitution, but only a practical condition upon its successful operation" (25).

Neither Hand nor Hamilton referred to the obvious — that the courts are but another department of government. The Bill of Rights was added to the Constitution to protect the people from the whole government, not just two-thirds. Here we might again note Jefferson's quote above on the need to bind *men* down from mischief by the chains of the Constitution. Jefferson extended this concern to the judiciary when he stated in his autobiography: ". . . our Judges are effectively independent of the nation. But this ought not to be. . . . It is not enough that honest men are appointed judges. All know the influence of interest on the minds of man, and how unconsciously his judgement is warped by that influence" (26).

From time to time justices have been aware of this problem undermining the ideal of a perfect judicial process. The human element of bias and response to an emotional issue can discolor a sincere effort to be guided by the Constitution. Justice Felix Frankfurter made crystal clear the need to separate personal leanings and cleave solely to constitutional principles in judicial decision: "As a member of this Court I am not justified in writing my private notions of policy into the Constitution, no matter how deeply I may cherish them or how mischievous I may deem their disregard. . . . It can never be emphasized too much that one's own opinion about the wisdom or evil of a law should be excluded altogether when one is doing one's duty on the bench" (27). In the same decision he refers to "the uncontrollable power wielded by the [Supreme] Court" and ". . . judicial restraint becomes more and not less important." In *Griswold* (28), in dissent, Justice Black reaffirms this: "Repugnance and evil qualities in the eyes of the Justice have no bearing on a judicial decision of what is the law." He repeats it later with: "He [J. Goldberg] also states without proof satisfactory to me, that [in subsequent cases] in making decisions on this basis [Ninth Amendment] Judges will not consider their personal and private notions" (29).

The Watergate experience awakened the country to how deeply the Constitution had been eroded by the government. The highest officials, sworn to defend those principles, were the most flagrant and deliberate violators of the Bill of Rights. The office of the Presidency and the Department of Justice have the greatest authority and responsibility for protecting those rights, and for punishing willful transgressors. The excuse that it was done to save the country aggravated the affront, already intolerable, because of the secrecy and lying that characterized the early stages of the crisis. Little has been said of less obvious erosions of the rights in the other two sectors of government. What did result was a nationwide rash of legislation to protect the rights of the individual from invasion by government and private organization wherever there existed detailed record keeping which had been used against individual's interests. Federal legislation for protection in credit transactions and Freedom of Information laws were soon joined by the Federal Privacy Act of 1974, limited to federal agencies. The detailed spelling out of protection in gathering, storing, and particularly in use of private information is so complex that it probably creates a field day for the legal profession and eventually headaches for the courts. All these acts contain exceptions by mandating that the new laws must not interfere with governmental function and that invasion of the rights is acceptable on court-issued subpoenas and search warrants — including wire tapping. Little has been said on how easily these writs have been obtained.

A new development is where the right to know is exercised by the patient. New legislation affirms the right of an individual to know what of his private information is stored, creating a separate problem for medical records. First, experience has shown that some patients cannot tolerate emotionally some aspects of their recorded data. This is most evident with psychiatric treatment records, but not restricted thereto. Second, such confidential records may include confidential material of third parties which may not be disclosed safely to the patient of record. A suggested compromise is that medical records, on request of the patient or patient's authorized representative, will be released to a physician of requestor's choice. This selected physician will take the responsibility of determining whether either or both of the factors described are in the records to be released. The physician will determine what can be released, and will interpret the record so that it is not misunderstood by the patient. This suggestion has been incorporated in some of the recent legislation introduced.

While these current developments have made more specific rights that were already protected by the Constitution, they will not eliminate the problems in organizations' misuse of privacy factors either through conviction or rationalization of overriding needs. Already existing examples are the regulations announced in the *Federal Register* for implementing some of these laws (30). Those from HEW specifically weight their implementation for disclosure on the need to oversee their vast empire of welfare and medical care. One HEW series was a demand that hospitals use Social Security numbers as a common identifier (31) — one of the first line of prohibitions in all such legislation.

Some legislation requiring strict judicial checks of invasion of Fourth Amendment rights inadvertently increases the risks. H.R. 214 of the 94th Congress, first session, included medical records in those that would require a court order, based on probable cause, for any "surreptitious entry." In the light of Congress' failing to provide for federal medical privilege, the wording in effect legalized procedure for invading medical records that otherwise would have been protected by a constitutional base for claiming privilege from such writs (32). Congressman Kastenmeier's Judiciary Subcommittee, which held the hearings on the bill, did delete "medical records" from H.R. 214.

All of which brings us back to judicial determination as the final arbiter in the right of privacy vs. the right to know. Developments in California have played a key role in affecting these decisions nationwide. As a guideline, it would help to know certain California statutes governing the issues. The series for *psychotherapist-patient privilege* is in the Code of Evidence beginning with Section 1010 (33). Section 1016 is the exception for the patient-litigant, when the patient injects his "mental or emotional condition" into issue, or his condition has been tendered by plaintiff for damages for injury or death of the patient. Section 1024 — "Dangerous Patient" — states "there is no privilege . . . if the psychotherapist has reasonable cause to believe that the patient is in such mental or emotional condition as to be dangerous to himself or to the person or property of another and that disclosure of the communication is *necessary to prevent the threatened danger*" (emphasis added). Do recall the definition of "privilege" as restricted to governmental (judicial) demand to know. This "privilege" is further supported by the sections cited above in the Code of

Evidence. A general rule in the Code of Evidence, Section 912(a), reads: "[the privilege] is waived if holder, without coercion, has disclosed a significant part of the communication or has consented to such disclosure made by anyone" (34).

The California Business and Professional Code includes the laws for certification of health practitioners. For dentists, it lists a number of factors that represent unprofessional conduct for which the possible penalties range from revocation of license to probation (35). Number 3 in this section is "Willful betrayal of professional secrets." For physicians, this same "Willful betrayal of professional secrets" is an entire separate section (36). No exceptions are given. Thereby any such willful disclosures are legally labeled malpractices, and would add civil and financial hazard to the penalties already listed (37). For reference later, it is well to note that "willful" is defined in the California Penal Code (38) as "A purpose or willingness to commit the act. It does not require intent to violate law or injure another or to acquire any advantage."* This will be referred to in discussion of the *Tarasoff* case (39).

The most important governing California law is the 1969 revision of the Welfare and Institutions Code beginning with Division 5, officially designated "The Lanterman-Petris-Short Act" (L.P.S.) (40). Section 5001 is *Declaration of legislative intent.*" Subsection (a) reads: "to end the inappropriate, indefinite, and involuntary commitment of mentally disordered persons and persons impaired by chronic alcoholism and to end legal disabilities." Subsection (c) is "to *guarantee and protect public safety*" (emphasis added); (d) "to safeguard individual rights through judicial review"; (f) "to encourage

---

* A commentary under Section 2379 (of physician's obligations) records that a Minnesota court (under their code) ascribed "bad purpose" to "willful." But the California Penal Code is quite precise. Even so, a California court has ruled similarly to the Minnesota decision in spite of the preciseness of Penal Code Section 7.

the full use of all existing agencies, professional personnel and public funds to accomplish these objectives. . . ."

Section 5005 provides immunity for any "person complained against in any petition or proceeding initiated by virtue of the provisions of this part. . . ." (41).

Section 5150 describes in extreme detail the legal procedure to follow "when any person is a danger to others or to himself" (42). Do note here as elsewhere the language consists of "*is* a danger," not "*will be.*" Note that Section 5001 (c), in contrast, states "to guarantee and protect *public* safety" *after* (a) to guarantee the civil rights of *patients*; and then (d) is added to "*safeguard* [these] *rights through judicial review*" (when there is a conflict between [a] and [c]?)

Section 5201 (43) indicates that *any* individual may apply to the legal machinery to consider involuntary hospitalization because of dangerousness (emphasis added). This suggests that "any person" involved would be covered by immunity of Section 5005.

Section 5203 (44) prescribes criminal or civil liability, including damages to person outraged, if a petitioner (of Section 5201) does so with knowledge that person is not a danger to self or others.

Sections 5328 (45) and 5330 (46) contain the most stringent demands for confidentiality and penalties for violation. Section 6006 extends the same civil rights to voluntary patients including those treated by private mental institutions (47). Throughout L.P.S. are references to strong admonitions against release of information "with penalties of $500, or triple actual damage, whichever is greater." Note these for later reference.

The legislature went through a long, extensive review of problems before codifying the detail of L.P.S. Special attention was paid to the problem of the potentially dangerous patient (48).

The above is the legal basis on which the California

Supreme Court gave its decision in the *Tarasoff* (39) and *Lifschutz* (13) cases.* In the latter, the court affirmed that, based on the U.S. Supreme Court's decision in *Griswold* (28), there is a constitutional right for protecting confidentiality in psychotherapy if such treatment is to be sought by those who need it, and if the treatment is to succeed (49). No mention was made of "Life, Liberty and the pursuit of Happiness." Nevertheless, the court upheld the waiver of privilege because the patient: (1) had sought damages for his emotional condition; and (2) had waived his privilege by having publicly admitted he had sought treatment from the plaintiff (50). However, the court indicated the waiver was limited to that disclosure for its reason (2) and that for its reason (1) waiver of privilege should be narrowly construed to mean disclosure of mental conditions disclosed by the patient in the suit (51). Here the court itself recognized the effect of broad disclosures.

> If the provision had as broad an effect as is suggested by the petitioner it might effectively deter many psychotherapeutic patients from instituting any general claim for mental suffering and damage out of fear of opening up all past communications to discovery. This result would clearly be an intolerable and overbroad intrusion into the patient's privacy, not sufficiently limited to the legitimate state interest embodied in the provision and would create opportunities for harassment and blackmail [52].

The court did not give recognition to another frequent occurrence, that of injured parties suing for emotional damage, needing treatment for those emotional damages, and avoiding treatment because they fear disclosures of intimate life will be forced from the therapist.

---

* For a summary of these cases, as well as *Griswold* (28), see Appendix.

The court rejected the existence of the therapist's right to claim privilege independently of the patient. Actually the privilege stems from the *patient's* right to privacy.* In rejecting the absolute right, Justice Tobriner, who wrote the decision, added, "The question whether such a ruling would have the medical merit claimed by the petitioner *must be addressed to the Legislature* [emphasis added]; we can find no basis for such a ruling in legal precedent or principle" (54). (I shall consider this later in reviewing *Tarasoff.*) He then denied that the clergy-penitent privilege provided such a precedent. Nowhere was there any consideration that the evidence required could be obtained from other sources, thereby excluding the need for testimony from the therapist.

In *Griswold* (55), Justice Goldberger called attention to the fact: "These statutes demonstrate that means for achieving the same basic purpose . . . are available . . . without need to invade the area of protected freedom." In refuting Dr. Lifschutz's reference to the *Griswold* case as supporting his independent right to the privilege for the protection of all his past, present, and future cases, the court indicated the *Griswold* decision was based on the patient's right of privilege (56). The court overlooked the U.S. Supreme Court's reference in *Griswold* to 346 US 249 that a white defendant had standing in matters affecting blacks, even though no black was a party to the suit: "The white defendant had standing to raise issues that it violated the Constitutional rights of Negroes" (57). Therefore, using the analogous reasoning, the psychotherapist needs the independent right of privilege, exercising the rights of other present and future patients whose therapy could be affected, particularly given the California court's own recognition that the threat of disclosure would intimidate patients (58). The court's specious argument that the law with its

* For reasons suggesting a need for an independent claim of privilege by the psychotherapist, see testimony, June 5, 1974, before the U.S. Senate Judiciary Committee hearings on proposed Federal Code of Evidence (53).

exceptions had not interfered with the growth of psychiatry (59) overlooks the court's own reasoning. Other factors may explain the "fact" of therapist confidentiality and/or disclosure more rationally.

The ultimate view of the California Supreme Court's *Lifschutz* decision can best be judged in subsequent cases. In the *Robertson* (60) and *Caesar* (61) cases, the all-important dictum that disclosure under Section 1016 must be limited to protect the constitutional rights of the patient, but that the limited disclosure is necessary, could not be applied in the opinion of inferior courts. In the absence of legislative and judicial guidelines, total disclosure remained in demand and was so ordered by appellate courts. For some unclear reason, the California Supreme Court agreed to review the *Robertson* case, but refused to review the *Caesar* case. It never did get to the *Robertson* case, because the defendants settled out of court for the full amount of damages claimed before it could be heard in the California Supreme Court. The difference between the two cases might be considered in understanding the California Supreme Court's views as they affected its *Tarasoff* decision.

A digression will illustrate the problems created by Section 1016—the patient-litigant exception to privilege. Insurance companies demand full details—sometimes the entire record —before considering payment of health care insurance claims. In refusing to give them such revealing material which could be destructive to the patient, and is also not truly essential to establish the validity of the claim, frequently therapist and patient are inviting refusal of payment. The only recourse is to initiate court action for payment. To file a suit injects the mental condition into issue because it is for that condition that treatment was needed. Section 1016 then opens all the confidential data to disclosure in public court hearing when it was necessary to guard it in the first place from limited but still unsafe disclosure to the insurance company—a regular Catch 22 situation.

The *Tarasoff* case in California demonstrates most graphically the multiple factors that influence the right to privacy versus the right to know. It encompasses the primary factor of two conflicting constitutional rights; the role of the judiciary in weighing these rights; that the judiciary is answerable neither to the other two branches of government nor to the public, in contrast to the legislative and executive branches; that Jefferson's aphorism applies to the judiciary (especially since they are answerable to no one); and the different attitude of the law toward the legal profession than to other segments of society.

The story as it unfolds in the introduction of the California Supreme Court's first decision of December 23, 1974 (39), begins with a patient, Prosenjit Poddar, receiving outpatient psychotherapy at the Cowell Memorial Hospital of the University of California at Berkeley. The date on which he began therapy was not available to the court. On August 20, 1969, Poddar's therapist determined that Poddar, in his threats to kill Tatiana Tarasoff, had become a great enough risk to warrant starting proceedings for involuntary hospitalization and did so. At the time Tatiana was visiting in Brazil for the summer and did not return for approximately two months. In accordance with L.P.S. procedure (described above), the therapist, Dr. Moore, applied to the campus police to take Poddar into custody pending the issuance of a 72-hour hold for observation, also in accordance with L.P.S. (A complicating factor is that at that time the campus police were not "peace officers" legislatively, but since have achieved that status.) L.P.S. dictates that the party to whom application is made must determine independently that the patient presents evidence of being dangerous. The police did take Poddar into custody, decided he was not dangerous, and freed him with a warning to stay away from Tatiana. A complication, clouding the issue further, was the absence of the director of the clinic at the time; on his return days later he demanded that all records of the attempt to secure involuntary hospitalization be destroyed. (Not in the record are two factors that may be involved. First, the University had previously been sued for imprisonment following successful attempt for commitment [62]. Second, openly known and widely reported in local newspapers was an ongoing feud between the director and the therapy staff.) As might have been expected, Poddar thereafter refused to return for further therapy.

Nowhere in the court's decision is there any linkage between these factors although all are taken up individually. Even Justice Mosk in his forceful criticism of the majority's reasoning, in his concurrence of ordering the case to trial, bases his concurrence on the "fact" that the therapist had decided "Poddar was *planning* to kill . . . Tatiana" (emphasis added) (63). And he concurred in the majority's major determination that there is a duty to warn under *Tarasoff* conditions.

Tatiana did not return home until October 1969. In the two-month interval Poddar was free, caused no problems, showed no evidence of violence, and in fact became a roommate of Tatiana's brother. We must assume he voiced no threat against Tatiana during this time, otherwise it would have constituted a warning. On October 27, 1969, shortly after Tatiana's return, Poddar killed her. Apparently the plaintiff's statements seeking damages went into inflammatory detail of the violence, giving the multiple number of stabbings and shooting.

Tatiana's parents sued the psychologist treating Poddar, Dr. Moore, the physicians with whom the latter consulted for seeking the involuntary hospitalization, the police who failed to carry through with the custody proceedings, the director of the clinic, and primarily the Regents of the University of California who employed all the others. The suit was on four grounds of causing or contributing to the wrongful death of their daughter. The lower courts dismissed the action outright on the basis of immunity for the multiple defendants and the psychotherapist's need to preserve confidentiality.

On appeal, the California Supreme Court agreed with the lower courts on all counts except one entered by the plaintiffs as the second of the four causes of action: failure to warn Tatiana's family of the "danger" — "since they *knew* that Poddar was at large and dangerous" (emphasis added) (64). In dismissing the need for confidentiality, the summation of the court's argument rests in one sentence: "*The protective privilege ends where the public peril begins.*" It is interesting to note that this sentence in the original December 23, 1974 decision (p. 21) is repeated verbatim in the July 1, 1976 post-rehearing decision (65), and has proven a catch-phrase used as precedent in country-wide hearings after the original order was made to return the case to the lower court for trial.

This sentence based on an uncontested premise that society needs protection obscures the processes within the decision that led to this basic assertion. When two conflicting constitutional rights are presented, a judgment must indicate which takes precedence. Usually legislative examination and debate will decide by statute. In the *absence* of legislative guidelines courts must then ascribe precedent values.

Justice Frankfurter in *Gobitis* (66) reminds: "Judicial review itself as a limitation on popular government is a fundamental part of our constitutional scheme. But to the legislatures no less than to courts is committed the guardianship of deeply-cherished liberties . . . to fight out the wise use of legislative authority in the forum of public opinion and before legislative assemblies rather than to transfer such a contest to the judicial arena seems to vindicate the self-confidence of a free people." Two years later, in *Barnette* (67), he quotes Justice Oliver Wendell Holmes, Jr., to the same effect. Learned Hand quotes Marshall in *Ware v. Hylton* (68): ". . . the judicial authority can have no right to question the validity of a law unless such jurisdiction is *expressly* given by the constitution" (69). The California Supreme Court affirmed this thesis in *Lifschutz*, as noted above, when it stated: considering whether "the benefits to be derived from a broadening of the existing privilege would outweigh the detriments resulting from a narrowing of evidence available in litigation, the balancing of those alternatives remains in the legislature" (70).

To clarify the concepts involved, it should be noted that the court's *Tarasoff* decision starts with the *duty* to break confidentiality where danger to society demands informing about the patient to prevent a danger. It switches somewhere to equate protecting society with warning a supposed victim. The catch-phrase sentence referred to previously applies to the former. Nowhere does the court demonstrate, let alone prove, that the two concepts are equivalent; nor do Fleming and Maximov (71) in their study on which the court heavily relied. (This aspect will be discussed later.)

The court also keeps using statements such as "to *predict* that Poddar presented a serious danger of violence . . . [and] did in fact *predict* that Poddar *would* kill" (emphasis added) (72). It indicates that the *amicus* brief introduced by national professional organizations did bring to their attention from the authoritative source of the treating professions that therapists can *not* predict a violent act. The statistics of studied experiences ran approximately one eventual violent act out of 100 "predictions." None of these studies compared these to the average population incidence of violence. Nor was mention made that therapists can detect thought and emotional processes having a violence theme. At times they may detect a weakening of the ordinary restraints that keep such themes from overt expression, but they certainly cannot predict the future external events that may trigger such an increased weakening of control of the violent emotion or thought that leads to either a verbal or physical assault. They cannot predict whether an act that may take place, should control break, will be verbally or physically assaultive. The statistics all demonstrate that while therapists in the main take no chances with public safety, this stance is based on their recognizing an intensification of violent *thought*, not on their predicting an act of violence. They do not, and cannot foresee a violent act, so that rarely, and certainly not in *Tarasoff*, is there a foreseeable danger. The court's quoted precedents of requiring warning are not applicable because they represent actual foreseeable dangers where simple warning against an avoidable danger applies for protection. In *Tarasoff*, an after-the-fact incident is of no help in judging the imminence of danger before the fact. In this case, the eventual victim was absent for two months after "the duty to warn." The court's conjecture that had Poddar been confined "Tatiana might be alive today" (73) is reflected in the court's assumption that "Tatiana might be alive today" if a warning had been given.

The court overlooks facts. When interviewed by the police, Poddar showed no evidence of abnormal behavior, let alone any violent tendencies. It can be assumed that while living with Tatiana's brother, he neither showed nor threatened violence against Tatiana. (If he had, it would have been a warning.) L.P.S. would have *required* his release, even if he had been held for 72-hour observation, because in all probability he would have continued to show an absence of any behavior or threat to warrant further confinement. Parenthetically one might ask: If so released, on what grounds would a warning be given that violates California's code on medical ethics (36, 45, 46), and upon whom would fall "the duty to warn"? The fact that others disagreed with Moore,* added to the profession's experience that a prediction of a violent act cannot be made, weakens the court's conviction that Moore's original opinion, not strengthened by

---

* In addition to the police who interviewed Poddar in August 1969, at Poddar's criminal trial (10 Cal. 3d 750-1974) prosecution experts found him not insane, and the jury found him not insane at the time of the murder, in finding him guilty of second-degree murder.

clairvoyance equivalent to the court's hindsight, was a valid prediction "that Poddar would kill."

The court, as noted, continually equates "warning" with protection of society, and does not differentiate a viable, uncontestably present danger, such as a communicable disease, a washed-out bridge, dangerous machinery left with a key available to a child, an uncovered manhole in a frequented walkway, or a patient who has previously committed violence or shows unmistakable loss of control (the opposite of Poddar), from a possible threat that *might* become a danger and therefore is not truly foreseeable. The court's note that a physician is obligated to warn a patient about driving when prescribing medication that might affect his driving ability is an example of the court's stretching of analogies. The physician is not obligated to, and would do his patient a disservice if he notified the Department of Motor Vehicles of the *potential* danger. And if he did, would the Department of Motor Vehicles suspend the patient's driver's license? How would society be protected by the warning? And the patient would have grounds for relief from unprofessional conduct as defined in the statutes.

It is not acceptable to have the court merely assume "a warning" is equivalent to "a protection" when it uses that as a reason for violating the constitutional rights of untold numbers of present and future patients—directly in California and already by court action in other states. The need to break confidence is only to protect society from a foreseeable danger, and the degree of foreseeability must also be measured with due regard for the risks. Hand in his Oliver Wendell Holmes Lecture states that in exercising rights to make determination one "must be sure it isn't merely a personal bias and that the decision really addresses itself to avowed purpose of the law"—in this case to protect society (74). Hand refers to a basic principle in judging two conflicting constitutional rights. When a legislative act, or executive directive is based on one constitutional right, in conflict with a basic inalienable right of the people, the issue must go beyond the existence of that legislative or executive right. It must include the factor whether the challenged violation of the public's right has substance to carry out the legislative or executive intent. A corollary is there must be proof that there is a real need for involving that questioned act. The latter was illustrated in *Griswold* [28]" (74).

About two weeks before the court's first opinion of December 13, 1974, an incident took place in Seattle, Washington. A man who had already assaulted his estranged wife and threatened her with a knife in September 1974 was held for trial, released on low bail on recommendation of the prosecution, and (reminiscent of *Tarasoff*) warned to stay away from his wife; he then killed his wife on December 6, 1974 — a little over two months after his wife had warning (75). In San Francisco, December 27, 1974 — four days after the original *Tarasoff* decision — a man killed his former wife and when a police car appeared, killed himself. The wife had been warned. Appeal to the police led to a statement that "we cannot intervene because he may be threatening but he has not done anything." Friends had advised her to leave the country (76). So much for "warning" equating protection. Add to this score the destructive effect on the "victim" warned (plus studies that the warning would be mistaken 99 times out of 100). A physician friend told me how a family, openly threatened with killing by a burglar who was arrested after being shot by the home owner, lived in terror with devastating effect on every member — they all feared the man's escape from prison. This continued for several years until the burglar died of natural causes in prison. The *San Francisco Chronicle* (77) reports that a woman found guilty of trying to hire an assassin to kill her husband's ex-wife was then found not guilty by reason of insanity. The judge released her because "at this time [she] does not present a danger to herself or others" — a prediction, even though she had just been found guilty of conspiracy to kill. The defense attorney was given custody of three guns owned by the defendant and her husband. The district attorney notified the judge that the intended victim phoned him after the verdict and told him "she was frightened of her life and wondered if she should move elsewhere." The newspaper reports the judge replied, "Well, the world is full of frightened people and I guess she is just added to that list."

Approximately 50 people interested in *Tarasoff* were informally asked, "If you were warned under these circumstances — a psychiatric patient on the loose, who had threatened your life during therapy — how would you protect yourself?" Most first answered, "I'd call the police." When told of the above cases, they gave one of these replies: "I would hate going into hiding"; "I don't know"; and "I'd kill him if he came near." The warning offers no protection and may well harm the supposed victim. The intended victim will be harmed 99 out of 100 times through disclosure, and a warning given could lead to the patient's murder. The possibility that public disclosure might lead to some patients' suicide is not merely a psychiatric experience. In a case seeking damages for the suicide of a patient (78), the court quoted Schwartz (79), a legal authority, in giving three circumstances where a psychotherapist could be considered liable. One was violating confidentiality negligently or intentionally, so that the released information drove the patient to suicide. The news media is replete with stories of suicide following public disclosure about the victim who may or may not have been in treatment. Psychiatrists can document their experience of it happening to patients. The California Supreme Court takes a cavalier attitude to those unfortunates who need the help we label psychotherapy. They blind themselves to all the ramifications of warning. It does not occur to them that the content of the warning might be more devastating than the public fact that hospitalization and treatment were needed.

Ayers and Holbrook (80), who advocate a warning as "affirmative action," and the court in *Tarasoff* show a total disregard of what "affirmative action" is required to be; a flawed assumption that "a warning" offers any protection; and a total disregard that the error odds are 100 to 1 and that the disclosure could lead to more damage, including possible death to the patient, than would be saved by a procedure for which no evidence of efficacy is supplied, and evidence of failure is available. Relatively slight cost indeed!

Compounding this unwarranted, judgmental assumption by the court is its stepping out of its judiciary role. As noted previously, in *Lifschutz* the court was aware of its limits against stepping into the jurisdiction of the legislature. Reference was made to the restricting declaration of Chief Justice John Marshall, who is better remembered for extending the bounds of the Supreme Court's authority. Learned Hand supported Marshall's position when he stated: "It was altogether in keeping with established practice to assume [by the Supreme Court] an authority to keep the State, Congress and the President within their prescribed powers" (81). On the next page he asks a question: "is this a government of law as we have always supposed, or in the end, only one of men?" We must not forget the judiciary is also part of government that must not arbitrarily violate the rights of the individual; nor should it invade the realm of the legislature.

In *Tarasoff* we have a court that either overlooks or ignores the background of L.P.S., that tries to balance the civil rights of patients — so long ignored — and the needs and safety of society. In the report of the California Assembly first printed in 1966 as the background for L.P.S., the legislature paid special attention to "Potentially Dangerous Persons" (82). They started with the recognition that there are those patients *proven* dangerous, those *potentially dangerous*, and those *assumed to be a danger* to themselves or others (emphasis in original). The same evidence made available to the court was independently used by the legislature to conclude that in the "probably dangerous person, the evidence available indicates that there are no tests that can predict an individual's capacity for dangerous behavior." They recognized that the release or holding of such patients will be done "in theory only."

No definition is given of "proven dangerous" — probably because the only proof is an actual *act of violence*. On this basis even the attempted commitment of Poddar was stretching things to the limit. But apparently the legislature recognized a border zone between "proven" and "potentially" as reflected in L.P.S. (40).

The court made reference to the danger's being increased when Dr. Moore broke confidentiality to the police and Poddar terminated treatment. It is in keeping with the court's entire approach to omit this acknowledgement in the decision after the rehearing.

Taking all the preceding into account suggests the court did in fact go beyond legislative intent and act, and assumed an unwarranted legislative role. It in fact orders that every therapist practice his art and skill in defiance of the law protecting the civil right of patients, by the therapist's independently determining that a patient's condition warrants violating those constitutional rights without following the due process created by L.P.S. to stop therapists from doing just that.

The court's references to professional and legislative permission for this command are faulty. First the court makes reference to Section 1026 of the Code of Evidence, which deals with "privilege." Both by its definition of "privilege" and its place in the Code of Evidence, this section is applicable only in situations of governmental demands for testimony. It would be applicable only during the following of due process under L.P.S. and not independent of a court action. Section 2379 of the Business and Professional Code (36) is the only one applicable. This states that "willful betrayal of a professional secret constitutes unprofessional conduct within the meaning of this chapter."

The court in referring to the American Medical Association's Code of Ethics (83) ignores that Section 9 of that code not only refers to violating confidentiality if necessary to protect others, but also indicates the physician may do so if demanded by law. Section 4 of the code demands physicians obey the law. From the preceding it would appear the court demands the therapist take the law in his own hands. As a matter of fact, the Code of Ethics of the American Psychiatric Association (84) has the same wording. In its annotation of Section 9, there is a special section having to do with court orders: the physician "may ethically hold the right to dissent within the framework of the law. When the psychiatrist is in doubt, the right of the patient to confidentiality and by extension to unimpaired treatment should be given priority."

The court also made reference to the report of the Task Force on Confidentiality of the American Psychiatric Association. Apparently it did not read that section carefully. The report emphasizes the need to protect society, *but stresses that the best protection is to keep the patient in treatment and not violate confidentiality*. The task force did recognize that treatment at times will seem to be failing and breaking confidentiality, while destructive, might be necessary to protect society (85). What is overlooked by the court is that this refers to taking steps to follow due process that results in hospitalization — involuntary if necessary — and not extralegal efforts to disclose the fact in manners that offer no protection and do additional harm.

The adversary rather than judicial role of the court is best exemplified by Justice Mosk's own remarks in the dissent portion of his decision (63). Justice Mosk raises the question by comparing the diametrically opposite position of the majority in *Burnick* (86)* to that in *Tarasoff* and disputes the contention the cases are not similar. Yet the crucial point Justice Mosk selects from *Burnick* is the fact obvious to all

---

* For a summary of this case, see appendix.

authorities, psychiatric and legal, that contrary to public expectation (or wishful thinking?) psychiatrists do not have the ability to predict dangerous behavior. And the majority agreed that psychiatrists cannot predict future destructive acts. This raises the question why Justice Mosk agreed in the decision for a lower court hearing based on the fact that Dr. Moore did so predict. Even Justice Mosk is demanding that a therapist compound one error ("predicting") against a patient by committing a second error.

The 4-3 majority opinion in *Burnick* was written by Mosk. He wrote: "We reject the asserted right of the state to publicly brand a man as a mentally disordered sex offender and lock him up for an indeterminant period in a maximum security mental hospital on a mere preponderance of the evidence. We hold rather that in order to comply with the requirement of the due process clauses of the California and Federal Constitutions, so drastic an impairment of the liberty and *reputation* of an individual must be justified by proof beyond a reasonable doubt" (emphasis added) (87). How even Justice Mosk can then in *Tarasoff* advocate a duty to warn, affecting the reputation and probably other rights of the patient, based on one person's admittedly "inherently unreliable" *prediction* —not even a preponderance of the evidence—without any of the judicial due process dictated by L.P.S., is difficult to understand and accept. There are additional references throughout the opinion on *Burnick* emphasizing the need to protect the constitutional rights of such patients, and not to impair them in any way "without due process guaranteed [both] by Article 1, Section 7, subdivision (a) of the California Constitution and the Fourteenth Amendment of the U.S. Constitution" (88).

And Justice Clark in his dissent in *Tarasoff* makes it very clear that the court in ignoring the clear mandate of L.P.S. as an expression of due process to be followed for potentially dangerous mental patients is not constitutionally establishing due

process with its "duty to warn." He specifically points out the
majority have gone beyond their judicial prerogative and invaded the legislative responsibilities that were clearly directed
to the problems at issue in *Tarasoff* when L.P.S. was enacted.
Justice Clark continues to support the concept, agreed on in
Lifschutz, of how important the patient's confidence in his
therapist is to successful therapy, and that successful therapy is
the best protection of society. He also emphasizes that L.P.S.
"established the therapist's duty to *not* disclose" (emphasis in
original). His reference to warning when federal and state
elective constitutional officers and their families are threatened, as required by a 1970 amendment to Section 5228,
should be considered in the light of these officials being able to
ask state and Federal agents to supply personal protection in
contrast to others who will not be protected by peace officers on
request.* He notes that in 1970, the legislature, *considering a
potentially dangerous patient who has disappeared from a
hospital,* enacted a warning, and quotes Section 5328.3: ". . .
notice of such disappearance *may* be made to *relatives and
governmental law enforcement agencies*" (emphasis supplied
by Justice Clark) (89). He also views the exception to psychotherapist-patient privilege on which the majority depended as
not relevant to the *Tarasoff* situation. While Justice Clark
includes Dr. Moore as covered by Section 5005 immunity, he
does not add the fact that "any person" can initiate the L.P.S.
procedures under Section 5201 and therefore is covered by the
L.P.S. immunity from civil suit by acting in honest conformity
to the statute, contrary to the majority's opinion. The majority
becomes technically literal on issues that support them, and
incredibly loose on codes, e.g., privilege exceptions, when it
suits them.

---

* With Poddar as one example, and patients released from state hospitals as other examples, there is still the question of how long this governmental, 24-hour protection can be maintained.

In view of the general restrictions on the judiciary from countermanding legislative solution of a problem, there can be intrusion by the court only if it can clearly prove—allowing for the broad leeway allotted to legislation—that the legislative act is unconstitutional.

Even Justice Clark overlooks the fact that police officers made a determination that there was no evidence of psychosis or danger and therefore there was no confirmed evidentiary basis for violating Poddar's constitutional rights—the parties in question not being blest with clairvoyance to match the court's hindsight, as noted before. Concurrence by the psychiatric consultants runs up against the obstacle of ability to predict a violent *act*.

Why the shift in opinion from *Burnick* to the opposite in *Tarasoff*, as pointed out by Mosk? Why the inconsistency of Justice Mosk in his stated position in *Burnick* as then applied in his concurring decision in *Tarasoff*? Some of the clues available are the differences in the original opinion of December 23, 1974, as compared to that of July 1, 1976, after the rehearing. In the original opinion the court admitted that the warning involved in the attempt for commitment increased the hazard. This acknowledgment that warning might add to the hazard is missing in the second opinion. In the first the court used the adjective "bungling" to describe the attempt at commitment. On page 2 of the 1976 decision, the court notes: "Defendants, in turn, assert that they owed no duty of reasonable care to Tatiana," and the qualifying phrase, later actually stated as implied, "because Tatiana was not their patient," was omitted. Even more inflammatory is the court's statement on page 8 of the same claim: "Defendants, however, contend . . . they owed no duty of care to Tatiana or her parents and that in the absence of such duty, *they were free to act in careless disregard of Tatiana's life and safety*" (emphasis added). In view of the former statement it would appear this is an addition by the court. These pejorative additions by the court might also be viewed in the context of statements made by two justices at the rehearing May 5, 1975. Justice Tobriner stated, "If someone were threatening me, I would want to be warned!" The transcript of the rehearing would confirm the wording was used, but could not convey the vehement emotional quality with which the justice colored the statement. Justice Sullivan, on the other hand, stated that all the expert psychiatric testimony, and actual statistical findings that 99 times out of 100 "predictions" of violence were wrong, carried no weight with him because they were not present in any legal decisions or precedents.

The court misused the reference to the AMA Code of Ethics and the APA's Task Force Report, and in its research failed to find the APA's Code of Ethics or decided it was better not to use it. If the 180-degree shifts between *Burnick* and *Tarasoff* and the inflammatory language slipping through in wording are added to the court's different handling of *Robertson* (60) and *Caesar* (61), a developing pattern begins to appear. The court is influenced by the emotional impact of the victims in the case involved. For example, in *Robertson* the plaintiffs lost family in the accident, and suffered emotionally from that. In *Caesar* it was only a young woman who, troubled to start with, but beginning to rehabilitate herself through therapy, was dashed back down again to an earlier condition by repeated accidents in which she was blameless. In *Burnick* there were no inflammatory images of victims as there were in *Tarasoff*. The personal biases of the judges showed through as noted. The court apparently forgot Justice Black's admonition quoted previously (28): "Repugnance and evil qualities in the eyes of the Justices have no bearing on a judicial decision of what is the law."

All in all the court violated the stricture emphasized by the authorities quoted throughout this presentation, from Thomas Jefferson to Justice Hugo Black: that the courts should guard against misuse of the judicial process by exercising

self-policing and self-restraint to conform to their constitutional duties.

A final consideration. The U.S. Supreme Court has ruled
that a prosecuting attorney is immune from civil liability even
if he deliberately violates the civil rights of the defendant —
specifically, if he knowingly used perjured testimony in a murder trial (90). In spite of Justice Powell (91) quoting Section
1933 of the Civil Rights Act — "every person who acts under
cover of state law liable for depriving another of a
constitutional right, shall be answerable to that person in a suit
for damages" (and admits for no immunities) — the U.S.
Supreme Court in *Imbler* stated: "The common law immunity
of a prosecutor is based on the same considerations that
underlie the common law immunity of judges and Grand
Juries acting within the scope of their duties" (92). The Court
concluded "that if prosecutors knew they could be sued years
after a criminal trial, that would impose unique and intolerable burdens." Even if the California Supreme Court ignores
the therapist's claim for immunity, which is justified by the
general immunity provision of L.P.S. (or even adding Section
5201 that makes "any individual" a part of the L.P.S. process),
equal rights under the Fourteenth Amendment should make
the *Imbler* decision applicable to psychotherapists. This
immunity provision would not be based on the common
law, a carryover from prerevolutionary days, which favored government over individuals. Rather the intent
of that common law applied through the Bill of Rights
should prevail. That intent is that any functions serving a vital
need of our society, functions requiring independent judgment, cannot be exercised effectively "if constantly under the
cloud of later civil liability." Here we might again review the
New York Commentary of 1836 on medical privilege given
above (11) by paraphrasing that comment for "immunity."
The basis for that immunity is the need to protect the vital
function of the prosecution in our system of law — "that if

prosecutors knew they could be sued years after a criminal trial, that would impose unique and intolerable burdens." But surely a need to protect a physician in his task of making judgments and taking actions when life itself may be in jeopardy is still stronger. The *Tarasoff* decision places the psychotherapist in double jeopardy, as Justice Clark pointed out. Equal rights should apply the *Imbler* decision to the *Tarasoff* defendants, were it not for the prejudiced attitude of the law toward the legal profession as compared to other vital functions in society.

Recent laws affirm that minors have civil rights independent of their parents (93, 94, 95). These include the right to have treatment without disclosures to their parents, e.g., in pregnancy, prescribing contraceptives, abortions, and treatment of venereal disease, and they compound the problems of the right to privacy versus the right to know. Should the treatment turn out disastrously, and the parents were not notified, application of the *Tarasoff* decision would truly make a medical, surgical, as well as psychotherapeutic therapist's life a nightmare. This has been discussed in greater detail in the 1977 *Annual Review of Medicine* (96).

The legal processes of eroding confidentiality will continue. The patient-consumers are just now beginning to be aware of the attacks on their civil rights, but are too unorganized to be effective. As in the past, the medical profession as a whole has a duty to act for their patients. The psychiatric sector has been active in promoting this cause mainly because the consequences there are more drastic and apparent. In 1976, under the encouragement of the American Psychiatric Association, an organization to support the right to privacy against the unwarranted attacks via the right to know was incorporated. This National Commission on the Confidentiality of Medical Records includes representatives of medical groups, legal groups, consumer groups, and the insurance industry. The struggle to balance the right to privacy against the right to know might reach a reasonable compromise if such an organization flourishes and grows effectively.

Suggestions for strengthening the side of the right to privacy might be reviewed in light of the above. As to the patient-litigant exception to psychotherapist-patient privilege, it would be fruitful to pursue the question of its being unconstitutional. The grounds might be that it is too broad, without guidelines, so that it leads to results violating constitutional rights unnecessarily. The California Supreme Court in *Lifschutz* has documented that broad disclosure is unconstitutional. Its remedy has proven impractical in lower court application. One suggestion was recommended to the U.S. Senate (97). Others might be even more precise.

As to the impossible dilemma created by the *Tarasoff* decision, there may be multiple grounds to test the decision's constitutionality based on the citations given. The first problem is that the Regents of the University of California, as the defendants, must file the suit to permit joining as *amicus curiae*. An exception might be made by citing *Griswold* (57) as establishing a base for a peripheral defendant status.*

The direct grounds could start with the California court's having exceeded its constitutional authority in ignoring due process established clearly by the legislature. U.S. Supreme Court justices and other legal authorities have been quoted as establishing such guidelines, not spelled out in the Constitution itself.

A second ground would be that the court's decision forces therapists illegally to ignore due process and violate patients'

* It is understood that in *Griswold* the peripheral defendant was a party to the original trial. Psychotherapists and their patients were not involved in the Tarasoffs' suit against the Regents of the University of California. However, the California Supreme Court, by their broad dictum that imperils all psychotherapists and their patients in effect added these others to the defendants of the court's attention. To wait for actual damage to these others before a suit can be entertained would be to subject them to an unnecessary and unconstitutional hazard.

constitutional rights. This not only creates illegal harm to patients, but places therapists in positions of legal jeopardy.

A third ground is that in weighing one constitutional right (privacy) against another (protection of society) the court not only has ignored the legislature's solution, but has supplied a solution that will not bear scrutiny whether it does in fact protect society. In this, the court has failed in balance to justify the extreme violation of the first right.

A fourth ground would be equal protection under the Fourteenth Amendment. The court failed to extend the immunity protection of the *Imbler* decision (90) to psychotherapists who serve a public function no less important than prosecuting attorneys, as references given make clear. This ground merits seeking a stay of execution of *Tarasoff* to prevent damage, until the U.S. Supreme Court can hear the issues. If this ground is upheld, the lower court's dismissal of the action would be upheld.

Failing an appeal to the federal courts, again it might be well to quote Jefferson from his autobiography: ". . . our judges are effectively independent of the nation. But this ought not to be. . . . It is not enough that honest men are appointed judges. All know the influence of interest on the mind of man; and how unconsciously his judgment is warped by that influence" (26). In a letter to James Madison, on January 30, 1787, Jefferson wrote: "I hold that a little rebellion, now and then, is a good thing and as necessary in the political world as storms in the physical" (98).

The entire psychiatric community should publish a manifesto in rebellion against the *Tarasoff* decision. It should state that the usual standard of care would condemn any psychiatrist who abandons the due process for dealing with a potentially dangerous patient; that it would condemn any psychiatrist who unilaterally divulges such derogatory information about a patient outside of legal or quasi-legal machinery. The burden of proof of the necessity for warning would be on the psychiatrist. Even in extreme circumstances, the representatives of the due process machinery are reachable by telephone, and they can exercise the judgment of warning if indicated. This is supported by the 1970 L.P.S. amendment referred to previously. There are only conceivable instances where such an urgent step might be needed. One would be when a patient leaves the presence of a psychotherapist in an uncontrollable rage with a weapon in hand (or where the therapist knows a weapon is easily available) and a potential victim is also relatively immediately at hand. The L.P.S. amendment noted the other instance — where a patient potentially dangerous has left custody and his whereabouts are unknown. There the legislature has dictated whom to notify, and it would apply to all truly immediate hazards.

The contest between the *right to privacy* versus the *right to know* should not be permitted to slip into imbalance by default.

APPENDIX

In re Lifschutz on Habeas Corpus*

After Joseph F. Housek, a teacher, allegedly was assaulted by John Arabian, the former sued the latter on June 3, 1968, for "physical injuries, pain, suffering, and severe mental and emotional distress." In a deposition Housek stated that he had received psychotherapy for approximately six months, ten years earlier, from Dr. Joseph E. Lifschutz. When Dr. Lifschutz was subpoenaed, he refused to testify, even as to whether or not he had treated Housek. Lifschutz claimed privilege both for the patient and especially for himself. Lower and appellate courts ruled he was in contempt because the

---

* Cal. S. Ct. Crim. 14131; 2 Cal. 3d 415, 467 P.2d 557, 85 Cal. Rptr. 829 (1970).

psychotherapist privilege, Article 7 of the California Code of Evidence, does not apply when the patient injects into issue his emotional or mental condition as a claim or defense (Section 1016, the patient-litigant exception). In addition, the privilege is that of the patient and not the therapist. When the California Supreme Court refused a hearing and Lifschutz still refused, he was jailed for contempt. The Court then ordered him released pending a hearing. In the decision of April 15, 1970, the court reviewed the facts and law. They emphasized that Section 1016 did apply and that the privilege was that of the patient. They pointed out that the patient did waive the privilege in openly testifying that he had been treated by Dr. Lifschutz. They dismissed Lifschutz's contention that the disclosure, interfering with psychotherapy as all acknowledged, if maintained, would interfere with his livelihood; that the clergy-penitent litigant act did not constitute unequal protection for psychotherapists; and that the *Griswold* protection for physicians did not apply because in *Griswold* the federal court was relying on the protection of husband-wife as well as the patient's protection. The California court then ruled that disclosure, based on Section 1016, need not be absolute and must be limited to bare essentials, because in truth, society would be hurt by interference with psychotherapy if patients felt that what they disclosed in therapy could be opened up in court without any protective limits. They also indicated that if it was important for the therapist to be able to claim the privilege independently, the law would have to be changed, and the legislature would have to do so. Dr. Lifschutz then testified that he had indeed seen Housek ten years ago in treatment. The judge of the trial court ruled that what transpired ten years ago would be immaterial to the present issue, excused Dr. Lifschutz from further disclosure, and ruled that the latter had purged himself of contempt.

A commentary that has been alluded to in the main presentation is that this ruling was pleaded in the *Robertson* and *Caesar* cases. In the former the trial judge ruled for the plaintiff in restricting disclosure. In the appeal to the Court of Appeals, this decision was reversed because there was no standard for applying limits without access to the whole record. In *Caesar*, after the *Robertson* ruling, the trial court ruled for the defendant, requiring the disclosure of the record, or complete disclosure beyond the testimony Dr. Caesar had willingly given. An appeal sustained the lower court. Although the Supreme Court agreed to hear an appeal from Robertson from the adverse appellate court decision, it became moot when the defendant settled as soon as the higher court accepted the case. The Court refused to hear an appeal from Dr. Caesar, leaving him in contempt. History has demonstrated that the *Lifschutz* decision has not held up in subsequent court practice.

Vitaly Tarasoff et al. v.
The Regents of the University of California et al. *

Prosenjit Poddar, a student of University of California at Berkeley, was in psychotherapy on an outpatient basis at Cowell Memorial Hospital of the University of California in 1969. When Poddar began making threats to kill a fellow student, Tatiana Tarasoff, Poddar's therapist, Dr. Lawrence Moore, believed the threats constituted a possible danger and asked the campus police to take his patient into custody incident to pursuing the legal machinery for involuntary hospitalization. This request was made on August 20, 1969. At the time Tatiana was in Brazil for a summer-long visit. The police did take Poddar into custody, but released him when they found no sign of abnormality, or of dangerousness.

Poddar caused no problems even though he terminated

* S.F. 23042; Super. Ct. 405694 (Dec. 23, 1974 opinion 118 Cal. Rptr. 129), Rehearing May 5, 1975 opinion filed July 1, 1976.

treatment after his therapist took this step. He even became the roommate of Tatiana's brother. Shortly after Tatiana reurned, Poddar did kill her on October 27, 1969. Tatiana's parents filed suit against all individuals involved, and the Regents of the University of California as their employer, for a wrongful death. The plaintiffs gave four legal grounds in support of their claim. The second was based on the defendant's failure to warn the parents of the danger to Tatiana.

The lower courts dismissed the action without a trial because of the legal immunity of the defendants, plus the overriding need to maintain confidentiality in psychotherapy. The dismissal was appealed to the California Supreme Court which reversed the lower courts and ordered the case to trial in a decision filed December 23, 1974. The court stated that psychotherapists had a duty to warn potential victims when they determined a patient was dangerous. Professional societies joined the defendants in a petition for a rehearing that was granted, with the hearing being held May 5, 1975. The basis for the *amicus curiae* intervention of the professionals was that violating confidentiality under those circumstances would be a major impediment to effective treatment for all patients; and that in approximately 99 cases out of 100 the judgment of dangerousness would be invalid, as proven by repeated studies. The court filed its revised decision on July 1, 1976, which did not alter the first decision in its essential feature obligating the warning.

Griswold v. Connecticut*

The State of Connecticut convicted physicians and those involved in public clinics of giving instruction to married couples on contraception and fitting the wives with

---

* 381 U.S. 479, 14 L.Ed.2d 510, 85 S. Ct. 1678.

contraceptive devices. This was held in violation of a statute making such activity a criminal violation. The defendants' appeal to the U.S. Supreme Court was that the Connecticut statute violated the constitutional rights of the convicted and was therefore unconstitutional. The State pleaded that the law was necessary to control illicit sexual activity and was required for the overriding need of legislating protection of society from activity that would destroy the family foundation of society. The majority of the U.S. Supreme Court ruled the Connecticut statute unconstitutional on many grounds, but primarily established a right of privacy as an unlisted but essential element protected by the Bill of Rights from governmental interference. Justices Black and Stewart dissented because there was no right of privacy explicitly stated in the Constitution. Justice Black indicated that use of the Ninth Amendment to cover privacy would lead to many judges' stretching the boundary of that amendment to whatever suited them personally. (Parenthetically note that in the main presentation the Ninth Amendment is "stretched" to cover "unalienable rights" listed in the Declaration of Independence.) The majority, basing their decision on the First, Fourth, Fifth, Ninth, and Fourteenth Amendments, stated that the freedoms of the First extended to all the rights of learning as exemplified by the broad concept of learning, teaching, and practicing what is learned that is utilized by a university; that an invasion of the rights of the husband-wife relationship, as confided to their physician, was an invasion of the Fourth both in respect to the marital functions and the rights of privacy of what husband and wife confide to physicians; that these rights were threatened by the state without the due process of the Fourteenth Amendment; and that the state invaded the Fifth's protection against self-discrimination. They quoted several sources that indicated that the physicians could plead the rights of their patients. "The rights of husband and wife, pressed here are likely to be diluted unless those rights are considered in a suit involving those who have this kind of confidential relation to them" (U.S. at 481, L. Ed.2d at 513). Justice Black in dissent also stressed that the decision was an unwarranted judicial invasion of the rights of legislatures to determine how they protect society. This was answered by the majority by pointing out that Connecticut already had adequate legislation against illicit sexual activity, and that the application of the law in question was against activity specifically available only to married couples and therefore the reasoning was specious. Since the law in question does not itself differentiate and deprives married couples of resources necessary for their private needs, it in effect has an unconstitutional effect and was so considered by the majority opinion.

*People v. Burnick**

Burnick was found guilty of homosexual activity with minors of adolescent age. The court hearing without jury elected to commit him to the State Hospital at Atascadero as a habitual sex offender. Burnick appealed because he preferred to be sentenced under the criminal code for two reasons. For commitment under the Welfare and Institutions Code, guilt may be a decision on the preponderance of the evidence and so elected by the court. Under the penal code guilt must be decided beyond a reasonable doubt. Furthermore, if convicted, as a first offender, he would probably at most be confined for several months. As a habitual sex offender his stay by commitment would be indeterminate. The majority 4-3 decision agreed with Burnick against the lower courts. Their grounds were that psychiatric judgments of future acts based on observable psychological study and tests are totally unreliable. To deprive an individual on such predictions is to

---

* 15 Cal. 3d 306, 121 Cal. Rptr. 488, 535 P.2d 352.

deprive him of his liberty without due process. The grounds of preponderance of the evidence are far less exacting than "beyond a reasonable doubt." Reference was made to the one state expert witness who affirmed that the one episode presaged that the defendant would be sure to repeat the acts and fit the description of a habitual offender. The two defense witnesses very emphatically denied that there was any reason to believe there would be future attacks on children as claimed by the prosecution. They pointed out that the age of the minors was more apt to suggest an act between consenting adults, and the activity did not fit the law's definition of "being dangerous to the health and safety of others," as required for the commitment route. Justice Mosk, who wrote the majority opinion, emphasized the horrendous consequences to the liberty and reputation of the person involved, the rights to due process, including "beyond a reasonable doubt," and the need to bear in mind the inability to predict future occurrences from a one-time act. "Neither psychiatrists nor anyone else have reliably demonstrated an ability to predict future violence or 'dangerousness'" (p. 327 of 14 Cal. 3d). It is well to note that the majority are the same who formed the majority in *Tarasoff*.

REFERENCES

1. Brant, I. *The Bill of Rights*. New York: New American Library, 1967, p. 223.
2. Rossiter, C. *1787—The Grand Convention*. New York: Macmillan, 1966, p. 302.
3. Wigmore, J. H. *Evidence in Trials at Common Law*, McNaughton rev. ed., vol. 8. Boston: Little, Brown, 1961, sec. 2285, p. 527.
4. Slovenko, R. *Psychiatry and Law*. Boston: Little, Brown, 1973, p. 435.
5. Wigmore, sec. 2380, p. 818.
6. Slovenko, pp. 62, 437.
7. Plucknett, T. F. T. *A Concise History of the Common Law,* 4th ed. London: Butterworth, 1948, pp. 111-114.
8. Wigmore, sec. 2192, p. 72 n. 1.
9. Ibid., sec. 2291, pp. 545-546.

10. Ibid., sec. 2190-2396, pp. 62-877.
11. Ibid., sec. 2380A, p. 828.
12. Ibid., sec. 2380A, pp. 830-831.
13. *In re Lifschutz.* 2 Cal. 3d 415, 467 P.2d 557, 85 Cal. Rptr. 829 (1970).
14. *California Code of Evidence.* St. Paul: West, 1966, sec. 1016, p. 624.
15. Committee on Rules of Practice and Procedure, Judicial Conference of the U.S. *Preliminary Draft of Proposed Rules of Evidence for the U.S. District Courts and Magistrates.* Washington, D.C.: Administrative Office of U.S. Courts, March 1969, Rule 504, p. 53.
16. Howard, E. R. (Executive Vice-President AMA). Letter to Congressman Rodino. Jan. 31, 1973.
17. Committee on Judiciary, U.S. Senate, 93rd, 2nd. *Hearings on Federal Rules of Evidence, H.R. 5463.* June 4-5, 1974. Washington, D.C.: U.S. Government Printing Office, 1974.
18. *Hickman v. Taylor.* 329 U.S. 495, 67 S. Ct. 385 (Jan. 1947).
19. Grossman, M. The psychiatrist and the subpoena. *Bull. Amer. Acad. Psychiat. Law,* 1:245-254, Dec. 1975.
20. Jefferson, T. Autobiography. In: *Writings of Thomas Jefferson,* vol. I, ed. A. J. Lipscomb. Washington, D.C.: Thomas Jefferson Memorial Association, 1903, p. 49.
21. Jefferson, T. The Kentucky Resolutions, 1798. In: *Writings of Thomas Jefferson,* vol. XVII, ed. A. J. Lipscomb. Washington, D.C.: Thomas Jefferson Memorial Association, 1903, p. 389.
22. Hand, L. *The Bill of Rights.* Cambridge, Mass.: Harvard University Press, 1958, p. 2.
23. Ibid., pp. 3-4.
24. Ibid., p. 7.
25. Ibid., p. 15.
26. Jefferson, Autobiography, p. 121.
27. *West Virginia State Board of Education v. W. Barnette.* 319 U.S. 624 at 647, 87 L.Ed. 1628 at 1642 (1943).
28. *Griswold v. Connecticut.* 381 U.S. 479 at 507, 14 L.Ed.2d 510 at 529 (1965).
29. Ibid., 381 U.S. at 519, 14 L.Ed.2d at 536.
30. Department of Health, Education and Welfare. Protecting confidentiality in alcohol and drug abuse patient records. *Federal Register,* 39 (164) Part II:30426-30437, Aug. 22, 1974.
31. Cooper, T. (Assistant Secretary for Health). Letter to hospitals. Dec. 30, 1975.
32. Grossman, M. Testimony for APA, Subcommittee on Courts, Civil Liberties, and Administration of Justice, H.R. Committee Judiciary, H.R. 214, July 25, 1975.
33. *California Code of Evidence,* Art. 7, sec. 1010-1026, pp. 616-632.
34. Ibid., sec. 912 (a), p. 491.

35. *California Code of Business and Professions.* St. Paul: West, 1974, sec. 1680, p. 262.
36. Ibid., sec. 2379, p. 493.
37. Ibid., Art. 13, p. 466.
38. *California Penal Code.* St. Paul: West, 1970, sec. 7, p. 19.
39. *Vitaly Tarasoff et al. v. The Regents of the University of California et al.* 118 Cal. Rptr. 129 (1974) (Decision of Dec. 23, 1974).
40. *California Welfare and Institutions Code,* Division 5 (Lanterman-Petris-Short Act). San Francisco: Deerings, Bancroft & Whitney, 1969, p. 77.
41. Ibid., sec. 5005, p. 79.
42. Ibid., sec. 5150, pp. 91-92.
43. Ibid., sec. 5201, p. 100.
44. Ibid., sec. 5203, p. 102.
45. Ibid., sec. 5328, p. 150.
46. Ibid., sec. 5330, p. 152.
47. Ibid., sec. 6006, p. 235.
48. California Legislative Assembly. *The Dilemma of Mental Commitment in California.* Sacramento: Assembly Rules Committee, 3rd Printing, April 1972.
49. *Lifschutz,* 2 Cal. 3d at 431-432, 467 P.2d at 567, 85 Cal. Rptr. at 839.
50. Ibid., 2 Cal. 3d at 434, 467 P.2d at 569, 85 Cal. Rptr. at 841.
51. Ibid., 2 Cal. 3d at 430, 467 P.2d at 566, 85 Cal. Rptr. at 839.
52. Ibid., 2 Cal. 3d at 435, 467 P.2d at 570, 85 Cal. Rptr. at 842.
53. Grossman, M. (Chairman). *Confidentiality and Third Parties.* Task Force Report 9. Washington, D.C.: American Psychiatric Association, 1975, p. 45.
54. *In re Lifschutz.* Calif. S. Ct. Criminal 14131, p. 44.
55. *Griswold,* 381 U.S. at 498, 14 L.Ed.2d at 523.
56. *Lifschutz,* Calif. S. Ct. Criminal 14131, p. 11.
57. *Griswold,* 381 U.S. at 481, 14 L.Ed.2d at 513.
58. *Lifschutz,* Calif. S. Ct. Criminal 14131, pp. 35-36.
59. Ibid., p. 17.
60. *Robertson, Murphy v. Penny.* Super. Ct. Cal. Alameda, No. 385947.
61. *Caesar v. Mountanos.* U.S. Ct. Appeal, 9th, No. 74-2271.
62. *California Welfare and Institutions Code,* p. 93n.
63. *Tarasoff,* Mosk dissent and concur., p. 1, July 1, 1976 opinion.
64. Ibid., July 1, 1976 majority opinion, p. 4.
65. Ibid., Dec. 23, 1974 opinion, p. 21; July 1, 1976, p. 24.
66. *Minersville School District v. W. Gobitis.* 310 U.S. 586 at 600, 84 L.Ed. 1375 at 1382 (1940).
67. *Barnette,* 319 U.S. at 647, 87 L.Ed. at 1642.
68. *Ware v. Hylton.* 3 Dallas 199 at 211 (1976).
69. Hand, p. 9.
70. *Lifschutz,* Calif. S. Ct. Criminal 14131, p. 19.

71. Fleming, J. G., & Maximov, B. The patient or his victim: The therapist's dilemma. *Cal. Law Rev.,* 62:1025-1068, 1974.
72. *Tarasoff,* p. 18 (Dec. 23, 1974 decision).
73. Ibid., p. 58.
74. Hand, p. 49.
75. Re McCoy. *Seattle Times,* Dec. 7, 1974, p. A3.
76. Re Cordero. *San Francisco Chronicle,* Dec. 28, 1974, p. 1.
77. Re Olivier. *San Francisco Chronicle,* May 24, 1975, p. 3.
78. *Runyon v. Reid.* Okla. 510 P.2d 943 at 950-951 (1973).
79. Schwartz, V. E. Civil liability for causing suicide. *Vanderbilt Law Rev.,* 24:217-256, 1971.
80. Ayers, J., Jr., & Holbrook, J. T. Law, psychotherapy and the duty to warn: A tragic trilogy. *Baylor Law Rev.,* 27:677-705, 1975.
81. Hand, p. 15.
82. California Legislative Assembly, p. 143.
83. American Medical Association. *Principles of Medical Ethics of the American Medical Association.* Chicago: American Medical Association, 1957.
84. American Psychiatric Association. *Principles of Medical Ethics with Annotation Especially Applicable to Psychiatry.* Washington, D.C.: American Psychiatric Association, 1973.
85. Grossman, *Confidentiality and Third Parties,* p. 28.
86. *People v. Burnick.* Cr. 16554, 14 Cal. 3d 306 at 326, 121 Cal. Rptr. 488 at 501, 535 P.2d 352 at 365 (1975).
87. Ibid., 14 Cal. 3d at 310, 121 Cal. Rptr. at 490, 535 P.2d at 354.
88. Ibid., 14 Cal. 3d at 314, 121 Cal. Rptr. at 493, 535 P.2d at 357.
89. *Tarasoff,* J. Clark dissent, pp. 6-7, July 1, 1976 opinion.
90. *Imbler v. Pachtman.* 96 S. Ct. 984 (March 2, 1976), West's S. Ct. Rptr. (Apr. 1, 1976).
91. Ibid., pp. 988-989.
92. Ibid., p. 991.
93. Slovenko, p. 500.
94. Peers, I. N. Confidentiality and consent in psychiatric treatment of minors. *J. Leg. Med.,* 4:12-16, 1976.
95. Modlin, H. C. The discharged patient in the community. *Psychiat. Dig.,* 37:13-22, June 1976.
96. Grossman, M. Confidentiality in medical practice. In: *Annual Review of Medicine,* vol. 28. Palo Alto: Annual Reviews, 1977.
97. Grossman, *Confidentiality and Third Parties,* pp. 48-52.
98. Jefferson, T. Letter to James Madison, Jan. 30, 1787. In: *The Papers of Thomas Jefferson,* vol. 11, ed. J. P. Boyd. Princeton: Princeton University Press, 1955, p. 93.

Chapter VIII

Confidentiality: The Myth and the Reality

JOHN DONNELLY, M.D.

Only in the 1960s did psychiatry as a medical discipline emerge on the public scene as a significant segment of the practice of medicine. A derivative of the experiences of both World War I and II, the National Institute of Mental Health was established and enthusiastically funded by the federal government. The necessity of expanding vastly and quickly the number of psychiatrists available to treat adequately the emotionally disturbed segment of the population was met by the appropriation of ever-increasing amounts of taxpayer dollars for the specific purpose of training psychiatrists and other mental health workers. The number of psychiatrists increased from approximately 3,000 in 1945 to over 25,000 today.

In order to maintain perspective on the ever-expanding role of psychiatry on the public stage, psychiatrists should remember that they owe the prominence of their specialty to the support provided them by public funds both directly and indirectly via their teachers. These funds were appropriated not for special interests, but for the general public welfare.

While "confidentiality" is a professional article of faith, it is wise not to forget the origins of the principle. The psychiatrist reasons that the basis of treatment lies, in large part, in the patient's confidence that his innermost secrets and fantasies shared with the therapist will not be communicated to others. From this pragmatic experience the argument is derived that the public welfare is enhanced because more individuals will thus seek psychiatric treatment, presumably with a favorable outcome. And, as a result of this favorable outcome, both individuals and society will benefit by a more healthy and contented population, as well as an economically less costly and more productive one. This reasoning is no more or less valid today than it was when the advocates of increasing the numbers and the professional qualifications of psychiatrists first sought the support of a receptive Congress.

What must be taken into consideration, however, are the enormous changes within the structure and organization of society in the past 25 years and those which are inevitable in the next ten. Some 25 years ago, when psychiatry was emerging as a potent public force, its advocates tended to be themselves professionally oriented to the psychoanalytic model. Indeed, a large majority of them were psychoanalysts or psychodynamically oriented psychiatrists whose advocacy was effective because of the public health appeal. Consistent with the models they provided, the fruits of their labors were evidenced by the evolution of the psychoanalytically oriented and the psychodynamically oriented psychiatrist, that is, a professional who utilized in therapy concepts derived from the psychoanalytic model.

As time passed, the underlying public health motivation, which had from the beginning stirred the legislators, resulted in the emergence of the concepts underpinning the establishment of the community mental health center. Thus, the primacy of psychoanalysis as the model for future practice was replaced by that of psychodynamically oriented psychiatry, which in turn has, in recent years, been challenged by public health or community-oriented psychiatry. Inevitably, the vital importance of the concept of the absolute confidentiality of the patient-psychiatrist relationship has been eroded in the eyes of the public, as represented through the legislative and judicial segments of government.

This evolution of psychiatry is important to keep in mind because of the almost revolutionary changes in the societal environment in the past two decades. The successful avant garde leaders of the past have themselves become the defenders of the status quo. Previously current ideals which were pertinent to the times have ceased to be completely applicable as the public environment in which psychiatry is practiced has become more complex. For example, the ideal of a relationship with complete confidentiality which existed in the one-to-one relationship of patient and physician was sacrificed when third-party coverage of psychiatric treatment made sharing of information essential to payment. The entrance of a third party, which two to three decades ago was nonexistent, has become a major force today in determining future directions of psychiatric practice.

Prior to 1945, the vast majority of psychiatrists practiced within the confines of governmental institutions and a few private, nonprofit psychiatric hospitals. The concerns of psychiatrists with respect to confidentiality were, by and large, contained within the very defined area of forensic psychiatry. They were primarily concerned with the issue of privilege, that is, with the limitations on confidentiality imposed by the law in respect to compulsory testimony in a court of law about information obtained in the therapeutic relationship. Their disquiet—when they were disquieted—arose mainly around the principle of self-incrimination in criminal cases.

Confidentiality, as an important public health issue in the practice of medicine in the United States, dates back to 1828 when privilege for all physicians was first enacted in New York State. Indeed, as a specific issue with respect to psychiatric patients, there was, prior to the 1950s, little concern other than in criminal cases. Today, the emotions associated with the possibility of self-incrimination have been displaced to much broader areas in the public arena where the intensity of these feelings is perhaps unwarranted and certainly, at least, inconsistent with public programs pushed by psychiatrists. For most mental health professions, the issue of psychotherapeutic confidentiality is one of absolute observance. But, is this equally true for the majority of patients?

This displacement of affect is quite consistent with the development of myths. A social myth is, after all, the enshrining of a value socially important at a particular time in history so that it becomes ensconced as part of the traditional folklore despite changes in the society which make it less relevant. The strong emotions with which confidentiality is debated would appear to be warranted only in situations in which the principle of self-incrimination is involved. When displaced to other issues, an element of paranoia may seem to emerge.

Despite the many areas in which the affect associated with confidentiality arises, there often appears to be a lack of recognition of the very real distinction between confidentiality, which is one aspect of the right to privacy, and privilege, which is a very specific variety of confidentiality. Privilege is a specific exception to the customary rules of evidence in the administration of the judicial system whereby one individual may prohibit the testimony of another with whom he has had a strict professional relationship recognized by law. The basic reason for privilege is that it advances the ultimate public welfare. Privilege is not a constitutional right per se. It is a special exemption legislatively enacted by a state or the federal government. While privilege, which springs from the issue of self-incrimination, has usually been enacted with respect to criminal trials, it has also been extended in many jurisdictions to civil actions. But, even in those states in which privilege has been conferred on patients, there are many differences in the extent to and circumstances in which privilege can be invoked, as well as in the specific exceptions to its exercise.

With rare exceptions, where privilege has been enacted, it has been granted only to the individual at risk. On that person, the patient, falls the responsibility of deciding whether or not to assert privilege. There has been much discussion within mental health circles, and even a case or two, with respect to whether the privilege belongs, or should belong, to the psychiatrist (1). This claim appears to originate in the realm of the therapist's fantasy in which the psychiatrist is endowed not only with guardianship but also judicial powers. In a patient, comparable claims would be interpreted as having the elements of a messiah complex or at least a demand for a role outside the real life environment of all other individuals in the society. One may justifiably speculate about the psychodynamics of such claims. This is quite appropriate when one considers that the patient litigant has a legal representative, with an officially recognized, special confidential relationship within the system of administration of justice, who is more knowledgeable about the system as it pertains to the patient's welfare. The attorney has the legal responsibility for presenting the best case for his client. While it may be true that a patient waiving privilege may not know the consequences of the information that may be brought out in testimony by the psychiatrist, he does have a very good idea about what he has told the therapist. While he may not be competent to decide whether or not it is to his advantage to waive privilege, certainly his attorney is. In any case, reality would require that the decision be made by the attorney for the patient, and he should be advised prior to trial of all the information the psychiatrist may be forced to provide. For psychiatrists to claim that, even with the patient's authorization, communication of confidential information to the attorney is a breach of confidentiality also appears to be in the realm of unreality.

It may be pointed out that these extraordinary claims for special privilege for the psychiatrist may actually result in erosion of the privileges already enacted for psychiatric patients. Thus, the tremendous importance attributed by psychiatrists to the rights of a patient may lead to challenges by persons concerned with the rights of others on whom the patient has a noxious impact. The legal decisions and public reactions in the *Tarasoff* (2) case offer an instance of such an outcome.

The final decision of the California Supreme Court in *Tarasoff* cannot fail to raise speculation. To many psychiatrists, it appears to be based not on the reality of the way society normally protects its citizens, but rather on emotional identification with the helpless victim—a process comparable to the identifications and value system of most psychiatrists.

Despite the furor which has arisen in psychiatric circles regarding this divided decision, it should be pointed out that the California Supreme Court did not establish a precedent with regard to the absolute legal responsibility of a therapist to warn a third party directly about his or her potential danger at the hands of a patient. Rather, this responsibility arises only if the exercise of reasonable care to protect the threatened victim requires the therapist to warn the endangered person or those who can reasonably be expected to notify him. This responsibility in fact arises only when the probability that violence will occur is actually predicted, as evidenced in this case by the notification of the campus police. Furthermore, the decision only declared that in this case there was sufficient evidence to warrant a trial as to whether there was negligence or malpractice involved on the part of the therapist in not exercising "that reasonable degree of skill, knowledge and care ordinarily possessed and exercised by members of [that professional specialty] under similar circumstances" (2).

A more fundamental issue has been obscured by discussion of these important but largely irrelevant questions, which would not arise in the customary practice of psychiatry: The usual course, and indeed the duty of a psychiatrist who has formed a definite opinion that a patient is likely to inflict bodily harm on another, is to protect his patient from his hostile impulses by hospitalizing him immediately, preferably voluntarily, but involuntarily if necessary. Although the therapist in *Tarasoff* did follow the procedure under the Lanterman-Petris-Short Act in recommending involuntary commitment, this did not occur. Notification of the police transfers the primary objective of the responsibility for protection of the patient to the secondary objective, albeit equally important, of responsibility for the protection of the potential victim.

The reasoning of the California Supreme Court does appear illogical. While at law the police may be immune from damages, this immunity does not *ipso facto* release the police from their responsibility for public safety, nor does it automatically shift the responsibility of protection of the potential victim back to the therapist. For these reasons, much of the discussion on the court's decision appears to me to be irrelevant.

There is, however, another aspect of the *Tarasoff* case. Many psychiatrists in and out of psychiatric hospitals have been faced with comparable situations. They have decided that protection of the patient has required taking steps to warn potential victims or law enforcement authorities (3). I have no reservations about discussing the potential dangerousness of a patient with his next of kin and of securing informed consent to notify the police. This action is taken while the patient is in hospital in anticipation of the patient's escaping, despite the tightest precautions to prevent this.

Moreover, it is rare that the potential victim is not aware of the patient's feelings, and the warning, while distressing, is not a surprise. Where possible, the warning is conveyed by a member of the patient's family which is as concerned as the psychiatrist. Finally, when the patient recovers and is advised about the actions taken, the reaction is a positive one.

Another area of ever-increasing erosion of the myth of confidentiality is in the matter of insurance coverage for psychiatric illness. Again, it is illuminating to look at the historical context. Prior to a couple of decades ago, private health insurance for coverage of private psychiatric hospitalization was practically nonexistent. The principle underlying any kind of insurance is that the risk be shared by a large number of participants. Insurance companies are organized to accomplish this purpose by individuals who are prepared to undertake the task and risk their capital in hopes of gaining economically by their efforts. The success in establishing insurance coverage depends on the ability of the company to collect the necessary information on which the financial risks or exposure can be calculated and premiums acceptable to potential policyholders established.

In the practice of medicine outside psychiatric illness, this is made possible by the cooperation of physicians and hospitals providing that data. Psychiatric illness was totally excluded in the past and is generally quite limited today for a variety of reasons. These include lack of reliable data, the secretiveness about mental illness, and public attitudes to it. There are close parallels in the cases of tuberculosis and venereal disease, though mental illness has an additional burden of its association in the public mind with irrationality and violence. In the past three decades, major changes have been effected with respect to all three categories. Those committed to the welfare of patients with these conditions have organized public support and public programs to remove the fear, rejection, and previously held myths. All three groups have had outstanding success in these efforts.

But psychiatry alone has been inconsistent and contradictory in its demands and practices. Psychiatrists have stridently insisted that psychiatric illness is no different from physical disease and that, therefore, coverage for mental disorders and for physical illness should be equal. The growth of private insurance coverage for psychiatric illness, and certainly for hospitalization under group insurance policies, would indicate that neither insurance companies nor private employers are inherently opposed to providing such protection.

It is true that both these groups have been cautious about providing equal coverage. Both groups are justified in this caution because they are legally, morally, and economically responsible for the moneys involved. If equal coverage is to be justified, it is obvious that all the data necessary to make accurate actuarial calculations and forecasts must be collected. The prime source of such data must be the psychiatric profession and hospitals treating mentally ill patients.

But, despite the clamor for equal coverage, equal treatment, and abolition of discrimination, within the profession there are equally loud demands that psychiatric illnesses and patients must be dealt with very differently from physical illnesses and physically ill patients (4). The bases of these arguments cover a number of areas, the most important of which is that of confidentiality. Psychiatrists, for example, do not want to furnish specific diagnoses, on the basis of the potential harm to an individual should breach of confidentiality occur in the offices of the insurance company. They demand, for example, that code numbers be substituted for actual diagnoses on insurance forms.

Here, too, there is an element of fantasy. With the ever-increasing numbers of subscribers being covered, increasing numbers of individuals in the employment of the carrier will have to be involved in the processing of claims. Many individuals will have to translate the code numbers into the actual diagnoses to make them meaningful — unless a new category of the human species can be found. In practice, they will be provided with, or can easily obtain from the American Psychiatric Association, copies of DSM I or II or III or whatever classification system is used. Curiosity, if aroused, will have little difficulty in finding satisfaction. Persons intent on obtaining information for illegal or other purposes will encounter little more in the way of impediments than at present.

Psychiatrists also want different processing procedures for psychiatric patients. For example, they urge that *all* the insurance forms be processed only by the medical director of the carrier in order to ensure confidentiality. If millions of Americans are to be covered, surely reality will impose restrictions on this approach. How many medical directors are going to be necessary and how are they to be recruited — not to mention the enormous additional costs this would create? Is it fantasy to extend this concept to the logical conclusion, namely, that physicians also man the typewriters, filing cabinets, duplicators, computers, etc.? If that is unrealistic, where does confidentiality start and where does it end?

Reality also requires that the treatment of patients involve large numbers of professionals and nonprofessionals, including those processing forms and records, such as personnel in the medical records departments of hospitals and in the offices of psychiatrists. The occasion for a breakdown in confidentiality is equally possible in any of these situations (5). In the future, as in the past, the preservation of confidentiality lies in the imposition of responsibility on all individuals handling not only psychiatric but medical records.

In the hospital with which I am associated, strict rules are enforced. For example, records transported from the medical records department to the offices of psychiatrists are carried in locked containers. Breach of confidentiality, for example, identification of names of patients outside the hospital, is cause for immediate dismissal. This rule applies to all categories of personnel.

Another aspect of the confidentiality issue is the demand that insurance processing for psychiatric illness, provided through employer group plans, be handled differently from that used for physical illness. It has been urged that forms completed by psychiatrists be sent directly to the insurance carrier. One reason given is to protect the employee from the possible loss of his job or adverse effects on him. Yet, reality once again raises its head to ask some very important questions. It is true that the Health Insurance Council has agreed to a coding system and to seek quarterly aggregate cost reporting, so that the employer is told only how much psychiatric coverage costs his company (6). If the psychiatrist does not trust the insurance carrier with respect to confidentiality, why should an employer trust the carrier in the financial aspect of the transaction?

There are other important reality factors, even if they are less obvious to the psychiatrist. First, the cost to the employer of providing health insurance is less if his personnel department performs routine processing, including certification that the claimant is (a) an employee and/or (b) eligible for health benefits. Psychiatrists do not demand that all claims be so processed — only psychiatric ones. Since the carrier would have to check with the employer if the psychiatrist's certification went directly to the medical department of the carrier, the employer, if interested, would know immediately that the employee had a psychiatric rather than a physical illness. The secretiveness involved would create and intensify the very fears associated with mental illness that the profession has, for the last 25 years, been trying to overcome. To claim that the employer would not know the diagnosis, thus providing protection for the employee, is of dubious validity. The natural

reaction of any employer—including those who are themselves psychiatrists—would be to place the employee in a
category of personnel about whom there were unanswered
questions with respect to reliability, responsibility, etc. This
would certainly apply in such situations as consideration for
advancement to positions with increasing responsibilities.

There are two other reality factors. Unless the psychiatrist
is willing to treat the patient outside the latter's working hours,
the patient would require time off to go for treatment. While
therapy itself may require only one hour of the physician's
time, for the employee perhaps double or more than that
amount of time off is required. Since psychiatric treatment
customarily is carried out over long periods of time, which
would be recorded as "sick time," the employer would rapidly
identify the type of condition. In other words, the sympathetic
cooperation of the employer is a *sine qua non* for successful
treatment.

Another reality factor is that employees cannot, and
usually do not want to, be completely secretive about seeing a
psychiatrist. They talk freely with their immediate associates
and friends. In any organization the grapevine is capable of
reducing to a sieve the most complex barrier erected to
preserve complete confidentiality regarding treatment by a
psychiatrist in his office. Where hospitalization is concerned, it
is completely impossible.

The final outcome, thus, would be detrimental to many
patients from their occupational standpoint. How much
healthier it is to work toward the time when mental illness no
longer is regarded in a different way from physical ills. As with
tuberculosis, familiarity would provide not fear or contempt
but respect for the individual and sympathetic support in
helping him benefit from those modern therapies so widely
publicized.

With respect to third-party coverage by employers, the
recent experience of government employees covered by Blue

Cross under the Federal Employees Health Benefits Program is most disheartening on the issue of confidentiality. This appears to be the only major health insurance program in which legitimate claims have been consistently denied and in which copies of complete records have been demanded. If, indeed, these records were reviewed by psychiatrists only, the practice might be less objectionable. However, they are reviewed by nurses and physicians, whose qualifications in the vast majority of cases appear to be notable in their lack of any kind of psychiatric training or experience. One cannot help but wonder whether all private insurance carriers, given the same number of psychiatric claims, would or could adhere to the medical director procedure referred to earlier.

Given the views and opinions expressed at the recent meeting of mental health professionals and legislators held in the halls of the Congress (7), the advocates of equal coverage for mental illness under National Health Insurance legislation should deeply ponder which of two principles should be given priority—coverage without confidentiality or confidentiality without coverage. From statements made at that meeting, it is evident that these are seen as mutually exclusive in the realities of federal expenditures and controls.

Yet another fantasy appears prevalent in the mental health field. For many psychiatrists, the issue of absolute confidentiality is paramount, to be defended to the hilt—short of going to prison. For the vast majority of patients, this is not the number one priority. Their priority is securing financial reimbursement for the charges made by the psychiatrist. In my experience, only rarely does a patient raise the issue of confidentiality. In this respect, the patient seems in pragmatic contact with his environment. For hospitalized patients, there is a simple choice and only extraordinarily rarely has any serious conflict arisen. Most patients accept the need for therapy for which they must pay, either out of their own pockets or from other sources—usually insurance. Very few patients are reluctant to waive confidentiality. Indeed, those who do usually fall into the group of patients covered as dependents in someone else's program. In some of these cases, the motivations for refusal to waive confidentiality often arise from hostility to the person who otherwise has to pay the bill.

Licensing and accreditation of psychiatric facilities provide yet another problem area in the maintenance of absolute confidentiality. Because the quality of the medical records is judged — perhaps accurately, perhaps erroneously — so important in the evaluation process, inspectors and surveyors, who often are not psychiatrists, review sample records to ensure compliance with bureaucratic regulations. Here the confidentiality problem is not loudly argued because the stark reality is that resistance leads automatically to loss of a license or accreditation.

Yet another area is developing in which the inconsistency in the psychiatric profession's approach is evident. As part of the right to know and freedom of information movement, some patients are demanding, and some psychiatrists are urging, that patients have access to their records. A recent guest editorial by the Committee on Public Information of the American Psychiatric Association seems to support this stand (8). The thrust of the reasoning here is that psychiatrists devote their "lives to helping patients gain a greater sense of control over their destiny — helping them free themselves from those wishes of their early childhood. This contrasts with the traditional physician-patient relationship that has fostered dependency, encouraged the patient to view the physician as a powerful authority figure. The growing assertion by the public (as patients) that this traditional relationship is no longer appropriate to our society is a development that psychiatrists should be encouraging."

The editorial points out that absolute confidentiality cannot be guaranteed. There are too many occasions when it is already compromised. The editorial appears to suggest a series of records on every patient, each of which would be accessible to the appropriate parties.

There are, however, difficulties in the implementation of such a system; for example, when the record is subpoenaed, all the records must be presented. Is it possible to train psychiatrists in the proper content of the different, separately maintained portions of a psychiatric record? What will psychiatrists record if patients have the right to see the records? Meaningless generalities? Information given by others who are promised confidentiality of their communications?

A major area where such a procedure would have a tremendous adverse effect is in the training of psychiatric residents. These programs are, for the most part, based on inpatient psychiatric facilities. Many of the patients are psychotic when admitted and some do not recover quickly. In order to obtain information about the patient, relatives and close friends are interviewed. All training manuals of worth advocate that all important dates and opinions be recorded. Granted that such information is hearsay and may be biased, but an essential part of good teaching is to instruct the resident always to keep this in mind in the diagnostic evaluation. To grant access to the record by the patient would in many, many cases be both countertherapeutic and detrimental to the training process.

This "solution" is but one additional example of the fragmentary and unrealistic approach to highly emotional issues, apparently without due deliberation, for the establishment of the priorities that serve the best interests of all patients. In reality, double-entry record keeping, besides being unmanageable, is not permitted when records are required in a court of law. Even if permissible, double-entry records, one of which would be available to the patient, would actually defeat the philosophical intent behind the advocacy of free access.

Because psychiatrists are human, it is understandable that they become involved in the emotionally charged issues of the current social scene. But they are also dedicated and trained to help patients review the broad range of their lives, to relate the emotional impact of past events and issues on their current thinking and behavior, and to assist them to resolve the emotional conflicts that incapacitate and/or impair their relationships and performance in the real world in which they live. If this is their function, it would appear incumbent upon them to be consistent and to have the same broad viewpoint in matters of concern to their patients and their profession.

That there are, and will be, conflicts between professional ideals and the pragmatic reality of the environment in which they practice is inevitable. As with patients, recognition of these conflicts is imperative if the priorities relating to the optimum welfare of patients are to become standard practice. With this in mind, the following positions are offered.

Accepting the basic principle that success in treatment (in many but certainly not the majority of cases) depends on the confidentiality of the psychiatrist-patient relationship, it is vital that there is a clear understanding of what is the proper subject of confidentiality. All too often, the principle of confidentiality is asserted to cover every contact with the psychiatrist, ranging from acknowledging that the patient was seeing the psychiatrist to *every* communication by the patient. This is impractically broad and unworkable in practice. For the patient, what is important is any communication which, if it were shared with others, would be injurious either to his own self-esteem or to his relationships with others, or to his disadvantage occupationally, economically, or socially. It is such items of information that are the proper subject of confidentiality, and they obviously vary from patient to patient. Assertion of confidentiality as a pure and absolute professional ideal may be, in fact, injurious to the patient because it is not consonant with the reality of the environment in which the patient must live and survive.

Second, a profession dedicated to enabling individuals to deal with the external real world, rather than dealing solely with the patients' intrapsychic problems, must operate in such a way as to recognize the independence of the competent patient in decision making, arising out of his involvement in a psychotherapeutic contract. From this it follows that he may assert or waive confidentiality when to do so is in his opinion to his benefit. The psychiatrist may offer his opinion as to the wisdom of such action but the decision must be that of the patient, guided by his legal representative.

In cases involving actual litigation, counsel for the patient has a legal responsibility far beyond that of the psychiatrist and it is the duty of the psychiatrist to communicate to the patient's designated attorney all information, including that potentially detrimental to the patient. Psychiatric records should also be made available to the attorney with the request that the attorney use the utmost discretion in communicating to his client sensitive information in the record.

When testifying in court, the psychiatrist is obligated to present specific information communicated to him by the patient only when requested in either direct or cross-examination. He is required to express his opinion only when he has arrived at a definite rather than just a tentative opinion. He does not have to, and should not, present his own speculations. Rarely, if ever, are communications about erotic fantasies and other sensitive areas necessary or relevant in a court of law. Nor is detailed recording of them necessary.

When the psychiatrist has listened to verbalizations regarding potential violence, it is his ethical responsibility to form an opinion about the risk of danger to the patient and/or others and to take such action as is necessary to protect the patient, including involuntary hospitalization. In court, such communications are usually relevant to the proceedings, insofar as the therapist is concerned, only in the context of whether the psychiatrist's action or lack of action was consistent with his judgment.

Third, the public welfare is best served by making psychiatric treatment not only readily accessible, but also acceptable to all segments of society as a usual, unremarkable part of the practice of medicine. This is likely to be best achieved not by legislation or by claiming special interests, but by education of the public. In the past, the fears of mental illness were generated and intensified by the secretiveness associated with it. As with tuberculosis, the development of modern therapeutic measures has removed the fears of the inevitability of deterioration, while further educational efforts will ameliorate stigmata associated with a genetic inevitability. A most important factor in promoting public acceptance, in addition to increasing information, has been the actual personal acquaintance of large numbers of individuals with psychiatrically ill persons other than their own family members. While necessarily rejecting, on the basis of scientific studies, the claims of the advocates of megavitamin therapy, one must recognize the educational impact of the various schizophrenia movements to defuse the once universal fears about this disorder. Indeed, many psychiatrists appear to continue to have more emotional reactions to the diagnosis of schizophrenia than large segments of the public.

Counterconstructive to the ultimate acceptance by the public of mental illness on the same level as a physical illness are the professional demands for secrecy and special measures in the handling of psychiatric illness, such as the differences in the processing of health insurance claims in the name of confidentiality. This advocacy by the profession only reinforces the belief that psychiatric illness is, indeed, different and is the occasion for justifiable fears on the part of the public.

In the face of the argument that actual occasions of loss of job or other adverse effects on a patient have resulted from disclosure of a psychiatric condition, it is recommended that the profession follow the lead of the mental health professions in Connecticut. There an amendment to the antidiscrimination statutes was enacted, prohibiting job discrimination on the basis of a psychiatric diagnosis (9).

Finally, while there are other broad areas of conflict meriting discussion, such as research, data banks, reporting to state and federal agencies, etc., the whole range of the purposes of psychiatric records requires clearer definition. Psychiatric records serve two vital functions and several subsidiary purposes. From the viewpoint of benefit to the patient, medical records are well recognized as the only universal means of providing for continuity of care. This is true not only when the patient later requires treatment by another physician, but also for the physician treating the patient over a long period of time. The second vital function is the one of professional training. This is particularly true of hospitals and other facilities engaged in residency training. In the better training programs, the residents (and the staff) are required to develop very detailed information regarding all aspects of the patient's history from birth on and, indeed, of familial and prenatal influences, noting the source. Much of the data must necessarily be secured from family members who are, of course, not disinterested persons and who give very private information on the assumption that it will not be available to anyone outside the therapeutic team.

Much of the affect associated with confidentiality appears to arise from regarding the physical record, and not what it contains, as the important issue. In the future, as in the better programs today, stress will be placed on training the resident and the psychiatrist on the selection of material to be placed in the record and the importance of language used in noting data and concepts. Data should be recorded always with the possibility in mind that the record may be open to inspection by other persons, including those in a court of law, so that statements potentially damaging to the patient in any of a range of circumstances will be avoided.

Thus, from the viewpoints of both patient care and training, there is no need to record the innermost secrets of the patient nor to detail fantasies, erotic or otherwise, about which so much concern is expressed. The English language is particularly suited to the selection of words which, while vague and nonspecific to the nonprofessional, alert a psychiatrist to areas he may wish to explore with the patient.

Despite the wrongs and injuries that have occurred as the result of breach of confidentiality, whether through leak of information via insurance claims, by presentation in court or other media, or by illegal actions, it is evident that there are so many more professionals and nonprofessionals becoming involved in the periphery of the psychotherapeutic process that neither legislation nor special security measures will, in fact, solve all the problems in the field. As with the chastity belt of old, successful achievement of purpose only comes about when virtue arises within the individual or is stringently imposed from without. One alternative, as with the chastity belt in the course of time, is acceptance of the imperfections of human nature. Another is the modification of the professional value system to bring it into harmony with the times.

There is thus an urgent need for a major effort on the part of the profession to look at the issues of confidentiality on the broadest canvas. This examination should include its origins and purposes in the context of past, present, and future social, health, legal, occupational, and other developments. It should cover the short- and long-term effects of adhering to concepts and practices not necessarily in the best interests of patients. There should be recognition that the ultimate decision-maker is the patient, and, above all, that while being of service to him, psychiatry must conform to meeting his needs in the context of the real world. Within such a framework, the profession must develop principles and guidelines that preserve confidentiality in the degrees the welfare of the patient demands.

Ageless as the conflict between idealism and reality is, it is much more intense in the United States than elsewhere. But it was, after all, an American philosopher, William James, who enunciated the doctrine of pragmatism by which the truth of an idea depends on whether its consequences lead to useful results or help resolve a problem.

REFERENCES

1. *In re Lifschutz.* 2 Cal.3d 415, 467 P.2d 557, 85 Cal. Rptr. 829 (1970).
2. *Vitaly Tarasoff et al. v. The Regents of the University of California et al.* S.F. 23042 (July 1, 1976).
3. Slovenko, R. On confidentiality. *Contemp. Psychoanal.,* 12:109-139, 1976.
4. Herrington, B. S. Legislators meet psychiatrists on NHI. *Psychiat. News,* 11:1, 18-21, July 16, 1976.
5. Baldwin, J. A., Leff, J., & Wing, J. K. Confidentiality of psychiatric data in medical information systems. *Brit. J. Psychiat.,* 128:417-427, 1976.
6. American Psychiatric Association. *Confidentiality and Third Parties.* Task Force Report 9. Washington, D.C.: American Psychiatric Association, 1975.
7. Herrington, B. S. Legislators urge unity of professions. *Psychiat. News,* 11:1,24-25, Aug. 6, 1976.
8. American Psychiatric Association Committee on Public Information. "Confidential?" [editorial]. *Psychiat. News,* 10:2, July 2, 1975.
9. Connecticut General Statutes, Title 17, Sec. 17-206j (Rev. 1975).

Part V

Competence and Responsibility

Competence is a legal concept concerned with the mental capacity of an individual to perform a transaction or make a contract. In each situation, the level of judgment required to make a decision may vary. One must ask: "Competent to do what?"

Every adult is assumed to be competent and the contrary view requires proof. We also believe that society should not, under ordinary circumstances, interfere to protect fools from their folly. When mental illness is present and, as a result of mental illness, there is a defect in judgment that impairs the ability to act, the individual may be incompetent in that particular situation.

Competence to stand trial requires the individual be able to comprehend the nature of the proceedings to conduct a rational defense and to cooperate with his or her attorney. There are other criteria as well, such as to follow the testimony and correct for errors, to testify, and to tolerate the stress of trial without disturbing behavior. A Joint Information Service survey (1) of mentally ill offenders found 52 percent of those referred incompetent to stand trial, but only 4 percent not guilty by reason of "insanity."

Crime is an act that violates a law and does injury to others. There is an overt act and the intent to commit it. Responsibility is answerability for one's conduct. For centuries, society has recognized that all are not equally accountable for their acts and some lack the intent to commit a crime. Children, the mentally ill, and mentally retarded may not be accountable and may be unable to formulate an intent.

The judicial system is adverse to enlarging the scope of the "insanity defense." Through the years it has attempted to specify the basis for determination in *M'Naghten*, the *Freeman* rule, the *Durham* decision and the formulation of the American Law Institute (ALI) rule. The latter states: "A person is not responsible for criminal conduct if, at the time of such conduct, as a result of mental disease or defect, he lacks substantial capacity to either appreciate the criminality of his conduct or to conform his conduct to the requirements of the law."

Psychiatrists and mental health professionals have contributed to the problem through their careless use of labels. "Any" impairment is not sufficient, it must be significant or substantial. "Total" impairment is also unnecessary. Antisocial conduct alone is not mental disease.

The real question boils down to: How much pathology or mental illness is necessary to escape responsibility for one's acts?

Irwin N. Perr is one of the rare individuals doubly trained in both psychiatry and law. He states: "When an individual is found to be incompetent there is deprivation of some authority and power to exercise choice." The ultimate decision as to competence is made by legal authorities. Mental health professionals' opinions are subject to legal ratification. Mental illness or defect when present is related to the issue at hand. Perr shows how the varying levels of impairment are relevant to: contracts, marriage, making a will, testimonial capacity, consent to sexual relations, care for children, minors, experimentation and research, and the death penalty.

Jacques M. Quen is an academician and medical historian with an interest in forensic psychiatry. He seeks to reconcile the administration of justice for the individual and for society with the determination of responsibility in those with mental illness or defect. His is a historical approach to the development of legal concepts. The influence of Isaac Ray on American forensic psychiatry and on the law is noted. Underscored are the major legal rules: *M'Naghten*, *Durham*, and the American Law Institute.

REFERENCE

1. Scheidemandel, P. H., & Kanno, C. K., *The Mentally Ill Offender: A Survey of Treatment Programs.* Washington, D.C.: Joint Information Service, American Psychiatric Assn., 1969.

Chapter IX

The Many Faces of Competence

IRWIN N. PERR, M.D., J.D.

Competence is a legal concept dealing with the mental capacity or ability of a person to perform an act. Mental capacity or ability is broadly reflected in the cognitive-affective-behavioral pattern of the person, depending on the specific legal act at issue. Physicians and psychiatrists as well as laymen often use the word "competence" to describe a level of judgment sufficient to make decisions. In this sense, the meaning is quasi-legal, for if a physician denotes someone as incompetent, he will be deprived of some authority as to his power to exercise choice, and this will have legal implications as well as practical everyday ones which may not be the subject of formal legal review.

The concept of capacity or ability is based on the unitary, integrated functioning of a person, which encompasses the traditional psychiatric triad of cognition, feeling, and conation and which may be affected by what we consider mental disease or defect.

The phrase "performance of an act" has many meanings depending on the context. Performance very frequently deals with the ability to assent or consent; here the act ultimately is one of adequate intellectual comprehension unaffected by significant factors which would interfere with decision-making powers. Performance may refer to a physical act involving purposeful use of the bodily musculature. Performance may also refer to the ability to understand and appreciate an act being directed toward the person.

The issue of competence is ultimately a legal one in that the law may make the final determination as to a person's ability to make decisions or to be responsible for acts or judgments. Unofficially the determination often is that of the person with whom the party at issue deals. However, this is almost invariably subject to the ultimate authority inherent within the legal process. Thus mental health professionals must keep in mind their limited role as advisors and the fact that their own decisions are subject to specific legal guidelines and review. This concept of competence refers to all interpersonal relationships—lawyers, businessmen, and citizens at large all may encounter situations where the question of competence may determine the validity of a contractual or any other type of relationship involving a give and take of communication or performance for which the person at issue assumes a legal responsibility. Because of the nature of their work, mental health professions need, more than others do, to understand fully the ramifications and complexities of competence.

The Role of the Law in Competence

Because competence at its hard core is a legal concept, psychiatrists and others would be best advised not to use the word other than to express an opinion directed to a legal issue. The use of the word is necessary for purposes of communication, and the psychiatrist should feel free to specify an opinion as to competence within the legal framework, recognizing that the opinion is often advisory and subject to ratification by a legal authority.

In the law itself, however, there is no single meaningful concept of competence. Competence refers to the authority to function within a specific legal context and is defined differently by law according to the specific legal situation at hand. Thus, in order to respond to a question about competence, the opinion-giver must have a clear understanding of the specific legal issue and the criteria for competence delineated by law for that issue.

One area of competence is that of "responsibility" or "criminal responsibility" which is based on a specific capacity to be held blameworthy for acts committed which are otherwise classified as criminal. Responsibility is thus a specific area of competence; it is discussed in Chapter X.

There are innumerable other areas of competence, several of which will be explored at length. The basic substrate in all issues involved in competence is: Is there a mental disease or defect which affects judgment, decision making, or behavior? And if there is, is it such that it meets the criteria of the law regarding the specific issue? The psychiatrist's or other mental health expert's professional background enables him to be a crucial advisor on the answer to the first question. The one who makes the ultimate legal decision, usually a judge, will incorporate that information and opinion in order to determine the answer to the second question.

THE PROFESSIONAL EXPERT

An expert is one who on the basis of skill, education, and experience is entitled to offer an opinion on matters not within the realm of the average person's knowledge. The law generally has been quite liberal in allowing a wide variety of persons to offer opinions as to mental functioning. Thus one does not encounter the exclusion of opinion in this area that one does in other areas of law where expertness is in question. On the other hand, the credibility or value placed on testimony or opinion by the ultimate decision-maker as to competence, the judge, will be affected markedly by the background of the person claiming such expertness. For some legal purposes and in some jurisdictions, the law may place by statute limitations in this regard. For some purposes, the use of a physician is required; for others a psychiatrist may be the only one allowed by law to offer an opinion; in still other situations, opinions may be restricted to psychiatrists or psychologists. Thus each profession must be aware of the rules within its own jurisdiction.

For practical purposes, many of the issues involved are based on medical-psychiatric parameters where purely medical information is the most appropriate. Accordingly, the opinions of others will carry little weight or may even be considered not relevant. The background of the psychiatrist is such that he is often uniquely qualified to give an opinion. For example, in a study (1) of involuntary commitment, I have noted the medical-psychiatric substrate of many of the cases that reached judicial review. On the other hand, the case at hand may involve matters of intellectual functioning which can be appropriately measured by pertinent psychological tests (2), and at times data from other sources may be helpful, even though they are not likely to be determinative. Regardless of the philosophical schisms between the medical-psychiatric model and the social-environmental one, most of the situations involving competence deal with determinations most appropriately evaluated in terms of the medical frame of reference.

AREAS OF COMPETENCE

The general principle of the law regarding consent demands that a person has the right to keep his body inviolate and that violation of this right may involve assault and battery or negligence. In other than emergency situations, a person must consent to hospitalization and treatment and to do so, he must have an understanding of what is involved. In regard to specific diagnostic procedures and treatments, particularly surgery, he must be able to understand the nature of the treatment, its benefits, and the risks. Every time a physician has a patient sign a release or permission form, he is in essence making a judgment that the patient is mentally capable of doing so. In the past, if a person was obviously not competent to sign because of some defect in understanding, the nearest relative would be asked to give such permission. However, increasingly, if there is any question, further procedures may be necessary.

Specific cases have involved elderly patients with severe physical illnesses that necessitate drastic surgery (with perhaps limited hopes of improvement or even survival) or younger persons with disfiguring or disabling conditions that can be alleviated by surgery. The patient either is clearly incompetent to make a decision or makes a decision that the treating doctors feel is inappropriate. A psychiatric consultation is requested. The psychiatrist may find that the person indeed cannot make a rational judgment because of the effect of a concurrent psychiatric disorder. A court, on reviewing the data, may then authorize treatment. Similarly, cases have arisen where a blood transfusion is needed and the patient expresses a death wish or a desire to leave the matter in the hands of God. Court decisions in such instances vary widely with a few courts stating that there is no right to die.

In some chronic disease hospitals or in situations involving disability or other benefits, the paying agency may ask the treating doctor if the person is competent to handle financial affairs. The decision may involve only whether the patient or an assigned family member is to receive the check.

Admission to and treatment in psychiatric hospitals may

involve more direct questions about competence to consent (3). In view of the litigation epidemic in the United States, the physician is best advised to assume a conservative stance in dealing with a voluntary patient. Increased use of the courts and commitment to state hospitals with their limited programs seem to be the current trend, though such social policies would scarcely seem to be in the best interests of patients.

Handling One's Affairs and Guardianship

Adults are assumed to be able to handle their ordinary business affairs and to be responsible financially for obligations incurred. Parents may face the problem of having a retarded or chronically mentally ill child who reaches adulthood and may seek advice on the future care of the child. They may wish a judgment by a physician or psychiatrist as to the child's ability to handle his affairs. One method for handling such a problem which does not involve a judicial determination is the creation of a trust for the care of the disabled person; termination of a trust may be stipulated in case of recovery (if the person has a reversible condition).

In many cases, particularly with the elderly, a person gradually loses intellectual capacities which may be related to the handling of business affairs. A businessman in a manic phase of a manic-depressive illness may become a financial menace within a very short time. If a person, for whatever reason, begins to dissipate his financial resources or to neglect responsibilities for family, the law may intervene to declare the person incompetent, impound his resources, and place him under guardianship. A guardian may be authorized to handle financial affairs and to handle decisions as to care of the person (guardian of the body). These functions may be separated, according to the jurisdiction.

For purposes of guardianship, a typical statute may read: "Incompetent means any person who by reason of advanced

age, improvidence, or mental or physical disability or infirm-
ity, chronic alcoholism, mental deficiency, lunacy, or mental
illness, is incapable of proper care of himself or his property or
fails to provide for his family or for other persons for whom he
is charged by law to provide, or any person confined to a penal
institution or any person indeterminately hospitalized and not
subsequently found competent."

Brackel and Rock (4) have reviewed the legal criteria in
various states. Many have little to do with judgmental capacity
related to traditional concepts of mental illness. If one is a
spendthrift, that is to be determined by information from
other sources. This, however, is scarcely a psychiatric
concept. If one is an incarcerated felon, then the status is
factual and automatically operant by rule of law.

The commonest problems are those of the elderly where
organic brain disease due to arteriosclerosis or senile brain
disease creates an increasing deficit which impairs social
functioning. A typical case was that of an elderly single woman
with heart disease, diabetes, and hypertension who had a
stroke which left her confused, aphasic, and paralyzed. She
owned considerable real estate with much rental income. A
brother was appointed as guardian and handled the patient's
financial affairs. Though she was in her eighties, she gradually
regained both speech and movement and showed minimal
effects of the cerebral vascular accident in terms of cognitive
functioning. She asked her brother to return management of
her affairs to herself. When he refused, she entreated the court
to terminate the guardianship and restore her legal
competence. Examination showed a good ability to communicate, excellent memory, and overall good judgmental
capacity. She was basically a tight-fisted conservative person
unlikely to dissipate her resources. The guardianship was
accordingly terminated.

An elderly man had a chronic paranoid psychosis with
arteriosclerotic brain disease. He thought that his 75-year-old

wife was the neighborhood prostitute and was copulating on the back lawn with an 85-year-old neighbor. He hired private detectives to trail her and his children, running up huge expenditures. Guardianship removed him from financial control and allowed for maintenance at home, rather than commitment.

Another elderly lady, quite eccentric, had vast sums of money that she had hidden in the lining of clothes (either in cash or bonds). She gradually became physically disabled, and a niece had her forcibly taken to a private mental hospital on an emergency basis. The patient was a devout Christian Scientist who recognized her failing physical capacities and who wished to go to a Christian Science Nursing Home. The niece, perhaps to forestall an unfavorable will, brought action for a declaration of incompetence and guardianship. The old lady was a very compulsive, rigid person who characteristically was a saver, but she showed no deviations meriting a diagnosis of significant brain deterioriation. Guardianship was refused.

In another case, a quadriplegic woman volunteered for guardianship based on physical disability. When she wished to change guardians from one sister to another, the first sister brought action for a guardianship based on mental disease. Again, despite advanced age and a horrifying total disability, no mental disease was demonstrated.

In these cases, the physician often must consider a complex medical condition, carefully check mental status, and estimate the degree of deficit and effect on behavior in deciding on a recommendation. He must keep in mind that people are deemed competent until the preponderance of evidence indicates otherwise, and the burden is on the one who claims incompetence.

Contracts and Marriage

A contract requires a meeting of the minds; to be legally binding, both participants must understand the nature of the transaction and its implications. If one of the parties because of mental disease or defect cannot do so, the contract may be rescinded and declared void. For this to be done, the degree of deficit must be significant and relate clearly to an understanding of the contract. In such a case, the person will be found to have been incompetent to make that specific contract. Litigation in this regard usually occurs after the event with one who previously has not been declared to be mentally ill. On occasion, contracts have been declared void because of the intellectual limitation of one of the parties, usually a retarded person who has signed a purchase agreement. This does not mean that one must exercise the finest of business judgment in order to make a valid contract; in fact litigation to void a contract is quite rare.

Certain contracts are of such an essential nature that the law will not allow an attack upon them. Thus contracts by severely mentally ill patients for necessary items (or "necessaries") will be upheld because they would have been essential regardless of the person's status. These include reasonable costs for food, shelter, clothing, and medical care. Thus a person who buys a $100 coat for protection from the cold will have to pay for the coat, no matter how disturbed he is; a woman in a grandiose state who buys a $10,000 mink coat would be in a different position. A person who has been severely psychotic cannot state that he did not agree to and therefore will not pay for hospitalization and psychiatric care because of his confused state; fortunately for psychiatrists and other physicians medical care is considered a necessity. Thus situations involving necessities are not likely to come to a psychiatrist for an opinion as to competence.

If a person is under guardianship, contracts may be easily voided. Otherwise whether a contract is automatically void or subject to be declared void (voidable) is beyond the scope of this discussion.

Some examples of lack of competence to make a contract follow. A 35-year-old mentally retarded woman, on welfare, with six children, signs a contract for an expensive encyclopedia (total cost: $1,000) because she is told that the books will make her children successful in life and will cost but pennies a day. A public service law agency, to whom she is referred, finds that she had no comprehension of the cost of the contract. A woman who is manic-depressive is voluntarily hospitalized; while on ground privileges, she leaves the hospital, walks to a local commercial center, goes to an appliance store, and buys twelve color-TV sets which she has sent to her friends. The husband, to his distress, soon finds out about this largesse. After much communication, the appliance store, recognizing the situation, has the sets picked up and returned. A businessman with a long history of manic-depressive illness has been reduced to an $80-a-week income as a clothing salesman. Invited to Las Vegas by ex-associates and in an expansive mood, he is able with the persuasive affability of a manic episode to borrow and lose $25,000 in one night. Much to their surprise, his gambling friends find on investigation that he in fact had been severely mentally ill and, recognizing the realities of the situation, accept the concept of lack of competence just as courts might do in a comparable situation.

As in most issues involving competence, cognition is not the sole measuring rod. The expansiveness of the manic and the suspicion of the paranoid affect the quality of the judgmental function.

Marriage is simply a special kind of contract. The quality of mental functioning is related to an understanding of what marriage and its responsibilities are. Very little mental functioning is needed for such an appraisal; one eminent professor of domestic relations has stated that the measure is approximately that level of comprehension needed to buy an ice cream cone. Competence to marry does occasionally arise particularly when it involves someone either indefinitely committed or under guardianship. In some states such patients are unable to contract a valid marriage; in others it may be voided on request of the ill party. Legal oddities have occurred where a person, incompetent by law in one state, crosses a state line to marry in another state. Elderly confused people enamored of younger attractive parties allegedly attracted by monetary gain have been the subject of litigation regarding validity of a marriage.

Inasmuch as awareness of what is transpiring is obviously essential to a contract, factors that might negate such awareness may accordingly provide the base for a claim of invalidity. Typical examples are severe intoxications with alcohol or drugs. Occasionally claims of amnesia must also be considered.

Making a Will

A will is the legal means by which a person distributes property after his death; as a legal instrument it requires competence by the one making the will at the time of its making. The soundness of mind and memory required, primarily a cognitive function, is measured generally by the following standards: (1) does the person know that he is making a will?, (2) does he know the extent of his property or bounty?, and (3) is he aware of who the living persons are who would be ordinarily eligible for such bequests? Because of the relatively narrow definitions, it is possible for one to have significant mental deficit and yet be considered capable of making a will, or as the law puts it, to have testamentary capacity. Thus, on occasion, wills made by patients in state hospitals have been upheld. The law appropriately favors the validity of a will made in conformance with the law and does not lightly overturn the wishes of a testator for eccentricity or bizarreness of philosophy or cause.

Psychiatrists and physicians at large may be involved in the will-making process at many levels. A patient may be terminal or in threat of death and may decide to complete a will because of his recognition of this; family members and others may pressure a declining person to do so. An attorney may ask the attending physician his opinion about the patient's capacity to participate in a will-making process. Not only may a patient have a complex of diseases which can affect the judgmental process, but he may be under considerable sedation or taking mind-affecting drugs. The law in this particular area has frequently commented on the validity of wills made during a "lucid interval"—a period during the course of an illness otherwise disabling where lawyers rush in and obtain the necessary signatures. Obviously there is such a thing as a lucid interval; if a physician is an attending or evaluating doctor at such a time, he should prepare a detailed dated note describing the circumstances and the patient's clinical state. He should also be alert to fraud and to possible duress on a very ill patient.

At times psychiatrists are asked to make a retrospective evaluation of the patient's state of mind at the time the will was made, which may have been many years earlier. He will take into account his knowledge of the patient, clinical descriptions at the time, and medical records before and after the event.

In any case, the evaluator looks first for the presence of demonstrable mental illness and second for its effect on the criteria for testamentary capacity. While the process of questioning a will has been subject to attack, as has the psychiatrist's role, an organized society requires some reasonable system of transferring property. Where a psychiatrist offers an opinion about a dead person whom he has never seen, considerable conservatism and sophistication are required.

The most common area of difficulty in will making is the effect of organic brain disease, whatever the cause. On rare occasions frank delusional systems may be in evidence. The role of alcohol or drugs is at times implicated. Obviously alcoholism per se is not a handicap; most alcoholics have clear mentation in periods other than acute intoxication. Any mental health professional who has dealt with the testator around the period when the will was made may have information helpful to the judge in his decision. If a patient has progressive senile brain disease, then beyond a certain point, recovery of lucidity is doubtful. Cerebrovascular accidents, however, may result in a clinical course with marked changes in functioning; time considerations thus become a key element in evaluation. One problem area is that of the elderly person with delusions of infidelity on the part of the spouse. The factual situation is most important. A spouse may be unfaithful or may indulge in a behavior pattern which would not unreasonably lead to such a conclusion. An erroneous judgment is not necessarily a delusion. Mental retardation often will sufficiently interfere with cognitive functions as to negate testamentary capacity. Ordinarily neuroses, behavior disorders, and philosophies of life will not be accepted as being disabling in this regard.

On occasion, because of the large amounts of money involved and the likelihood of a family dispute, an attorney will seek a careful detailed examination to substantiate current capacity. Tapes, movies, and even television reels have been placed on record to ward off a later attack.

Testimonial Capacity

Another type of competence concerns the ability to give testimony, to be a witness. If a person has a significant deficit which would interfere with the relating of facts or communicating meaningfully, then a judge may rule the person to be incompetent as a witness. Such a determination may be made in the case of children of specified ages, usually under ten, who are questioned about the meanings of truth and lying and of an oath. It is a judicial determination not requiring special evaluation. At times, particularly in sex offense cases, a request may be made to have children examined to ascertain, if possible, any impediment to credibility.

I once saw an elderly lady charged in a personal injury suit. She had made an inappropriate left turn resulting in an automobile accident. By the time the case came to court a few years later, she had had progressive brain disease, was probably senile, and had no recollection of the accident. In another case, an essential witness for the state had had acute depressions and psychoses due to drug intoxication and was hospitalized during the pendency of the trial. Careful review of his status before trial was made as he was an essential witness whose testimony would be expected to be subject to attack. Another area of interest results from assaults in hospitals. In a famous Cleveland case, an elderly patient was beaten to death by two attendants before twenty other patients whose credibility was attacked.

A finding of testimonial incapacity or incompetence excludes all testimony. In addition, witnesses may be attacked in court for any condition that would affect their credibility. Unlike other legal situations, cases involving psychopathic traits have periodically occurred, the most famous being the Alger Hiss case where an effort was made to discredit Whittaker Chambers on the ground that he was a psychopath. This maneuver failed.

Performance of Duties of a Position

Under civil service law, the standards for hiring may be rigidly spelled out, limiting the power of a hiring authority to use its discretion, good or bad. If a candidate meets the job requirements, passes the civil service test at a sufficient level, and is physically capable, the hiring authority must select him if he is the only one on the list or the only one left. Generally an applicant can be denied a job if he lies about his background, has a sufficiently poor work record, or a criminal past. One other area of exclusion is based on mental unfitness to perform the duties of the position involved. In New Jersey such claims have dealt primarily with applicants for police jobs and have usually involved personality disorders and their measurement. Problems in psychiatric or psychological evaluation have been explored in a series of articles based on the experience of the Civil Service Medical Review Board (5, 6). Such screening may be found in other cases, as in those assigned to atom bomb work in the military, but it will not be involved in the legal process as it is in the ordinary civil service situation. Similarly, the question of competence to continue in a civil service job may arise, as it has with schoolteachers who otherwise are protected by tenure.

Consent to Sexual Relations

The essence of rape is forcible "carnal knowledge" or sexual penetration. Forcible means unwilling subjection by the victim. In addition, by statute, certain parties may be declared to be unable to give consent and are therefore "unwilling" regardless of overt behavior. This situation usually involves sex relations with a minor below a specified age who cannot give consent, and therefore the sex act becomes one of statutory rape. Statutory rape may also result where a person is incapable of consent by virtue of such a degree of mental illness or defect that the meaning and ramifications of the sex act are not comprehended. Obviously most people, no matter how ill, know what sex is and so this issue will rarely arise. A-buse of patients in state hospitals may result in such charges. In at least one state, the one charged with the crime must have reason to know that the consent is vitiated by mental dysfunction; after all, a person having sexual relations with an overtly willing partner will rarely conduct a mental status examination. One interesting case involving the degree of retardation relevant to such an issue has been described elsewhere (2); here a severely retarded woman with an IQ of about 40 was found incompetent to consent.

Care of Children

Competence to care for a child is not governed by rigid legal rules, but is determined by the facts. This issue may be involved in adoption, custody, or removal of a child for neglect or other reasons. There is ordinarily no necessary correlation between mental functioning and child care, unless there are extreme deviations. On the other hand, the essence of care is the care itself, the actual behavior. This is therefore one area where the information provided by the social worker is of extreme importance to a disposition. Psychiatrists and psychologists must be careful not to be seduced into an advocacy role in a bitter custody fight, particularly where their knowledge of the actual home situation is limited. The other side of the coin is the implication that some minor psychiatric aberration renders a person unfit to care for a child. The abuses in court hearings have been so great that many psychiatrists and psychologists refuse to be consultants in custody cases.

Consent by Minors, Particularly for Medical Treatment

In many areas of behavior, the legal capacity of a person to perform an act is spelled out by law based on chronological age. In certain medical situations the criterion is not age alone but comprehension and understanding — for example when an injured child requires amputation and his parents are unavailable, when a teenager requests an abortion, when an adolescent asks for treatment of drug abuse or venereal disease without his parents' knowledge, or when a sexually active 13-year-old girl asks for contraceptive advice. It is therefore possible that such capacity may be involved in legal review (7,

8). This is especially true now that the authority of parents to consent for their children is under attack.

Consent for Experimentation and Research

A very complicated area under review is the establishment of guidelines for consent either to experimentation or drastic, questionable, or extreme forms of treatment. The law itself in various states has set up cumbersome machinery which in many ways has vitiated the right to consent, for example, in the use of electroshock therapy. In research and experimentation, the risk-benefit ratio is a matter for consideration. In addition, the comprehension by the subject is of importance as is the possibility of duress based on the environmental circumstances. This has applied particularly to prisons and was the subject of the famous *Kaimowitz* case (9).*

Criminality

The subject of competence is applicable to many stages of the criminal process. In addition to the well-known subject of competence to stand trial, competence may arise as an issue at any step where legal procedure is involved. Thus, the issue of competence to fire an attorney, cop a plea, or even to be executed may be the subject of review.

Standing Trial. Competence to stand trial is a common issue. In some jurisdictions as many as 25 percent of those who were said to have committed murder and were examined psychiatrically were found incompetent to stand trial; one English study of the 1930s reported a rate of 38 percent. The criteria to stand trial are based on mental illness of such degree that the

---

* See also the discussion of informed consent in Chapters III and IV of this volume, which are concerned with the individual's ability to understand and exercise free choice.

defendant may .be unable to relate the events, cooperate with his attorney, and understand the nature of the charges against him and the possible penalties. Very severe disability is ordinarily required to show that a person is not competent to stand trial, the usual effect of such a finding being that he is incarcerated in a special institution, usually one for the criminally insane, until he is "restored to reason" and able to return for his trial. As a result of the Supreme Court decision in *Jackson v. Indiana* (10), a person may be held only a limited time for such purposes. If there is no prospect of return to competence, then the charges must be dismissed and the person handled civilly. In the past the concept of competence to stand trial has been misused for a number of strategic reasons with little publicity. In recent times the problems of amnesia and the use of drugs to control mental illness at the time of the trial have raised technical questions for judicial review. A recent G.A.P. report (11) has explored these issues, using the *Dusky* case (12) as a base for discussion.

Because of the uses and abuses of the concept, psychiatrists have been very critical of the plea. Many lawyers have felt that justice delayed is not justice at all, particularly where the defendant in fact did not commit the crime alleged. Halpern (13), in a thorough discussion of the subject, supports the elimination of the plea with intermediate steps to facilitate a speedy trial until public opinion can enforce such a major change in policy.

The issue of competence to stand trial is subject to many legal technicalities which need not be explored here — who can raise the plea, being one example. Regardless, the issue remains with us, and the courts continue to turn to psychiatrists for assistance in such a determination. The criteria are practical, everyday ones dealing with the ability to communicate and comprehend. It is not expected that the defendant will be a master of the legal process and its multifold technicalities. I recall one case of an illiterate black self-proclaimed minister with an IQ of 60 who was found to be able to stand trial. He had a lifelong history of borderline functioning, but earned a living, bought property, paid his bills, related in excruciating detail what had occurred, and comprehended the situation to a fair degree despite a bizarre religiosity which led one unsophisticated examiner to label him as schizophrenic.

In an attempt to quantify the criteria for competence to stand trial, Lipsitt, Lelos, and McGarry (14) have formulated a checklist and a numerical rating system; however, this arbitrary system has not found any wide acceptance.

Copping a Plea. Similar rules apply to competence to cop a plea although it is a rare event. Did the defendant understand the meaning of plea bargaining and how it would affect his position? A most interesting case I have described elsewhere (15) deals with constant delays and rehearings because of periodic raising of the issue. Such an issue may be raised as a tactical one by an attorney seeking to delay a legal disposition. In New Jersey it is within the discretion of the judge whether or not to accept a plea, and it is the judge's obligation to determine that the plea was voluntarily made. Thus, in an attempt to withdraw a plea, there will have been a prior review. In addition to "voluntariness," the issue of coercion may arise. Such an issue may arise much later, even years, after the event in question.

Death Penalty. Now that the trend has been established for a return to the death penalty, the psychiatrist, particularly the prison psychiatrist, may once again be faced with that legal rarity—deferment of execution because of mental illness. Ohio (16), for example, has had statutes that specified the procedures to be followed in such a case. A finding of "insanity" by the judge defers execution until the governor should find the convict to be of "sound mind." If he does so, he could then set a time for execution. Thus the mentally ill convict is confronted with the bizarre situation that, should he recover, he would then be in a position to appreciate the fact that he was being executed, hardly a motivating factor for improvement.

I testified at a trial involving a brutal slaying by a "pseudopsychopathic schizophrenic." After the usual conflicting psychiatric testimony, the defendant was found guilty of first-degree murder and sentenced to die. He was transferred to the state penitentiary where, within one month, the prison psychiatrists found him to be a blatant paranoid psychotic. He was then found to be incompetent to be executed and was transferred to the state institution for the criminally insane. Subsequently, before his recovery to a "sound mind," the state's capital punishment law was overturned. In this case at least, his psychosis was a life-saving event. Since then, he has been transferred back and forth between prison and hospital depending on the vagaries of his psychotic state. In Ohio, a similar rule applied to pregnant prisoners awaiting execution; pregnancy, however, is a much more easily definable state, albeit absolutely reflective of sex discrimination.

General Comments

The numerous examples described have been utilized to stress the point that there is no such entity as competence in a psychiatric or legal context. The word is used broadly to refer to a mental capacity that would allow one to operate in a certain fashion under the law or other authority. The broad use of the term, however, often tends to confuse because it refers to so many concepts. On the other hand, it conveys a very specific and understandable meaning if it is applied to a delineated circumstance. Thus, instead of commentary that a given person is competent, the communication should be that he is competent to stand trial or competent to consent to surgery or competent to make a will. The professional expert should further clarify what he means by specific reference to the disease or aberration present and its degree and its effect on the narrow area of competence in question. For example, if a patient is evaluated for will-making purposes, the examiner might note that the patient is confused and disoriented due to organic brain disease, that he recalls owning only a home on Elm Street when he in fact also owns an apartment house on Maple Avenue, that he talks of being penniless when he in fact has \$182,000 in cash assets according to his attorney, that he does not remember his oldest son who lives in California, etc. That is the kind of data that attorneys and judges can utilize.

The basis for incompetence is the presence of a disorder that affects functioning. As noted, such a determination is not based on cognitive elements alone, but in many cases cognition is the prime area for scrutiny in terms of legal relevance. Cognition is highly important in the making of contracts, wills, and marriages. It is not usually a major point of reference in competence to handle a child or competence to handle a delicate job where personality factors may be more important. In other cases, specific intellectual levels and functioning may be determinative.

The ultimate responsibility for a decision of competence in the legal context is that of the legal profession, usually a judge, or some governmental or administrative equivalent. In a general medical context, consent is judged by the attending professional and is usually not questioned, particularly if the patient attempts to give consent and the therapist or agency agrees. Consent does involve competence in the broad sense. Professional workers should be attuned to the occasional necessity of questioning ability to consent where the person seems to be incompetent; in that case a legal determination may be necessary for the protection of the patient and all involved.

As has been thus far implied, the status of the professional mental health worker in terms of advising in competence issues is not easily or dogmatically delineated. For practical

purposes, there is no such thing as a "mental health professional" as the term is used variably to describe all kinds of people of different educational, occupational, and technical skills.
Generally the psychiatrist is in a position to participate as an
opinion-giver or expert in these matters. Frequently psychologists by their training and experience are part of the
evaluative process. In certain circumstances, the input of the
social worker is most appropriate. The roles allowed may be
determined by law and custom in a given area. To the extent
that the mental dysfunction is related to medical-physical factors or biochemically and neurophysiologically related mental
disorders, the psychiatrist or other physician may be the only
person whose opinion will be accepted or at least relied upon
by a given court. Where a multitude of workers have engaged
in a team effort, each worker might possibly have input from
the standpoint of his particular work effort. If an electroen-
cephalogram report is relevant, it is so whether it was interpreted by a Ph.D. or an M.D., as long as the individual can
demonstrate adequate credentials as a basis for his being
accepted as an expert. Efforts have been made to broaden input by statute for certain purposes and in specific states.
Obviously local policy will be controlled by the law of the
locus.

Where an opinion is offered, whether in everyday records
or in reports to courts, the examiner is well advised to know the
criteria, to state his conclusion as definitively as possible in the
appropriate terms, and to buttress that conclusion with clinical data that have relevance to the specific legal issues. This
will lessen litigation and allow the appropriate legal bodies to
make their determinations with a minimum of time and cost.

Every psychiatrist should be fully aware of all these issues
as the very nature of the profession of psychiatry dictates his
participation in competence questions. As shown, competence
issues are involved in all areas of medicine, and any physician,
again by the very nature of his work, may be called upon to

offer an opinion because of his close, continuing contact with a patient. So may a psychotherapist. I might add that, regardless of the exact merits in a given case, courts and lawyers value highly the opinions of treating physicians. Often such a person is a most valuable informant. For example, an internist who has taken care of a patient for a prolonged period, may be in an excellent position to offer an opinion as to the functioning of a person who made a will during that period.

In many of these matters, communications are most appropriately made in terms of the medical model. In others, this is not so. The traditional concepts of medical disorder — brain disease, intoxications and addictions, neurosis, psychosis, personality disorders, and degrees of retardation — have become part of the everyday language, and the fact-finders can both understand and utilize this language in deciding on the legal criteria. Numerous problems have now arisen in terms of drug and alcohol effect, amnesia, stress, and overall integrative capacity. These may require special review by the examiner or opinion-giver.

In any event, the more all health professionals are aware of these issues, the more likely they are to be of use to their patients, the courts, and society at large.

REFERENCES

1. Perr, I. N. Independent examination of patients hospitalized against their will. *Amer. J. Psychiat.*, 131:765-768, 1974.
2. Perr, I. N. Statutory rape of an insane person. *J. Forensic Sci.*, 13(4): 433-441, 1968.
3. Perr, I. N. Incompetence and consent to psychiatric hospitalization and treatment. *J. Leg. Med.*, 5:16H-16K, 1977.
4. Brackel, S. J., & Rock, R. S. *The Mentally Disabled and the Law.* Revised ed. Chicago: University of Chicago Press, 1971.
5. Perr, I. N. The psychiatric screening of Civil Service candidates with particular reference to police applicants. *J. Forensic Sci.*, 20(1):176-180, 1975.
6. Perr, I. N. A review of rejected police candidates. *J. Forensic Sci.*, 20(4): 714-718, 1975.

7. Perr, I. N. Confidentiality and consent in psychiatric treatment of minors. *J. Leg. Med.,* 4(6):9-13, 1976.

8. Perr, I. N. Recent legal-psychiatric developments in the United States. *Bull. Amer. Acad. Psychiat. Law,* 3:139-142, 1975.

9. *Kaimowitz v. Michigan Department of Mental Health.* Civ. No. 73-19434-AW (Cir. Ct., 1973).

10. *Jackson v. Indiana.* 406 U.S. 715 (1972).

11. Group for Advancement of Psychiatry. *Misuse of Psychiatry in the Criminal Courts: Competency to Stand Trial.* New York: GAP Vol. VIII, Report No. 89, Feb. 1974.

12. *Dusky v. United States,* 271 F.2d 385 (8th Cir., 1959); 362 U.S. 402 (1960); 295 F.2d 743 (8th Cir., 1961).

13. Halpern, A. L. Use and misuse of psychiatry in competency examination of criminal defendants. *Psychiat. Ann.,* 15:8 ff., 1975.

14. Lipsitt, P. D., Lelos, D., & McGarry, A. L. Competency for trial: A screening instrument. *Amer. J. Psychiat.,* 128:105-109, 1971.

15. Perr, I. N. Competency to cop a plea. *Bull. Amer. Acad. Psychiat. Law,* 5:45-50, 1976.

16. Ohio Rev. Code, Sec. 2949.28-30.

Chapter X

Isaac Ray and Charles Doe: Responsibility and Justice

JACQUES M. QUEN, M.D.

The problem of reconciling the administration of justice for the individual and for society with the determination of the responsibility of the insane has been a difficult one throughout the recorded history of Western civilization. It was a problem for the ancient Hebrews as it is for twentieth-century America (1).

What do we mean by the responsibility of the insane? What do we mean by insane? Too few mental health professionals realize that insanity was a thoroughly proper medical term, at least through 1921, when the *American Journal of Insanity* changed its name to the *American Journal of Psychiatry*. The change appeared to have been a function of several factors, among which were the large influx of neurologists into the practice of psychiatry with the promise of making it more scientific, the development of neuropathology and psychology research laboratories, the introduction of Freud's psychoanalysis with its promise of cure by the resolution of unconscious conflicts, and the need for a new, socially more acceptable term to facilitate the enlistment of public support.

235

It was, in effect, part of an effort to change the public image of a rapidly changing profession (2).

Despite the effort at repudiating the word, "insanity" did describe a medical phenomenon which, like its contemporary medical term "consumption," included more than one discrete diagnostic entity. At the height of its medical usage, insanity included not only the psychoses, but compulsive syndromes such as kleptomania, pyromania, and dipsomania. It has also included idiocy, imbecility, and dementia, as well as postictal states.

What do we mean by responsibility? We mean, among other things, answerability for one's acts and their consequences. In the past that meant that if one did something harmful or damaging, one had to make material reparations to the victim or the victim's family. Responsibility also included eligibility for punitive measures by society. In this general area there were, in ancient Hebrew law, those exceptions who were excused from responsibility for their acts. These included the imbecile (or insane) and the minor.

In later English law one finds similar exceptions named by Henry Bracton. A judge of the Church courts and of the King's secular courts, Bracton is credited with having codified and integrated British law in the thirteenth century. He defined a common law crime as consisting of a material element (the *actus rea* or the criminal act) and a mental element (the *mens rea* or the criminal intent). In the absence of either, there is no crime. "We must consider with what mind or with what intent a thing is done. . . . For take away the will and every act will be indifferent, because your state of mind gives meaning to your act, and a crime is not committed unless the intent to injure intervene, nor is a theft committed except with the intent to steal . . . And this is in accordance with what might be said of the infant or the madman, since the innocence of design protects the one and the lack of reason in committing the act excuses the other" (3). Bracton saw the infant and the madman as sharing, not the same psychology, but the same incapability and the same exculpability before the law.

British legal commentators in subsequent centuries enlarged upon Bracton's view to include, as part of the mental component to be considered, the presence or absence of an understanding will, liberty of choice, and knowledge of right and wrong. In the seventeenth century, Matthew Hale (4) suggested, as *dictum*, that the dividing line between total and partial insanity, or exculpatory and nonexculpatory insanity, should be "as great understanding, as ordinarily a child of fourteen years hath." That is, anyone with less understanding than a 14-year-old, should be considered totally or irresponsibly insane before the law.

In 1724, Edward Arnold, known locally as "Crazy Ned," was found legally responsible in a trial in which the judge instructed the jury that if the defendant had no more reason than an infant, a brute, or a wild beast, he should be acquitted. This has been called the "wild beast" test, but not by any historian who knows that in 1724, "brute" referred to farm animals and that wild beasts in England were pretty much restricted to badgers, foxes, deer, and rabbits. The emphasis was on the lack of intellectual ability rather than the violently wild, ravenous beast image that the phrase calls to mind today. I think that if you read the original charge to the jury in its entirety, you will see that its spirit is consistent with the "lack of reason" interpretation.

In 1800, James Hadfield, an ex-soldier discharged from the army because of insanity secondary to skull wounds causing severe brain damage, became convinced that God was going to destroy the world, but that he, Hadfield, could prevent it by sacrificing his own life. However, he did not want to commit the moral crime of suicide. He knew that attempted regicide was punishable by death, and so he shot at the King, meaning him no harm. Thomas Erskine, either from ignorance or as an

intentional distortion, played with Hale's phrase "total insanity" to create a straw man. He then demolished the straw
man and suggested replacing it with the "delusion" test (with
or without loss of reason) and the product test. Presiding Judge
Kenyon, who had been a partner of Erskine's in an important
case several years earlier, apparently did not recognize
Erskine's distortion of fact to the jury; nor did he appear to
realize that he was writing new law when he told the jury that if
a man was in a deranged state of mind at the time he
committed the act, he could not be found guilty. Nor did he
seem to realize that, when he told the jury that the
"defendant's sanity must be made out to the satisfaction of a
moral man," he was assigning the burden of proof where it
belonged, on the shoulders of the prosecution (5).

In 1812, John Bellingham, a delusional businessman, shot
and killed Sir Spencer Perceval, Prime Minister of England, on
Monday, May 11. On Thursday evening, May 14, the court
notified two attorneys of their appointment to represent Bellingham. On Friday morning, May 15, the trial began after
refusal of a motion to postpone the trial to allow people from
Bellingham's home town to come to testify as to his mental history. In a charge to the jury that resembled Marc Antony's
inflammatory speech, Lord Mansfield added the finishing
touches.* The jury returned their verdict of guilty that same
afternoon and Judge Mansfield, perhaps concerned that
justice delayed is justice denied, immediately pronounced
sentence—hanging and dissection the following Monday

---

* "When he mentioned the name of a man so dear and so revered as
that of Mr. Spencer Perceval, he found it difficult to suppress his own
feelings. As, however, to say anything of the distinguished talents and
virtues of that amiable man might tend to excite improper emotions in the
minds of the jury, he should withhold those feelings which pressed for
utterance from his heart, and leave them to form their judgment upon the
evidence which had been adduced in support of the case, unbiassed by any
unfair indignation which they might feel against his murderer, by any
description, however faint, of the excellent qualities of the deceased" (6).

morning, May 18. Surgeons speak of rapid surgery, timing it from skin to skin — this instance of rapid due process, homicide to homicide, can be seen only as judicial murder. It is striking that while explicitly rejected as legal authority in 1840 in a high treason trial, and again in 1843 in the debate on M'Naghten's case in the House of Lords, our own Judge Cardozo, in his classic analysis of the meaning of "wrong" in *M'Naghten*, cited Mansfield's charge to the jury as one of the legal authorities on which he based his interpretation (7).

In 1840, in *Regina v. Oxford*, Chief Justice Denman (8) reached the high point of British law in this area by reaffirming the liberal position in *Hadfield* and adding what I see as "irresistible impulse" to the English common law. While my view of it is in direct opposition to the opinion of British judges, I would ask you to read Justice Denman's opinion and decide for yourself.*

By 1843, multiple, disparate, and occasionally discordant judicial decisions and traditions had developed. In that year, a paranoid Glasgow wood-turner, Daniel M'Naghten, fatally shot Edward Drummond, private secretary to Prime Minister Robert Peel (9). The myth that M'Naghten intended to shoot Peel grew out of an allegation which I believe was designed to convert a crazy, senseless act into a calculated, vicious crime. M'Naghten's statement on arraignment, referring to his delusion, contained absolutely no reference to Peel or indication of his involvement. Following the unanimous medical testimony that M'Naghten was insane, he was acquitted. This raised such a storm of protest that the House of

---

* Justice Denman wrote: "If some controlling disease was, in truth, the acting power within him which he could not resist, then he will not be responsible" (8). This is clearly a variant of the irresistible impulse, especially if one considers that in that period impulse meant not merely momentary thrust but motivating power as well. My view is that with this statement Denman introduced irresistible impulse into British law, although British judges refer to irresistible impulse as an American invention.

Lords called on the fifteen judges of the Queen's Bench to clarify for them the law of England regarding the criminal responsibility of the insane.

The House of Lords asked the judges five questions, none of which specifically mentioned M'Naghten's case, but which did refer to principles and concepts that had been raised in response to the trial outcome. The judges combined two of the questions and returned four answers. Of the four answers, the one generally referred to as the *M'Naghten* rule states that to acquit somebody of a crime "it must be clearly proved that, at the time of committing the act, the party accused was labouring under such a defect of reason, from disease of the mind, as not to know the nature and quality of the act he was doing; or if he did know it, that he did not know that he was doing wrong."

British lawyers and members of Parliament protested that the judges' answers were not clear as to the intended meanings of "wrong" and "know." British and American psychiatrists maintained that their asylums were filled with people who knew the difference between right and wrong, but who were unquestionably not morally responsible for their insane behavior. There was general dissatisfaction with the *M'Naghten* rule, which increased with the passing of time.

The judges' answers represented a remarkably simplistic and regressive interpretation of the law as it had evolved. The possibility that this was due to inadequate judicial learning is a necessary consideration. Certainly the judges were influenced by the fact that England was facing social, political, and economic crises. There were the radical Chartists and the Anti-Corn-Law League, the agitation for universal male suffrage, the radical demands for reform of abusive child labor practices and for expanding economic relief to the poor. It appeared that the basic structural foundation of England was threatened (9).

In 1844, in Massachusetts, Abner Rogers, an insane convict, was tried for the stabbing death of his warden. Chief

Justice Lemuel Shaw is credited with having introduced *M'Naghten* into America in this trial. This exemplifies the shoddy scholarship abounding in this area of legal history. The concepts, as well as the language used by Shaw, are clearly derived from *Oxford* and could not possibly be derived from *M'Naghten* and the judges' answers (10, 11).

By the 1860's, the *M'Naghten* rule was solidly entrenched in the common law tradition of England and appeared to be well on its way to universal acceptance in the American courts. I will focus on two Americans who were dissatisfied with the course of development of this area of the law. They were the physician, Isaac Ray, and the then Associate Justice of the New Hampshire Supreme Court, Charles Doe.

Isaac Ray was born in Beverly, Massachusetts, and received his medical degree from the Medical School of Maine at Bowdoin College in 1827 (12). Although he had no special training in either law or insanity, Ray became interested in the interface of these two areas while a general practitioner in Eastport, Maine. In 1838, Ray published *A Treatise on the Medical Jurisprudence of Insanity* (13). The following year, two separate editions were published in England and in Scotland. The book received prominent mention in the argument of the defense in the trial of Daniel M'Naghten. In 1962, more than a century later, Winfred Overholser, Superintendent of St. Elizabeth's Hospital, said, "We have not even yet fully caught up with the reforms [Ray] advocated" (14).

Ray went on to become Superintendent of the Maine Insane Hospital at Augusta, and then of the Butler Hospital in Providence, Rhode Island, as well as a founder and president of the organization now known as the American Psychiatric Association. His *Treatise* went through four subsequent American editions (1844, 1853, 1860, 1871).

A copy of the third edition was purchased in 1854 by Charles Doe, a young New Hampshire lawyer who was just starting his law practice. Born in Derry, New Hampshire, in 1830, Doe graduated Phi Beta Kappa from Dartmouth in 1849. His legal education consisted of three years in the office of New Hampshire lawyer Daniel Christie and one semester at Harvard Law School. Between 1859 and 1874, Doe served as Associate Justice of the New Hampshire Supreme Court, and from 1876 to 1896 served as its Chief Justice. Doe was an independent thinker with a remarkable devotion to the law and to legal principle as an instrument of justice. In 1938, Roscoe Pound (15) listed Charles Doe as one of the ten greatest judges in American history.

In 1866, Charles Doe began a correspondence with Isaac Ray which continued until 1872 (16). The preceding year, Doe had sat on a case involving the testamentary capacity of an individual of questioned sanity. Doe was disturbed by the multiplicity of tests or standards of insanity in criminal and civil law. He felt that there should be one consistent legal approach to the problem, based on legal principle rather than the state of medical knowledge of an earlier period. In his dissenting opinion in this case (*Boardman v. Woodman* [17]), Doe wrote a masterful scholarly review and analysis of the development of the common law responsibility of the insane. He interpreted the law to be that if an act was the offspring of insanity, the individual could not be held responsible for it. Thus, if a will was the act of the testator's insanity, it was no more his "will" than if he had been physically coerced into signing it, or if he had written and signed it while involuntarily intoxicated. Doe said that earlier legal tests of insanity dictated to juries constituted judicial error, perpetuating an illegal usurpation of the role of the jury by the court. Insanity, Doe maintained, was a matter of fact, definitions of it were matters of fact, and tests for it were, equally, matters of fact. In jury trials, all matters of fact are in the province of the jury and it is their role to determine the facts. As Doe (18) elaborated later, the New Hampshire doctrine "is, not that the common-law prescribes a test of any disease, physical or mental, but that an act caused by mental disease is not a crime, a contract, or a will."

In a letter to Isaac Ray, Doe wrote, on March 23, 1869, "I was led to examinations which produced [the *Boardman v. Woodman*] opinion solely by the copy of the 3rd edition of your 'Med. Jur. of Insanity' which I bought when I began the practice of law in 1854" (19). However, the correspondence makes clear that Doe arrived at his interpretation of the law on the basis of his own reasoning. Confirmation of this is found in the attitudes of these two men toward the jury system. Isaac Ray said, "That a body of men, taken promiscuously from the common walks of life, should be required to decide . . . a professional question of a most delicate nature and involving some of the highest interests of man [i.e., insanity] is an idea so preposterous that one finds it difficult at first sight to believe that it ever was seriously entertained" (20). It wasn't until the fifth edition in 1871 that Ray modified that statement to read "is an idea that is relieved of its apparent folly only by the reflection that it is inseparable from a judicial system which is regarded, as, on the whole, better fitted than any other to serve the ends of justice" (21). The New Hampshire doctrine is obviously based on a fundamental faith in the jury system, and it is clearly Judge Doe's creation. Ray's modified stand would appear to be a result of their correspondence and of Doe's influence, at least in part.

In 1869, in a New Hampshire murder trial (*State v. Pike* [22]), Chief Justice Perley instructed the jury that if the homicide was the offspring of insanity, the defendant must be found not guilty. He also said that the definition of insanity and whether the defendant suffered from insanity were questions of fact to be determined by the jury. "When Pike appealed his conviction, Doe wrote the opinion for a unanimous court sustaining Perley's charge. In *State v. Pike* Doe's dissent in *Boardman* became law and the New Hampshire doctrine was born" (23). In another murder trial in 1871 (*State v. Jones* [24]), Doe was the presiding judge and instructed the jury that "all symptoms and all tests of disease are purely matters of fact to be determined by the jury." This case, too, was appealed and once again a unanimous court sustained the instructions and confirmed the establishment of the doctrine as the law of the state.

The beauty of the ruling lay in its simplicity, its reliance on first principles, and its insistence on preserving the functional distinction between matters of law and matters of fact. If adhered to with reasonable and respectable professional competence by the presiding judge and the attorneys, it would not require the law to conform to changing medical theories. By basing New Hampshire doctrine exclusively on legal principle, Doe avoided the fatal defect of the *Durham* rule of 1954.* As one student of the New Hampshire doctrine pointed out, "*Durham* is a medical test. The jury must accept the expert testimony of the alienists, and if psychiatric opinion changes overnight, a person convicted as a result of the obsolete opinion may be entitled to another jury trial at which the jury cannot 'arbitrarily reject' the new opinion. Shifts in medical theory and even in medical nomenclature may determine the conduct of trials and the fate of defendants . . . . It is difficult to conceive of a test more unlike what [Judge Doe] had in mind" (25).

In a review (26) of the working of the New Hampshire doctrine since its formulation, Reid has concluded: "If the New Hampshire doctrine has any inherent weakness, it is that it is misunderstood. Psychiatrists have missed its implications [and testify in the language of *M'Naghten*]; defense counsel have not appreciated its full scope, and at least one [New Hampshire judge] has confused it with *M'Naghten*. Worst of

---

* The *Durham* rule holds that an accused is not criminally responsible if his unlawful act was the product of mental disease or defect.

all another court equated it with *Durham*. . . . This is unfortunate because New Hampshire has all the merits of *Durham*—but few of its faults" (27).

Durham is dead and *M'Naghten* is moribund; both have given way to the American Law Institute (ALI) rule which says: "A person is not responsible for criminal conduct if at the time of such conduct as a result of mental disease or defect he lacks substantial capacity to appreciate the criminality of his conduct or to conform his conduct to the requirements of the law. The terms 'mental disease or defect' do not include an abnormality manifested only by repeated criminal or otherwise anti-social conduct" (28). As *M'Naghten* brought with it interminable debate on the meaning of "wrong," "know," and "nature and quality," one can see that the ALI rule will bring with it equally interminable discussions on the meaning of "substantial capacity," "appreciate," and, perhaps, "conform." The history of the efforts to deal with the problem of the criminal responsibility of the insane has been characterized by a pathological obsession of the legal and medical professions with the magic of words.

The British Royal Commission on Capital Punishment (1949-1953) almost suggested that the jury should determine "whether at the time of the act the accused was suffering from disease of the mind (or mental deficiency) to such a degree that he ought not to be held responsible" (29). In *U.S. v. Brawner* (30), (which contains the official demise of *Durham*), in a concurring and dissenting opinion, Judge Bazelon suggested that the jury should be instructed to acquit the defendant "if at the time of his unlawful conduct his mental or emotional processes or behavior controls were impaired to such an extent that he cannot justly be held responsible for his act" (31). The New Hampshire doctrine mandates this as a jury function and has done so for more than a hundred years.

Earlier, I referred to the problem of reconciling the administration of justice for the individual and for society when trying to determine the responsibility of the insane. As a student of the developmental history of legal psychiatry, it is clear to me that a major contribution to the problem is made by the grossly inadequate knowledge of the history of the relevant law on the part of judges, lawyers, and mental health professionals. One forensic psychiatrist recently wrote: "Our courts had never considered that a man was innocent by virtue of insanity until psychiatry convinced them that it was so" (32). That was undeniably "eloquent testimony to the inadequate education in the history of legal psychiatry within the [medical] profession" (33). There are published examples of equally disillusioning ignorance on the part of judges and lawyers (34-36).

Another forensic psychiatrist recently wrote: "It is common knowledge that the insanity defense is largely a legalistic ploy, confusing to the jury and frustrating to the psychiatric profession. It does nothing to promote justice, damages respect for law, sustains the sham of the 'battle of the experts' in our courtrooms, and increases the cost of trying and defending allegedly mentally disordered criminals. It is a glaring example of the misuse of psychiatry in this country, common sense and justice cry for its abandonment" (37). One might contrast this statement about the "legalistic ploy" with the previous one damning psychiatry. As for the confusion of the jurors, there are several retrospective studies that indicate that juries appear to be less confused than jurists or psychiatrists by the insanity defense (26, 38, 39). As for the insanity defense's doing nothing for justice and justice's crying for its abandonment, I can do no better in a brief statement than to quote Professor Slovenko: "Evidence of insanity relates to the issue of intent. Any proposal to abolish the insanity defense, which has been urged from time to time, makes no vital change in the law as long as intent or a certain state of mind is a required element of crime. With moral guilt an essential ingredient of the criminal law, testimony in one form or another about the accused's state of mind would continue" (40). On a more subjective level, I think that it did quite a bit for justice that Hadfield and M'Naghten weren't hanged, as was Bellingham, just as I think that it was a gross injustice that the insanity plea failed in the case of Guiteau, President Garfield's assassin, and that he was hanged (41, 42).

As for the "battle of experts," I confess that I've never been able to understand why, when psychiatrists disagree, it is proof positive that they don't know what they're talking about and it demeans the profession; while, when our Supreme Court decides the law of the land by a disagreement of 5-4, they are scholars dealing with profound, difficult, and complicated issues and one must respect their differences in judgment. In fact, our Supreme Court has nine judges because we knew they would disagree and we didn't want tie votes. Our hierarchical court system is based on the expectation that judges, in their roles as law experts, will disagree, but they seem not to be demeaned by it.

In conclusion, I would like to call attention to an unacknowledged benefit of the continuing problem of determining the responsibility of the insane, for the behavioral and social sciences (and I include the legal professions in this group). It forces us to recognize the limitations of our knowledge, the deficiencies of our theories, and the need for specific and extended research studies. What are the psychological components and origins of malice, intention, and will? What is the method by which we as individuals estimate the relative responsibility of other individuals? How do we calibrate responsibility? What happens to those who plead irresponsibility but are found guilty? What are the later careers of those who commit criminal acts but are dealt with medically? What are their "recidivism" rates as compared with others? How do they differ from those pleading insanity but found guilty? Are there reliable "natural experiments" that we can study to help us answer these questions? Can we construct some procedure to study whether the current binary mode (guilty or not guilty) of the American law regarding responsibility is more desirable than a system that recognizes degrees of responsibility?

As long as the problem is with us, we must examine our theories, our practices, and our assumptions — the lawyers, the judges, and the mental health professionals. Isaac Ray and Charles Doe had the sense of responsibility to the insane and to society to do this. We would have difficulty finding better role models.

REFERENCES

1. Quen, J. M. Anglo-American criminal insanity: An historical perspective. *J. Hist. Behav. Sci.,* 3:313-323, 1974.
2. Quen, J. M. Asylum psychiatry, neurology, social work, and mental hygiene: An exploratory study in interprofessional history. *J. Hist. Behav. Sci.,* 13:3-11, 1977.
3. Bracton, H. *De Legibus et Consuetudinus Angliae.* Quoted in: F. B. Sayre. *Mens rea. Harvard Law Rev.,* 45:974-1026, 1932.
4. Hale, M. *The History of the Pleas of the Crown.* London: 1736.
5. Quen, J. M. James Hadfield and medical jurisprudence of insanity. *N.Y. State J. Med.,* 69:1221-1226, 1969.
6. Collinson, G. D. *A Treatise on the Law Concerning Idiots, Lunatics and Other Persons Non Compos Mentis.* London: W. Reed, 1812.
7. *People v. Schmidt.* 110 N.E. 945 at 947 (1915).
8. *Regina v. Oxford.* In: *The English Reports. Vol. 173. Nisi Prius IV Containing Carrington & Payne 7-9; Moody and Malkin.* Edinburgh: 1928.
9. Quen, J. M. An historical view of the M'Naghten trial. *Bull. Hist. Med.,* 42:43-51, 1968.
10. Bigelow, G. T., & Bemis, G. *Report of the Trial of Abner Rogers, Jr., Indicted for the Murder of Charles Lincoln, Jr., Late Warden of the Massachusetts State Prison; Before the Supreme Judicial Court of Massachusetts, Holden at Boston, on Tuesday, Jan. 30, 1844.* Boston: 1844.
11. Ray, I. The trial of Rogers. In: *Contributions to Mental Pathology.* Boston: Little, Brown, 1873, pp. 210-228. (Reprint ed. Delmar, N.Y.: Scholars' Facsimiles and Reprints, 1973.)
12. Quen, J. M. Isaac Ray and his "Remarks on Pathological Anatomy." *Bull. Hist. Med.,* 38:113-126, 1964.

13. Ray, I. *A Treatise on the Medical Jurisprudence of Insanity.* Boston: Little Brown, 1838. (Reprint ed. Cambridge, Mass.: Belknap Press, 1962.)
14. Ibid., p. vii.
15. Pound, R. *Formative Era of American Law* (1938). Cited in: J. P. Reid. *Chief Justice: The Judicial World of Charles Doe.* Cambridge, Mass.: Harvard University Press, 1967.
16. Reik, L. E. The Doe-Ray correspondence: A pioneer collaboration in the jurisprudence of mental disease. *Yale Law J., 63*:183-196, 1953. (The correspondence manuscripts are in the Isaac Ray Medical Library, Butler Hospital, Providence, R.I.).
17. *Boardman v. Woodman.* 47 N.H. 120 (1868).
18. Bell, C. Editorial: The right-wrong test in cases of homicide by the insane. *Medico-Legal J., 16*:260-267, n.d. (after 1896). (The editorial reprints a letter from Charles Doe to Clark Bell, 10 January 1889, from which the quotation [p. 264] is taken.)
19. Doe, C. Letter to Isaac Ray, 23 March 1869. Manuscript collection, Isaac Ray Medical Library, Butler Hospital, Providence, R.I.
20. Ray, *A Treatise,* p. 49.
21. Ray, I. *A Treatise on the Medical Jurisprudence of Insanity,* 5th ed. Boston: Little, Brown, 1871. (Reprint ed. New York: Arno Press, 1976, p. 71.)
22. *State v. Pike.* 49 N.H. 399 (1870).
23. Reid, J. P. *Chief Justice: The Judicial World of Charles Doe.* Cambridge, Mass.: Harvard University Press, 1967, p. 118.
24. *State v. Jones.* 50 N.H. 369 (1871).
25. Reid, *Chief Justice,* pp. 119-120.
26. Reid, J. P. The working of the New Hampshire doctrine of criminal insanity. *U. Miami Law Rev., 15*:14-58, 1960.
27. Ibid., pp. 43-44.
28. American Law Institute. *Model Penal Code.* Quoted in: R. Slovenko. *Psychiatry and Law.* Boston: Little Brown, 1973, p. 83.
29. *Royal Commission on Capital Punishment, 1949-1953, Report.* London: 1953, p. 116, #333 (iii).
30. *U.S. v. Brawner.* 471 F.2d 969 (D.C. Cir. 1972).
31. Ibid., at 1032.
32. Lewin, K. K. Insanity in the courtroom—whose? *J. Leg. Med., 2*: 19-21, 1974.
33. Quen, J. M. The insanity defense. *J. Leg. Med., 2*:8-9, 1974.
34. *U.S. v. Freeman.* 357 F.2d 606 at 616-618 (1966).
35. Quen, J. M., & Bazelon, D. L. Letters. *Sci. Amer., 231*:6-11, 1974.
36. Quen, J. M. Isaac Ray: Have we learned his lessons? *Bull. Amer. Acad. Psychiat. Law, 2*:137-147, 1974.
37. Halpern, A. L. Insanity defense argued. *Clin. Psychiat. News, 4*(8):6, 1976.

38. Barnes, H. A Century of McNaghten rules. *Cambridge Law J.,* 8:300-321, 1944.
39. Simon, R. *The Jury and the Defense of Insanity.* Boston: Little, Brown, 1967.
40. Slovenko, R. *Psychiatry and Law.* Boston: Little, Brown, 1973, p. 77.
41. Quen, J. M. Historical reflections on American legal psychiatry. *Bull. Amer. Acad. Psychiat. Law,* 2:237-241, 1975.
42. Rosenberg, C. E. *The Trial of the Assassin Guiteau: Psychiatry and Law in the Gilded Age.* Chicago: University of Chicago Press, 1968.

Part VI

Patient Rights and Involuntary Admissions Limited to Dangerousness

Injustices perceived eventually get transformed into rights. When freedom was sacrificed for hospitalization, more than custodial care was demanded. This was reflected in judicial decisions articulating a right to treatment and to a less restrictive environment when the original symptoms which led to involuntary confinement were no longer present.

Emphasis has been on procedural rights to substantiate the need for confinement. Two-thirds of the states have recently revised commitment laws. Dr. Beigel and his associates present the areas of debate and conflict around the implementation of Arizona's 1974 law, which requires a mental illness be present and that the individual be dangerous to himself or to others or gravely disabled.

It is a truism that the prediction of dangerousness cannot be made with accuracy. The current trend to limit involuntary admissions to those who are dangerous to themselves or to others assumes that involuntary hospitalization is the same as preventive detention. The application of criminal rules for the prevention of injury is not an accepted medical position.

There are persons with serious mental illness who can be helped—for example, the mentally ill person who haunts the office of public officials daily seeking redress from bodily

251

invasion by electrical rays; the excited person, who exhausts him or herself with sleepless days and nights in a never-ceasing frenzy of activity; the disturbed individual who each day places on the boss's desk a wrapped package of warm feces. Such individuals are grievously ill but may survive. The terrible cost to the individual denied treatment, the troubled family who can't understand the reason for barring a family member from treatment who lacks the ability to seek it, and the prolonged delays that are formidable barriers to essential therapy, distress everyone. The recommended approach to legislation noted by Robert L. Sadoff in the section that follows deserves careful study. The proposed remedy has four parts: (1) a serious mental disorder is present, (2) as a consequence the individual lacks the ability to make an informed judgment as to the need for treatment, (3) treatment will probably benefit the disorder, and (4) the illness is likely to cause imminent serious physical or emotional harm to self or others as evidenced by recent behavior.

Louis E. Kopolow serves in the National Institute of Mental Health. His interest is the constitutional rights of the mentally handicapped, the right to treatment, and the right to a humane environment. The legal relationship of doctor-patient has been abrogated. It has been replaced by the user of the service, the therapist, the insured, the government and the judiciary, each with different goals.

Recently judicial action has been the most prominent area. Discussion has concerned criteria for admission to hospital, procedural rights to protect patient freedom, and substantive rights such as the right to treatment. Noted also is the proposed patient-advocacy system.

Allan Beigel, Kenney Hegland, and David Wexler have worked with many organizations over three years to develop the Arizona Mental Health Statute. The authors define the areas of conflict and debate, and the opinions leading to a law that admits to involuntary status, those who have inflicted or attempted to inflict harm within the recent past to others or to self, or those so grievously ill as to be unable to provide essential food, clothing, and shelter for themselves. A definition of mental illness is offered as well as steps to policy development.

The authors add feedback on the performances over the three years the Arizona law has been in effect. The Arizona Psychiatric Association opposes the barriers to treatment that now exist, stating that it is impossible to admit a patient to hospital unless there is evidence a criminal act has been committed.

Robert L. Sadoff, an academician and a forensic psychiatrist, notes the shift from the presence of mental illness to dangerousness as the reason for involuntary hospitalization. Problems exist with the standards of dangerousness employed as a criterion. While the present trend to limit admissions brings comfort to civil libertarians, it is a millstone for patients, families, and mental health professionals. Sadoff would focus attention on patient welfare and the need for research on the predictability of dangerousness. He presents a reasoned approach to mental health statutes that is consonant with the objectives of mental health professionals and that could well become a model for future legislative reform.

Chapter XI

Patients' Rights and Psychiatric Practice

LOUIS E. KOPOLOW, M.D.

The interface between medicine and law has always been marked by controversy, and this situation is especially true today in the mental health field. In recent years there has been an upsurge of interest in the constitutional rights of the mentally handicapped individual, i.e., the right to treatment, right to least restrictive alternative to hospitalization, right to a humane environment, and right to services which are appropriate and adequate in quality to a patient's needs and wishes. As a result of this concern for patients' rights, the nature of the patient-therapist relationship has been greatly altered. The traditional dyadic has now evolved into a pentagonal relationship (see Figure 1) consisting of consumers, providers, insurance companies, government, and the judiciary. The interaction among these forces dramatically affects the availability, quality, and nature of mental health services in this country. The impact of the new fifth force, the judiciary, and the need to develop alternatives to litigation will be the focus of this chapter.

Each of the five pivotal forces brings into the arena differing values and goals. The consumer is primarily

Pentagonal Relationship

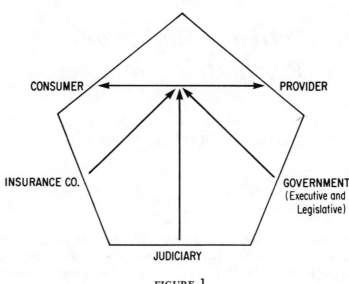

FIGURE 1

concerned that the services he receives are available when and where he wishes them, that they are appropriate to his needs, and that he is involved in establishing the priorities of a program. The provider wants to be able to "do his thing" with the fewest possible external encumbrances. If outside controls must exist, he wants them equitably applied, and he wants clarification of his specific responsibilities and liabilities. Insurance companies are concerned with making a profit or, if not a profit, at least making sure that coverage of certain high-cost "risks" does not endanger the entire program. They also seek assurance that they are only paying for covered illnesses and services, and that these services are delivered by appropriately licensed and credentialed professionals. Government concerns can be expressed by the phrase "best service at the least cost." In terms of provision of services, the government wants its citizens to have access to quality care which is cost effective, and wants the providers to be accountable for the treatments they provide. The fifth and final force acting on the relationship between patient and doctor is the judiciary. After years of all but ignoring the legal status of the mentally ill, the courts have recently assumed the role of guardian of patients' constitutional rights, and have begun to closely scrutinize all aspects of care and treatment (1).

The increasing role of insurance and government in the health care system during the 1950s and 1960s, and the recent activities of the judiciary, have dramatically affected the provider's role, diminished his flexibility in choosing treatment, and greatly reduced his powers. There are many explanations given for this phenomenon within the field of mental health. They include the growing public skepticism regarding the medical model of mental illness, the question of the efficacy of mental health treatment which has in the past so often been oversold, and the disillusionment bred of recent revelations of some of the more hideous abuses that have taken place in the name of institutional care (2).

A review of the evolution of the mental health system in this country provides a valuable perspective on present-day problems. It is important, however, to remember that throughout the history of the United States, the mental health profession has accepted responsibility for the care and treatment of a class of individuals abused and avoided by the general population and frequently ignored by the rest of medicine.

HISTORICAL DEVELOPMENT

During colonial times, as is frequently the case today, there was a two-tier system distinguishing the treatment of the rich from the poor. The insane rich were usually kept at home and concealed from society to protect the reputation of their families. The insane poor were left to the discretion of local communities. If they were seen as poor and harmlessly deranged, society's main fear was that they would become public charges. To prevent this from occurring, the mentally ill were subjected to whippings, banishment, and forced to wander and beg. If they remained in a community, incarceration in the local jails or poor houses was frequently their treatment (3).

The last part of the eighteenth century marked the development of new approaches to the treatment of the mentally ill. Philippe Pinel pioneered a more humane treatment of the patients at Bicêtre and Salpêtrière, and at York Retreat in England, under Samuel Tuke, moral treatment resulted in patients being treated with respect, kindness, but firmness in an atmosphere allowing them quiet time before their return to open society.

Moral treatment carried to America by a Quaker clergyman, Reverend Thomas Scattergood, became the dominant approach used in mental hospitals during the first half of the nineteenth century. Great success, as high as 90 percent improvement in conditions, was reported by early practitioners of moral treatment. This treatment was accomplished by removing the patient from his family and community at the onset of his symptoms and placing him in a peaceful rural retreat—the asylum—where, under the absolute control of his physician, he lived a tightly disciplined existence and engaged in useful employment (4).

This era of humane and hopeful treatment was short-lived as the resources of the asylum were soon overburdened by the great influx of impoverished immigrants from Europe and a growing population of chronic patients. Moral treatment began to fade and was replaced with custodialism. Overcrowding and disorder created justification for mechanical restraints and punishments which grew in usage and severity (4).

The failings and increasing harshness of public asylums, however, did not lead to their dismantlement. Overcrowding worsened as chronic patients remained indefinitely, and loose commitment laws facilitated the extrusion of the mentally disabled not tolerated by an increasingly urban society. Efforts to improve conditions were sporadic and progress was slow and uneven. Despite numerous books and exposés, including Clifford Beers's *The Mind that Found Itself* (5), Deutsch's *The Shame of the States* (6), and Marcy Ward's book *Snake Pit* (7), later made into a movie, the period of custodialism continued well into the first half of the twentieth century (4).

By the mid-1950s, discontent with the situation in state mental hospitals was widespread. The resident population soared to 550,000 and approximately two out of every five hospital beds were located in state and county mental hospitals. The President of the American Psychiatric Association declared in 1958: "I do not see how any reasonably objective view of our mental hospitals today can fail to conclude that they are bankrupt beyond remedy" (8).

The recognition that society was failing to provide an adequate or even humane system of services to care for its mentally ill citizens led Congress to establish the Joint Commission on Mental Illness and Health in 1955. This commission advocated the goal of community-based mental health care accessible and responsive to the needs of all citizens. Its report specifically attacked the philosophy of large state hospitals and recommended providing psychiatric services in the community to reduce the need for prolonged or repeated hospitalization.

Despite the growth of the community mental health center movement (there are now over 400 centers across the country), large state hospitals with all the old problems of dehumanization, inadequate facilities, and insufficient staffs continue to exist. In part, because of the abuses that have existed in such facilities, the psychiatric profession is increasingly finding itself the object of diatribes from various consumer and civil liberties groups. These groups, through the judicial and legislative processes, seek to alter the psychiatrist's powers and prerogatives in his relationship with his patient and to assure the rights of the mentally handicapped.

The short-term results of governmental and judicial activities in patients' rights have produced confusion and resentment among mental health professionals, and it is unclear whether these changes are truly beneficial to the individual patient. Since it is the judiciary which is presently having the greatest impact on the patients' rights and psychiatric practice, developments in this area must be closely examined. Court decisions have generally fallen into three broad areas: (a) criteria for commitment, (b) procedural rights, and (c) substantive rights.

COMMITMENT CRITERIA

Essentially there are two justifications for a state's power to confine a person in an institution against his will: the *parens patriae* doctrine and the police powers of the state. *Parens patriae* refers to the duty of the state to take care of those citizens who, it is thought, cannot sensibly take care of their own needs (in old English tradition, this would include widows, the insane, idiots, etc.). The second justification — police powers — refers to the obligations of the state to protect the community by confining people who would otherwise be dangerous.

American psychiatrists have traditionally accepted the role of instruments of the state's *parens patriae* doctrine. Such acceptance is consistent with the premise that life and health (physical as well as mental well-being) should be at the pinnacle of any hierarchy of values and should be maintained at any cost. A countervailing civil liberties philosophy has been that although a person's physical and mental health are important, they are not necessarily of the highest value, and that a person's freedom to place a higher value on other things should be respected.

The United States Supreme Court has given considerable boost to the civil liberties view by undercutting the *parens patriae* doctrine in its decision in the case of *O'Connor v. Donaldson* (9). This case dealt with an involuntarily committed, nondangerous individual who did not receive treatment during his 15 years of hospitalization. The court declared in this case that: "A State cannot constitutionally confine, without more, a non-dangerous individual who is capable of surviving safely in freedom by himself or with the help of willing and responsible family members or friends." This case raised three major issues of particular concern to psychiatrists: determination of dangerousness, physicians' liability, and the involvement of the courts in deciding what constitutes adequate treatment.

On the issue of dangerousness a recent American Psychiatric Association Task Force Bulletin, "Clinical Aspects of the Violent Individual" (10), noted that since prediction of dangerousness concerns rare or infrequent events, there are no reliable base rates. Even if an index of violence proneness could be developed so as to identify 50 percent of the individuals who will commit violent acts, the continued employment of such an index would identify eight times as many false positives as true positives. Thus, for the courts to continue to use the determination of dangerousness as a primary ground for involuntary commitment is to place a heavy burden on a slender reed, and will lead either to a total end of involuntary commitment, or possibly to changing the role of the mental hospital to that of a detention center for disturbed persons accused but not convicted of criminal acts against persons or property.

The second important issue raised by the *Donaldson* decision, i.e., physician liability, was of particular concern to

American psychiatrists because the nature of the charges (violation of a patient's constitutional right to liberty) would obviate any possibility that malpractice insurance could cover any part of the damages. Fortunately, the Supreme Court remanded the issue of damages to the lower court with the qualification: "An official has, of course, no duty to anticipate unforeseeable constitutional developments." Nevertheless, this decision must be taken as a warning to physicians that if they, now or in the future, confine or retain in custodial care a person who is not dangerous to himself or others, and is capable of living safely in an available community alternative, even if he requires some support, they may be held liable for money damages (11).

The Supreme Court in the *Donaldson* decision also examined matters of treatment which in the past the judiciary considered to be beyond their domain. The court noted that "where treatment is the sole asserted ground of depriving an individual of his liberty, it is plainly unacceptable to suggest that courts are powerless to determine whether the asserted ground is present." Such a view may reflect an increasing willingness of the judiciary to determine for itself what does or does not constitute adequate treatment. It therefore would behoove the profession to prepare for such a potentiality by developing nationally accepted standards, such as those of the PSRO, upon which it can rely in future court conflicts (11).

PROCEDURAL RIGHTS

In addition to examining the grounds for commitment, a number of courts and legislatures have sought ways of assuring procedural safeguards for patients prior to commitment. A major suit in this area was *Lessard v. Schmidt* (12). The court ruled in this case that the patient had the right to be present at the proceedings and be represented by counsel, cross-examine witnesses, and put on witnesses of his own. For the mental health professional, the imposition of these traditional adversary requirements will require greater amounts of time away from direct patient care, but will also lead to a careful assessment of the entire issue of "forced treatment."

Another highly significant case concerns the rights of parents to commit a juvenile for treatment against his will. In the *Bartley v. Kremens* case (13), the Pennsylvania Court ruled that juveniles essentially had the same rights as those mentioned above in the *Lessard* case. This case poses some very serious problems, for although some parents might be overly quick to seek hospitalizaiton of a difficult-to-manage youngster, the dilemma remains of what to do with the youngster who wins the right not to be hospitalized over the objection of his parents.

SUBSTANTIVE RIGHTS

The final area of court decisions to be reviewed involves the substantive rights of patients. These cover a broad range of issues concerning constitutionally established and court-enforced rights of patients.

The first of these concerns the Eighth Amendment — "right to freedom from cruel and unusual punishment." This was the grounds for outlawing some of the most abusive conditions existing in various institutions. In the Willowbrook decision (14) the judge ordered the State of New York to significantly upgrade the facilities based on the constitutional right of the residents (voluntary and involuntary) to be protected from harm. Although this decision applies to the mentally retarded, it can be expanded to the mentally ill as a means of attempting to assure dignified, humane conditions and respect for individual rights.

A second substantive right was enunciated by Morton Birnbaum (15) in an article suggesting a constitutional right to treatment for those involuntarily committed. This concept received judicial recognition in the landmark *Wyatt v.*

Stickney case (16). Judge Johnson in this case promulgated minimum standards for nearly every aspect of institutional care including the adequacy of the physical plant, appropriate staff-patient ratios, prohibition of institutional peonage, and the requirement that the least restrictive setting for patient care be selected. Even now several years after the ruling was laid down, the court-ordered programs are still not fully implemented. This case highlights some of the problems that the judiciary faces when it takes on the responsibilities of the State Department of Mental Health and it also raises the issue of comity, i.e., separation of powers within government.

A third right — "right to least restrictive alternative to hospitalization" — was included in the District of Columbia in the case of *Dixon v. Weinberger* (17). In December 1973, Judge Robinson ruled that patients in the District have a statutory right to confinement in the least restrictive facility. Responsibility was placed on the District of Columbia and the federal government to develop a plan to identify those that should be transferred to community-based facilities and the means for achieving this transfer, including the creation of alternative facilities if necessary. This suit, while not a constitutional ruling, is expected to have significant effect in litigation in other jurisdictions, and lead to increased judicial pressure for the establishment and upgrading of community-based facilities.

Fourth, one of the most troubling areas of patients' rights for mental health professionals concerns the right of patients to refuse treatment. If courts and legislatures should endorse the right of patients to refuse treatment, while at the same time endorsing the concept of involuntarily committing the dangerous mentally ill, psychiatrists will find themselves acting wonders for a totally unmanageable population. If a patient refuses treatment, a psychiatrist is faced with an excruciating dilemma. If he discharges the patient, the psychiatrist may be found liable for malpractice if the patient harms himself. If he continues to retain the patient, but gives no treatment, he may be found liable as a result of the *Donaldson* decision. A solution might lie in throwing the whole issue back into the courts and letting the judges decide.

Although this area of "refusal of treatment" is just emerging, some legislatures have actively entered the field by passing laws restricting the use of ECT (California), and some courts have begun to question the capacity of patients to give informed consent to irreversible procedures such as lobotomies. The most significant of the decisions in this area is *Kaimowitz v. Michigan Department of Mental Health* (18)—which essentially declared that Kaimowitz, faced with the choice of life-long commitment or lobotomy, could not make a truly informed and noncoerced consent.

The final substantive right to be discussed here concerns the right to confidentiality. It is important to note that this privilege of confidentiality of one's medical record belongs to the patient, not to the provider. The issue of confidentiality is an important instrument in assuring the essential right to privacy. There are, however, many conflicting concerns revolving around this issue. Employers, insurance companies, and government agencies frequently request information about treatments and past mental illness in making job decisions and in assuring that treatments provided have been necessary and proper.

The legal challenges to these practices have rested on the constitutional principle that even though government and other organizations may have a legitimate need to know about a person's mental health, they cannot unnecessarily impinge on the important individual rights of privacy and confidentiality. In several recent cases, concern about privacy and confidentiality has been the overriding issue. Two cases of particular interest are: *Joan Roe v. Jane Doe* (19) and *Tarasoff v. Regents of University of California* (20). The *Joan Roe* case concerns issues of informed consent and confidentiality. In this case, a patient sued her former therapist to prevent publishing of a book dealing with the patient's personal life, as told during therapy. The patient claimed that no formal consent was given. Many mental health practitioners feel that suits such as this, plus the court's expectation that patients be "fully informed" before consent is valid, create an adversary situation which may disrupt the relationship or impede treatment. Others have argued that the patients should no longer be treated as children who are incapable of knowing what they really want and must be shielded from facts that might distress them.

The *Tarasoff* case is another example of the difficulties mental health professionals face in preserving the confidential and trusting nature of their relationships with their clients. In this case, the court ruled that the psychotherapist had the responsibility to give warning that his patient was contemplating killing a California coed. The case was appealed, but if the decision is upheld many psychiatrists feel, as did the dissenting judge, that it will "cripple the use and effectiveness of psychiatry by destroying the assurance of confidentiality" (on which psychiatry depends). This case exemplifies the double-edged nature of the judiciary's involvement in the mental health system. While most suits have expanded the rights of the emotionally distressed, this suit has the potential of restricting them.

ALTERNATIVES TO LITIGATION

This review of the impact of patients' rights on the provision of mental health services has concentrated on the courts because it is there that the revolution in the nature of patient-therapist relationship is being fought. Despite its shortcomings, the civil liberties approach being enunciated in decision after decision is gaining social acceptance. Some of the reasons are that individual self-determination is rooted in our history; that economy-minded legislators and governors are often attracted by the appeal of deinstitutionalization because of its potential for reducing public expenditures; and finally, that courts are likely to prefer to order the release of patients, rather than taking on all of the administrative responsibilities of assuring adequate treatment for each person.

While the judiciary has served the useful function of initiating change, and providing momentary redress for abuses, it is clear that its general inflexibility and the difficulty in maintaining improvements necessitate the development of alternative methods. One such alternative to litigation is the establishment of patient advocacy programs. Such programs can protect the mental health system from being overwhelmed by arbitrary and inflexible judicial decisions, provide a mechanism for resolution of grievances outside the adversary arena, promote cooperation and resolution of disagreements between clinicians and patients, lead to a contractual rather than paternalistic dyadic relationship, recognize the rights of clinicians, and seek to assure that all of a patient's rights are respected — human and clinical as well as constitutional.

Advocacy models come in various shapes, sizes, and costs. While a Cadillac model might cost a state a lot in the beginning, it might tend to be far less costly than court-ordered changes which might also run counter to the state's mental health philosophy. Essentially two kinds of advocacy programs can be identified: legal advocacy (which exists) and service advocacy (which is only beginning to develop).

The legal advocate approximates most closely the activities of the mental health attorney — representing a client in commitment proceedings, advocating least restrictive alternatives to hospitalization, monitoring of various treatment regimes to assure due process has been followed and informed consent has been obtained, arranging for release at earliest appropriate time, etc. Legal advocacy inevitably assumes an adversary relationship between the patient, on one hand, and the psychiatric institution, on the other. In carrying out his role, the legal advocate will tend to use the skills of his profession: bringing court action on behalf of a patient against the institution, filing class action suits, and lodging complaints regarding specific violations of patients' rights in order to secure redress. Although the ability to gain judicial intervention is an essential aspect of any advocacy, it has been found to be neither the only, nor most significant function. The directors of the New York Mental Health Information Service (MHIS), which has had advocates working in both hospital wards and courtrooms since 1965, believe that the most important of all mental health reforms is the introduction of independent presence into the hospitals. They maintain that "advocates accomplish much more in the hospitals, where they serve as ombudspersons for patients and advisors on hospital policies, than in the courtroom where they fill the narrower role of legal advocates" (21).

These additional functions performed by the advocates of MHIS are part of the broader activities of service advocacy. Service advocacy duties require a departure from traditional legal roles. They include evaluating alternatives to confinement, helping the client examine the complex of potential services and select those that are truly helpful, aiding the client in legal issues such as property disposition, marriage, driver's license, etc., and helping the patient and staff in arranging aftercare programs.

In addition to these patient-related activities, the advocate may assume functions related to the institution in which he works, as an institutional change agent, an educator, and consultant. As an institutional change agent, the advocate acts as an ombudsperson or institutional superego. In this role the patient advocate would seek to identify problem areas within the institution, collect and analyze facts regarding these problem areas, and present these analyses to responsible staff with recommendations for solution (22).

By the very nature of his position within the institutional setting, the advocate has the opportunity to observe conditions and formulate a perspective not available to either patient or staff. In this role he can act as a transmitter of information to both groups—educating the staff about unmet needs of patients and informing individual patients or groups of patients regarding institutional practices and policies.

To fulfill the many tasks of patient advocacy described above, no one person or profession is sufficient. The medical profession which has the necessary clinical information for treatment alternatives may not recognize or give adequate importance to legal concerns and vice versa. It is therefore necessary that there be some reconciliation of the conflicts that arise in assuring patients' clinical and civil rights. The reconciliation can be at least partly resolved through the creation of an alternative approach, i.e., a citizen advocacy program which will have readily available access to legal and psychiatric consultants. Such a concept has been extensively described by Wolf Wolfensberger (23), but it will suffice to say that such a program of independent citizen advocacy offers the greatest hope in the cause of assuring appropriate care to all mentally disabled individuals.

Some psychiatrists have argued that patient advocates add an adversary element to what is essentially a medical treatment matter. Such an argument fails to recognize that an adversary situation is created the moment a psychiatrist begins to treat a resisting patient. A modified patient advocate model (including private citizens, lawyers, and mental health professionals) can become an important and more lasting alternative to litigation and helps to create a mediated, flexible system of care for the mentally ill. It is clear that the law is inexorably intertwined with the mental health system, and it is therefore essential and in the best interest of patient care for psychiatrists and other mental health professionals to work as a team with enlightened lawyers and concerned citizens (including former patients) in establishing programs recognizing the clinical, human, as well as legal rights of the mentally ill.

After more than 200 years of working to improve the condition of the mentally ill, American psychiatrists must not now abandon their advocate role to the legal profession, nor renounce their obligations as physicians to treat the whole patient and not just the disease. This latter feature requires psychiatrists to recognize the patient's right to be actively consulted and involved in his treatment program. While in the past the public has viewed the violation of patients' rights as an unfortunate but inevitable aspect of treatment of the mentally ill, it now considers such a situation as intolerable and unacceptable in a free society.

REFERENCES

1. Kopolow, L. et al. *Litigation and Mental Health Services.* Washington, D.C.: U.S. Government Printing Office, 1975.
2. Klein, J. Background paper on the civil rights of the mentally ill. Unpublished manuscript, 1976.
3. Deutsch, A. *The Mentally Ill in America.* New York: Columbia University Press, 1949.
4. Rothman, D. J. *Discovery of the Asylum.* Boston: Little, Brown, 1971.
5. Beers, C. *The Mind That Found Itself.* Garden City, N.Y.: Doubleday, 1936.
6. Deutsch, A. *The Shame of the States.* New York: Harcourt, Brace, 1948.
7. Ward, M. *Snake Pit.* New York: Random House, 1946.
8. Solomon, H. C. Presidential address. *Amer. J. Psychiat.,* 115:1-17, 1958.
9. *O'Connor v. Donaldson.* 43 USLU 4929 (1975).
10. American Psychiatric Association. *Clinical Aspects of the Violent Individual.* Task Force Report 8. Washington, D.C.: American Psychiatric Association, 1974.
11. Kopolow, L. A review of major implications of the O'Connor v. Donaldson decision. *Amer. J. Psychiat.,* 133:379-383, 1976.
12. *Lessard v. Schmidt.* 349 F.Supp. 1078 (E.D. Wis. 1972).
13. *Bartley et al. v. Kremens et al.* 402 F.Supp. 1039 (E.D. Pa. 1975).
14. *New York State Association for Retarded Children and Parisi v. Carey.* No. 72-C-356-357 (E.D. N.Y. March 10, 1977).

15. Birnbaum, M. The right to treatment. *Amer. Bar Assn. J.*, 46:499, 1960.

16. *Wyatt v. Stickney.* 325 F.Supp. 781 (M.D. Ala. 1971).

17. Dixon v. Weinberger. *No. 74285* [*C.D.D.C. Feb. 14, 1974*].

18. *Kaimowitz v. Michigan Department of Mental Health.* Civ. No. 73-19434-AW (Cir. Ct. July 10, 1973). Reported in part at 42 USLW 2063.

19. *Joan Roe v. Jane Doe.* 33 N.Y.S.2d 902, 307 N.E.2d 823 (1973); 41 L.Ed.2d 210, 94 US 2601.

20. *Vitaly Tarasoff et al. v. The Regents of University of California et al.* 529 P.2d 553 (Sup. Ct. Cal. 1974).

21. Rosenzweig, S. (Director of Mental Health Information Service, First Justice Department, N.Y.) Personal communication to Henry A. Beyer (Staff Attorney, Law and Health Science, Boston University School of Law). Nov. 14, 1975.

22. Stone, A. A. *Mental Health and Law: A System in Transition.* U.S. Department of Health, Education and Welfare Publication 75-176. Rockville, Md.: National Institute of Mental Health, 1975.

23. Wolfensberger, W., & Zauha, H. *Citizen Advocacy.* Toronto: Macdonald-Downie, 1973.

Chapter XII

Implementing a New Commitment Law in the Community: Practical Problems for Professionals

ALLAN BEIGEL, M.D.,
KENNEY HEGLAND, J.D.,
and DAVID WEXLER, J.D.

This chapter presents a discussion of some of the substantive issues which have arisen as Arizona has attempted to implement a new civil commitment statute. An examination of these issues in the context of the experiences of one state and its legal and medical professionals may provide guidelines to others in proceeding through the murky waters which recent changes in societal and judicial attitudes toward the process of civil commitment have engendered.

While some may consider Arizona, the land of "conservative" ideology, to be atypical and a poor choice for a field study, it can be categorically stated that, at least in the area of civil commitment, it most certainly is not. As elsewhere in the United States, differences of opinion regarding what is

medically sound, what is legally acceptable, and what is so-
cietally appropriate are found in Arizona.

BACKGROUND

In 1971, the University of Arizona College of Law
published a comprehensive study of practices then in vogue
regarding civil commitment. Entitled "The Administration of
Psychiatric Justice: Theory and Practice in Arizona" (1), the
report received favorable comments from the legal and psychiatric communities, both locally and nationally.

As a result of this report and national trends, reform was
in the air during 1972 and 1973. Legal, legislative, and
medical professionals (including the authors of this chapter)
successfully pursued large-scale revisions in the Arizona Civil
Commitment Law based primarily on progressive practices in
certain portions of the state identified during the 1971 study as
well as on legislative and judicial developments in other states.
Introduced initially in 1973, the proposed revision was passed
in 1974.

Immediately, it was clear that while all professionals had
agreed in 1972 that something had to be done, disagreement
was widespread about what actually had been done in the new
law. Throughout 1975, multiple concerns were voiced from all
interested parties—legal, judicial, legislative, and psychiatric.
In late 1975, in an attempt to ward off piecemeal revision of the
law by pressure groups, it was recommended to the Division of
Behavioral Health of the Arizona State Department of Health
Services that a comprehensive study of the new law and its
impact be commissioned from the University of Arizona
College of Law with a provision for substantive input from all
concerned parties. The ultimate purpose of this study was to
arrive at a proposed set of revisions to the Law of 1974 which
could be introduced during the 1977 legislative session and
which would be based on data and reason rather than conjec-

ture and bias. The material to be presented here regarding some of the substantive issues uncovered in the course of the study is drawn from this report (2).*

AREAS OF DEBATE AND CONFLICT

While numerous procedural issues arose during the study, they were not the principal sources of debate among legal, legislative, and mental health professionals. Rather, the primary conflict which arose regarding the Law of 1974 surrounded its definitional sections. Briefly, the statute requires, for court-ordered treatment to occur, a double showing: first, that the individual is mentally ill and, second, that he is either a danger to himself, a danger to others, or gravely disabled. The most common complaints, primarily from mental health and law enforcement professionals, were that the definitional standards in each of these areas were too narrow and failed to authorize forced treatment of those who, in the critics' opinion, require treatment. Specifically, it was alleged that the act was faulty in the following respects.

1. *Definition of danger to others.* The act is written to require as evidence for involuntary admission either the infliction of or the attempt to inflict substantial bodily harm. Critics believe that a serious threat should be allowed to trigger a commitment procedure and that the requirement of "substantial" bodily injury is being interpreted too strictly.

2. *Definition of danger to self.* The definition requires that the danger be purposeful and hence does not cover individuals who, due to an acute psychotic episode, are in danger of substantial harm.

* Professors Kenney Hegland and David Wexler of the University of Arizona College of Law are the principal authors of the full report; Dr. Allan Beigel served as a consultant to the study.

3. *Definition of grave disability.* The standard requires that the person be unable to provide food, clothing, *and* shelter. Pointing out that the lack of one is surely enough, critics suggest the disjunctive. In addition, the statute is faulted because it does not permit emergency admission of the gravely disabled.

4. *Lack of an "in need of treatment" category.* The act allows court-ordered treatment only if the individual is a danger to others or to himself as a consequence of physical harm. Critics argue that there are many who are in desperate need of psychiatric treatment because they are engaged in nonphysical destructive behavior which is causing or will cause them great emotional or financial suffering and which is contributing to family torment. One cannot give credence to their rejection of treatment because they are suffering from a mental condition which incapacitates them.

5. *Definition of mental illness.* The act excludes from the definition of mental illness, and hence from court-ordered treatment, individuals whose only mental problems are a direct consequence of alcoholism, drug abuse, mental retardation, or sexual deviance.

Before proceeding with a detailed discussion of these issues, these criticisms must be first considered in the light of emerging case law. Not all options are open.

The Legal Background

The Fourteenth Amendment prohibits a state from denying a citizen "life, liberty, or property without due process of law." Two questions arise. Is civil commitment such a denial? If it is, under what circumstances and by what methods can the state deny the individual his liberty because he is mentally ill?

If civil commitment is not a denial of liberty, the due

process clause should not apply. Some have argued that commitment is not a denial of liberty, that it is a civil rather than a criminal proceeding which is undertaken to help rather than punish the individual. The courts have rejected these arguments. As Chief Justice Burger has recently written: "There can be no doubt that involuntary confinement to a mental hospital, like involuntary confinement of an individual for any reason, is a deprivation of liberty which the state cannot accomplish without due process of law" (3).

Once it is determined that due process is required because the state is denying the individual liberty, the question arises as to "what is due?" Due process involves two distinct concepts: procedural due process — the right to a lawyer and so forth — and substantive due process — the circumstances under which the individual can be committed. It is the latter concept that is involved in the definitional dispute regarding commitment criteria.

There are two interests that the state can assert for treating an individual for mental illness against his will: that of protecting society from him — the police power — and that of helping the individual help himself — the paternalistic or *parens patriae* power.

Very briefly, the *parens patriae* rationale justifies forced treatment only upon a showing that the person is incapable of deciding for himself and that, if he were capable, he would probably choose treatment. Police power intervention is justified by a "balancing" process: the amount of harm suffered by the individual due to the state's intervention is weighed against the amount of harm saved by society due to the intervention — what kind of damage might the person do and how likely is he to do it?

There is surprisingly little case law defining the exact limits on these substantive standards. The only outer limit enunciated to date by the United States Supreme Court was rendered in the case of *O'Connor v. Donaldson* (3): "State cannot constitutionally confine . . . a nondangerous individual who is capable of surviving safely in freedom by himself with the help of willing and responsible family members or friends." However, the court also added: "We need not decide whether, when, or by what procedures, a mentally ill person may be confined by the State on any of the grounds which, under contemporary statutes, are generally advanced to justify involuntary confinement of such a person—to prevent injury to the public, to insure his own survival or safety or to alleviate or cure his illness."

Hence, there are no definitive answers to most of the legal issues to be raised in this chapter. For the present, in pursuing solutions to those definitional issues which have been the principal sources of debate and conflict among professionals in Arizona, only the lower courts have rendered any assistance in providing guidelines.

With this brief legal background, let us proceed to a more in-depth examination of the issues which have arisen in each of the five definitional areas as well as to a description of the proposals which have been recommended for legislative action based on the material collected during the study.

DANGER TO OTHERS

Court-ordered treatment and confinement of individuals thought to be dangerous to others are justified as an exercise of police power. To analyze the propriety of these commitments, from both a judicial and legislative point of view, the imposition on the affected individual must be weighed against the benefits to the public.

Arizona requires that the threatened harm be both substantial and directed at a person rather than at property. Hardly any dissatisfaction with the restriction against property was found during the study. The only example offered in support of an expansion of the law in this area dealt with a mentally ill individual who was observed kicking in the doors of a neighbor's Volkswagen. Yet, the criminal law can deal adequately with this situation. The current restriction to physical danger is consistent with other modern statutes and with the trend of recent cases (4).

Some critics have proposed an amendment that would drop the requirement of "substantial bodily harm" and substitute for it "bodily harm." They point out that the present criterion is vague and has apparently led some mental health screening agencies, set up by the 1974 law to screen applications for commitment, to a restrictive interpretation which equates "substantial" harm with maiming. This does not seem warranted since the statute clearly contrasts "substantial" bodily harm with "grievous or horrendous" harm.

This distinction suggests that it was the intent of the 1974 law to exclude an expansive reading of bodily harm. The deletion of "substantial" might lead to an expansive and inappropriate reading. If the societal harm is only inconsequential or symbolic, the drastic remedy of incarceration would not be justified.

At the same time, the use of the word "substantial" without further definitional explicitness is admittedly vague and language must be found to explain more specifically what is meant. The following definition is suggested:

> Substantial bodily injury means unjustified physical harm of such a magnitude that the physical confinement of the actor is justified to prevent it from occurring. More specifically, it means grave as opposed to trivial injuries and includes those injuries as give rise to apprehension of danger to life, health, or limbs. It is not, however, required that the injuries be such as may result in death.

The first clause of this proposed definition has the advantage of focusing decision-makers on the real issue involved — the kinds of potential harm that justify the state in confining a person for compulsory treatment" (5). The second part is an attempt to flesh this clause out and is taken from a case (6) attempting to define "serious bodily injury" with regard to aggravated battery. To facilitate utilization of this embellished, but more specific definition (and others which will be discussed), it is also recommended that a team of mental health and legal professionals draft illustrative (but not legally binding) examples which would clarify the distinction between substantial and insubstantial and which could be used in the training of various mental health and legal professionals.

Having considered what kind of harm we wish to prevent, we next consider how likely it is that it will come to pass if we do nothing.

Civil commitment of those who are dangerous to others is a form of preventive detention. At the same time, the literature (7-9) confirms the high rate of error in predictions of violence. Difficulties with prediction have caused some to question the advisability and indeed constitutionality of commitment for dangerousness. However, the legal worth of such claims has recently suffered a sharp devaluation in decisions handed down in death penalty cases. A Texas statute required the jury to find, prior to imposition of the death penalty, "whether there is a probability that the defendant would commit criminal acts of violence that would constitute a continuous threat to society." This standard was attacked as vague on the grounds that future behavior could not be predicted. Upholding the standard, the Supreme Court responded (10): "The fact that such a determination is difficult however does not mean that it cannot be made. Indeed the prediction of future criminal conduct is an essential element in many decisions rendered throughout our criminal justice system."

On the other hand, while no court or legislature has thus far been willling to go so far as to deny commitment based on dangerousness, many, in order to cut the rate of error, require a previous act of violence before an individual can be labeled "dangerous."

Arizona law requires that before an individual can be committed as dangerous, it must be shown that he has inflicted or attempted to inflict substantial bodily harm on another. By requiring the finding of dangerousness to be based on historical fact, rather than on mere psychological or psychiatric assessment, the statute reflects the recognition that previous acting out bolsters the validity of the prediction of future violence (9). Furthermore, the requirement of a historical event also reflects the simple yet profound notion that a person should not lose his liberty without having "done something."

Arizona's 1974 law conforms to other recent state statutes in this regard, and the requirement of a prior act may be eventually constitutionally mandated. Due to the problem of predicting violence without a historical event, a statute allowing for commitment based solely on psychiatric assessment could possibly be struck down as overbroad. A prediction of dangerousness without a prior act of violence simply casts the net too wide because it allows the capture of too many people who, although they may appear to be dangerous during psychiatric assessment, are not in fact dangerous. Yet even the requirement of a previous act is too broad if the act occurred in the distant past. It is then no longer indicative of present dangerousness.

One court has already suggested that narrow time frames are constitutionally compelled to avoid the problem of overbreadth. In *Lessard v. Schmidt* (11), a three-judge federal district court ruled that the Wisconsin commitment statute could withstand constitutional challenge only if construed to require a showing of "extreme likelihood that if the person is not confined he will do immediate harm to himself or others" based on a finding of a "recent overt act, attempt, or threat to do substantial harm to one's self or another."

The study concluded that the 1974 Arizona law is overbroad in allowing a finding of dangerousness to be predicated on an act that occurred as much as a year previously, as opposed to in the recent past, and in failing to impose a time frame in which the predicted violence may occur, such as "immediate danger." The study team recommended the following revisions: that the time frame for the historical event be shortened from one year to six months and that prediction of dangerousness in other than the immediate future be limited. Support for this conclusion is already present in California law (12) which requires an "imminent danger" and from the *Lessard* case which talks of "immediate harm" (11). The proposed language for Arizona, "in the near future," is taken from the tentative draft of the Mental Health Legislative Guide (13).

Thus far, in discussing dangerousness to others, we have been speaking of acts of doing or attempting substantial bodily harm. In Arizona, nowhere was debate more sharply focused in this area than in regard to the matter of "threat."

The 1974 Arizona law provides that threats alone are not enough. Critics argue that the statute as drafted requires the commission of a serious felony before commitment and this makes little sense when the goal is preventive. We agree and propose the following addition to the definition of "dangerousness to others":

Behavior which constitutes a danger of inflicting substantial bodily harm upon another person based upon a history of: (a) having seriously threatened, within 30 days previous to the filing of the petition for court-ordered treatment, to engage in behavior which will likely result in substantial bodily harm to another person, provided that the threat, when considered in light of its context and in light of the individual's previous acts, is substantially supportive of an expectation that the threat will be carried out; or . . .

A few points must be made in support of this decision. First, in including threats, the act would still require an objective historical event; the individual must still "have done something." Commitment would not rest only on predictions. Second, the trend in recent statutes is to include threats. California (12) and Michigan (14) include threats. The Mental Health Legislative Guide (13) authorizes the finding of dangerousness on "behavior threatening." Finally, an extension to include substantial threats seems clearly constitutional. Even language from the more restrictive courts condones the use of "threats." For example, the *Lessard* decision quoted earlier permitted "a recent overt act, attempt, or threat" (11). Unless it can be shown that threats are much less predictive of future violence than previous actions, there is no constitutional reason to allow commitment based on one and not the other.

There are three principal objections to extending the definition. First, the attempt to restrict the definition to only "substantial" threats could be easily circumvented. Second, even substantial threats may not be sufficiently predictive of future behavior, and hence many people who would never carry out their threats would be incarcerated. Third, as a matter of principle, no one should be committed who has not committed a criminal act.

There is little literature on the subject of the predictive significance of threats (15). The major reasons for justifying the extension of the definition to include threats, aside from no apparent constitutional objection, is frankly the intuitive feeling that threats can be a significant predictor of future behavior. Even if they are not, the limited social response of civil commitment is justified in the case of the mentally ill individual who is making grave threats as demonstrated by other laws which indicate that the state can legitimately protect its citizens against psychological terror. For example, some purely verbal threats are criminal. In Arizona, it is a crime to make telephone calls threatening to inflict injury or physical harm (16). Under the Model Penal Code, it is a felony to threaten to "commit any crime of violence with the purpose of terrorizing another" (17) and, if the threat is coupled with some overt act, the individual may be guilty of attempted assault or perhaps assault (18). Most importantly, however, even where a serious threat is not criminal, it can justify self-defense. It is cruel to both victim and aggressor to leave the matter there.

Finally, the validity of this intuitive approach appears to have been recognized even by one of the most ardent critics of the value of psychiatric assessment as a tool in predicting dangerousness (7). Ennis recommends that if dangerousness commitments are to continue, a return to a common-sense approach is dictated. He would require that a person have actually "done or threatened something dangerous in the recent past."

DANGER TO SELF

There are two kinds of individuals who present a physical danger to themselves: the actively suicidal and the gravely confused or withdrawn individual who cannot care for himself and, as a result, may come to great physical harm. The study found that the greatest controversy surrounded the latter group. Some of these individuals were covered under the definition of "gravely disabled," which we will discuss in a moment. However, the statute did not authorize involuntary *emergency* admission for this group and this was often needed for medical reasons.

Furthermore, neither the definitions of gravely disabled

nor of danger to self covered the individual who, as a result of an *acute* mental disorder, presents a passive threat to his own physical being, such as the person who, extremely disorganized, is found wandering in the desert. This person is not covered by the present statute since "gravely disabled" is limited to those who have a long-term or chronic mental illness and danger to self is limited to those with an "active" self-destructive desire.

Three possibilities for correcting this deficiency in the law suggest themselves. One is the drafting of a new category. The second is an amendment to "danger to self," and the third is an amendment to "gravely disabled."

In order not to prejudice a decision with regard to inclusion of a judgmentally impaired or an "in need of treatment" category, a discussion we will come to in a moment, it was decided that this problem could be dealt with most appropriately by an amendment to "danger to self." However, in drafting such an amendment, a few points must be kept in mind.

First, the danger presented must be one of great physical harm in the near future, consistent with previous statements related to physical harm to others. Without this requirement, we would be arriving at an "in need of treatment" standard through the back door. Second, the physical danger should be one that has been manifested by some historical fact. Again, the position is that commitment should not be predicated solely on a psychiatric prediction that the person will come to harm. Finally, there should be a showing that less restrictive alternatives such as guardianship are insufficient to solve the problem.

Consequently, the study recommends the adoption of the following amendment to the definition of "danger to self": " . . . behavior which indicates that the person, without hospitalization, will come to grave physical harm or serious illness in the near future."

GRAVELY DISABLED

Under the 1974 statute, the archetype of the committable individual is the elderly nuisance — crotchety, partially senile, "unable to provide for his basic personal needs for food, clothing and shelter" because of a mental disorder which has "developed over a long period of time" or as part of "degenerative brain disease during old age." Presently, there is no requirement that the condition be such that, without hospitalization, the individual will suffer substantial physical harm or come to serious illness in the near future.

Why should these people be confined against their will? Were they a danger to others, they could be committed under that standard; a danger to self, under that standard. Can one justify forced hospitalization with the paternalistic or *parens patriae* rationale? May we disregard a person's expressed objection on the grounds that he is incapable of making hospitalization decisions and then, exercising his will for him, conclude that hospitalization is in the person's best interest?

These questions highlight certain considerations particularly germane to this class of persons. First, are they incapable of deciding? By definition, these people are suffering from long-term illness. Consequently, it could be argued that had they wished hospitalization, they could have sought it earlier. Second, is it in their best interest to be taken from their community, perhaps to die in the state hospital? The prognosis in terms of "cure" is not certain — freedom and early death may be preferred to hospitalization and later death. Recall the issues in the Karen Quinlan case.

The study came to the conclusion that the category should be tightened so that the person's condition be grave in the sense, as with danger to self and danger to others, that very immediate serious injury or illness will occur without hospitalization. Tightening the requirement will make us more confident in our decision to override the person's refusal because it is more likely that he would choose hospitalization rather than suffer immediate harm; in addition, tightening of the requirement would assure that "grave disability" is not an easy way of warehousing elderly nuisances.

An "In Need of Treatment" or "Judgmentally Impaired" Standard

Arizona law authorizes court-ordered treatment only when an individual presents a threat of physical harm to himself or others. Should it be amended to include treatment for the nondangerous person who is in need of mental health services?

This question has clearly separated the civil libertarians from the physicians. Often one answers a question by the way it is asked. Is the proper question "who will be helped?" or "who will be denied liberty?" Just as civil libertarians have pointed out the severe deprivations that court-ordered treatment involves, psychiatrists can point to the serious problems that follow from the state's refusal to exercise its coercive power and to order treatment which the person would seek, the argument runs, but for the mental illness that prevents him from recognizing his own best interest.

The study heard many complaints from the mental health professionals that the rejection of an "in need of treatment" standard means that the law does not trust them. There is no doubt that great mistrust exists in some quarters. But to cast the debate in terms of trust overlooks a crucial point. Whether an individual is mentally ill is a professional question, but whether to commit him against his apparent will is a social question.

Should the statute be changed? Would the change be constitutional? Would it be good social policy?

Constitutionality

Although the Supreme Court has not answered the question and although some courts have clearly indicated that commitment can only follow from a showing of "dangerousness" (11), it is believed that a tightly drafted "judgmentally impaired" standard would be constitutional. Speaking of the state's general powers, Chief Justice Burger (3) has said:

> The States are vested with an historic parens-patrial power, including the duty to protect "persons under legal disabilities to act for themselves" . . . At a minimum, a particular scheme for protection of the mentally ill must rest upon a legislative determination that it is compatible with the best interest of the affected class and that the members are unable to act for themselves.

This would suggest that, to pass constitutional muster, any statute must conform to the two factors noted by the Chief Justice: the person must be unable to act for himself and it must be shown that commitment is in the best interest of the person.

To treat an individual over his objections first requires that he be found incapable of making a treatment decision for himself. There are two problems with the notion of capacity to decide. First is the equation of mental illness with incapacity—that is, the assertion that no treatment decision of a mentally ill individual should be respected because, ipso facto, the individual lacks capacity. This is in error since many mentally ill individuals have legal capacity (9).

The second problem is circularity: the individual has made a bad decision (one that is harmful to him) and thus he must lack capacity. Under this reasoning, individuals are denied the fundamental right to make "bad decisions." To protect an individual's freedom, it must be remembered that "capacity" refers to the person's understanding of the factors involved, not the weight he chooses to give them.

An example from medical treatment will clarify. Two individuals refuse to consent to a life-saving cancer operation. Upon questioning, one rejects treatment because "all doctors are out to kill me"; the other responds that, given the pain that will be involved and the prognosis for total recovery, he would rather take his chances without an operation. The first individual is incapable of making a decision while the second individual is capable since he understands the factors involved in the decision.

Those opposing an "in need of treatment" statute argue that in the real world it would automatically be assumed that the person lacks capacity if he makes a bad decision since it, in turn, would be defined as refusing the advice of his psychiatrist.

In addition to requiring incapacity, an "in need of treatment" statute would have to require a showing that the person, if capable, would probably want treatment. This determination requires the assessment of several factors.

First, it seems that the mental illness would have to be of recent and sudden origin — if the person has lived with it for a number of years, it is much less likely that he would desire "curing it." In the case of *In re Ballay* (19), the Federal Court of Appeals gave the example of a man who knew that he was subject to great fits of depression and that it was likely he would kill himself during such a period. The court favored the view that his decision not to seek treatment, made while he was free from depression and capable, should be respected.

Second, given the fact that forced treatment will cause the person detriment, the mental illness must be one which causes him great suffering or substantially impairs his ability to function in society.

Third, there would need to be a showing that hospitalization would probably benefit the individual in a relatively short period of time. Confinement without a good chance of improvement is not "in one's best interest."

Policy Arguments

The study found strong support, particularly among psychiatrists, for an expansion of the commitment standard to include individuals who are not immediately dangerous to themselves or others. The major argument made is the number of instances of human suffering that probably could have been avoided by a looser standard.

Supporting arguments for an "in need of treatment" standard were most often that a majority of people falling in this category would be "turned around" with two to three days of treatment and would be thankful for the forced intervention. One doctor estimated that 70 percent of individuals in this category would agree to voluntary treatment after two to three days of forced treatment. To critics of expansion, however, this is in itself grounds for concern with the spectre of personality reshaping by way of drugs or heavy psychological assault looming very large.

A final argument made in support of an "in need of treatment" ("judgmentally impaired") standard is that some people, while currently not an immediate danger to self or others, will become so in the near future. To wait will make eventual treatment more difficult.

There are also substantial arguments against expansion. Even if the statute were properly administered and if only those who truly lack capacity were committed, some would still be harmed as a result of the loss of liberty, the forced treatment, and the future stigma. All might outweigh any benefit associated with a possible cure.

Those in opposition also argue that the statute would be extremely difficult to administer properly and that people would be committed and "remade" simply because they are different. In support of this belief, it is pointed out that both judges and lawyers often give psychiatrists great leeway. If they continue to do so, commitment will really be based on a psychiatrist's opinion that the person needs treatment and this would be too subjective a standard.

Other opponents point out that alternative ways exist of dealing with people who might fall within a "judgmentally impaired" or "in need of treatment" standard. Some of course will eventually volunteer for treatment and others may possibly get better on their own. Furthermore, other legal devices are available.

A typical example is the manic-depressive who, during a manic state, goes through the family fortune. The family can take adequate steps to protect their finances short of civil commitment. For instance, with joint bank accounts or credit cards, a call from the "sane" partner will freeze them. For those solely in the manic's name, a temporary conservatorship may be available. With stocks, because the caller does not get his cash for about five days, there is adequate time to seek a conservator.

Criminal law may also provide an alternative remedy. One psychiatrist reported the case of a man masturbating in front of children. This is presumably a criminal offense. It may be said that this is a cruel alternative, but perhaps it clearly focuses part of the issue: in both arrest and civil commitment, "they" physically take you away.

Finally, opponents point out that the current strict standards are justified as they protect psychiatrists from undue family pressures, even though this surely may not be the view of many psychiatrists. It is argued that private psychiatrists, who are among the strongest proponents of an expanded definition that includes an "in need of treatment" standard, are often in a conflict position in that they are concerned with both the welfare of the patient and his family. If the standard were loosened, then the decision would rest more with the psychiatrist and hence he would be subject to great pressure. On the other hand, *private* psychiatrists and private facilities may be in a relatively strong position to meet the "best interest" test by the availability of treatment resources which may be in scarce supply—and which raise the possibility of "warehousing"—in the *public* sector.

In reaching a final conclusion as to whether commitment statutes should include an "in need of treatment" or "judgmentally impaired" standard, one final important point must be kept in mind. When Arizona and other state legislatures made a major policy decision to commit only the dangerous, the burden of proof for a major change from this policy decision shifted. The burden is now on those who advocate change. The question must be asked, "Have they made their case?" What has in fact happened to those who were unable to be confined according to the present "rigorous" standards? Have they eventually entered voluntarily? Have they undergone spontaneous remissions? How many have become therapeutic "disasters"?

One must also point out that many of the criticisms really addressed the definition of "danger to self." Consequently, it might be wise to counter many of these criticisms by a revision of that definition rather than to undertake a major shift in philosophy through the inclusion of a "judgmentally impaired" standard. Only after one sees clearly whether changes in the definition of "danger to self" and other definitions have alleviated the difficulties, debates, and conflicts, should any major policy change be considered. If a "judgmentally impaired" standard is eventually adopted, it should at the least have a short durational limit (30 days), and should be honestly applied to avoid definitional circularity and to ensure that such commitments are in fact in the patient's "best interests" (which would probably mean that commitments pursuant to the criteria should be to well-budgeted and well-staffed facilities).

DEFINITION OF MENTAL ILLNESS

The requirement of mental illness currently fulfills the vital function of limiting the kinds of people subject to civil court-ordered treatment. Arizona defines mental disorder (20) as a "substantial disorder of the person's emotional processes, thought content, cognition, and memory," thereby avoiding medical terminology and hence allowing the fact-finder to decide. No criticism of the definition was found during the study.

However, criticism focused on the following language in the statute (21):

"Mental disorder" is distinguished from:
(a) Conditions which are primarily those of drug abuse, alcoholism, or mental retardation;
(b) The declining mental abilities that directly accompany impending death;
(c) Character and personality disorders characterized by life-long and deeply ingrained anti-social behavior patterns, including sexual behaviors which are abnormal and prohibited by statute unless the behavior results from a mental disorder.

Most of the criticism found during the study involved the exclusion of alcoholism. Part of the problem may be how the act is interpreted: the statute does not automatically exclude all alcoholics. If the individual has mental problems in addition to alcoholism or if alcoholism has led to a mental disorder, then he falls within the definition of mental illness. What the act attempts to do is to exclude the commitment of alcoholics as alcoholics (similarly with drug addicts and the mentally retarded). Should they be excluded? It would seem that the burden is on those who would forcibly treat alcoholics. The decision to exclude them was made in Arizona in 1974 and in other states during the last five years. Furthermore, under the *parens patriae* rationale, intervention is not justified because alcoholics, at least when sober, have sufficient capacity to decide whether or not they wish treatment. Similarly, intervention under the police power does not seem justified as alcoholics are usually not sufficiently dangerous.

As for the exclusion of "character and personality disorders characterized by life-long and deeply ingrained anti-social behavior patterns, including sexual behavior," it seems that this, in many states, is part of a continuing fight between the state hospitals and the state prisons. As this group by definition appears to be dangerous, it was recommended to keep the exclusion and to move the psychiatrist to the prison rather than the guards to the hospital.

A final point about the definition of mental illness is in order. The exclusions go only to those people who can be committed; they do not prevent any state hospital from taking anyone as a voluntary patient. Alcoholics and those with sexual disorders can seek help at a state hospital. If they are denied it, it is not because of a statute.

SUMMARY

This paper has presented the findings of a study of Arizona's Civil Commitment Law of 1974. Substantive definitional issues have been discussed which were the principal sources of debate and conflict among professionals. Careful examination of these issues as they have arisen in Arizona and other states can serve as an appropriate method for arriving at a statute that is consistent with social policy and still reflects the legitimate concerns of those charged by society with providing care and treatment to the mentally ill. Only through a cooperative partnership, which this study represents, will both legal and mental health professionals be able to reach a resolution of those conflicts that have sharply divided them in the past.

REFERENCES

1. Wexler, D., & Scoville, S. The administration of psychiatric justice: Theory and practice in Arizona. *Ariz. Law Rev.,* 13:1-259, 1971.
2. Hegland, K., & Wexler, D. Report on the Mental Health Services Act. Unpublished report, 1976.
3. *O'Connor v. Donaldson.* 45 L.Ed.2d 396 at 410 (Concurring opinion) (1975).
4. *Dixon v. Attorney General.* 325 F.Supp. 966 (M.D. Pa. 1971).
5. *Humphrey v. Cady.* 405 U.S. 504 (1972).
6. *State v. Miller.* 16 Ariz. App. 92 (1972).
7. Ennis, B. J., & Litwack, T. R. Psychiatry and the presumption of expertise: Flipping coins in the courtroom. *Calif. Law Rev.,* 62:693-752, 1974.
8. Steadman, H. Some evidence on the inadequacy of the concept and determination of dangerousness in law and psychiatry. *J. Psychiat. Law,* 1:409-426, 1973.
9. *Developments in the Law—Civil Commitment of the Mentally Ill. Harvard Law Rev.,* 87, 1974.
10. *Jurek v. Texas.* 96 S. Ct. 2950 (1976).
11. *Lessard v. Schmidt.* 349 F.Supp. 1078 (E.D. Wis. 1972).
12. *California Welfare and Institutions Code.* No. 5300. San Francisco: Deerings, Bancroft & Whitney, 1969.
13. Model Statute #1 at 3c.
14. *Michigan Statutes Annotated,* Chap. 127, Sec. 14.800 (401), 1974.
15. Macdonald, J. The threat to kill. *Amer. J. Psychiat.* 120:125-130, 1963.
16. A.R.S. 13-895.
17. Model Penal Code Proposed Official Draft Revised, Sec. 2H.3, 1962.
18. A.R.S. 13-108, 13-241.
19. *In re Ballay.* 482 F.2d 648 (1973).
20. A.R.S. 36-501 (18).
21. A.R.S. 36-501 (18) (a)-(c).

Chapter XIII

Indications for Involuntary Hospitalization: Dangerousness or Mental Illness?

ROBERT L. SADOFF, M.D.

Until relatively recently people were hospitalized for treatment of mental illness when their physicians felt they were sufficiently disabled to require hospitalization rather than outpatient treatment. Voluntary admissions were encouraged, but involuntary hospitalization was deemed necessary in many cases when the patient refused to be admitted. Initially the signature of one physician was sufficient for such involuntary procedures. Gradually, however, as people began to mistrust the motives of some physicians who aligned themselves with families against the patient, stricter safeguards were instituted and implemented.

The first step was to require a two-physician certificate rather than a single evaluation. This, too, proved to be insufficient, and the matter was taken out of the hands of physicians and placed in the laps of judges, who could hear arguments from both sides in an adversary proceeding.

Theoretically, this policy would provide the potential patient
with the constitutional safeguards of due process of law.
Judges, however, were not experts on mental illness and more
often than not would agree to commit patients to the hospitals
against their will on the say-so of psychiatrists who would
testify that on a brief, and sometimes joint, examination they
found the patient to be "mentally ill and in need of
hospitalization."

A second step removed the responsibility for commitment
even further from the physicians by changing the criterion for
involuntary hospitalization from "mental illness" to mental
illness and "dangerousness." This measure appeared to be justified by continual reference to John Stuart Mill who said,
"The only purpose for which power can be rightfully exercised
over any member of a civilized community, against his will, is
to prevent harm to others. His own good, either physical or
moral, is not a sufficient warrant" (1). The state assumed
police powers over its citizens in place of the *parens patriae*
doctrine.

The question thus arises: Should dangerousness be the
criterion for involuntary hospitalization? The answer to that
question is obviously, and very clearly, a resounding "No"! The
reason is both very simple and very complex. First, and simple,
we do not hospitalize people who are dangerous; we don't even
put such people in jail unless they have committed a criminal
act that requires or allows for their incarceration. We may,
however, discriminate against the mentally ill who are also
"dangerous" and preventively detain them with some degree of
justification, though we would never think of doing so to a
person who is only dangerous and not mentally ill.

Now, the complex response: How can we utilize dangerousness, even in the mentally ill, as a criterion for involuntary hospitalization when we really don't have an
adequate definition of this condition? What is dangerousness?
Many have tried to answer this question. Kozol et al. (2) define

dangerousness as "a potential for inflicting serious bodily harm on another." Goldzband (3) considers that dangerousness is "the quality of an individual or a situation leading to the potential or actuation of harm to an individual, community or social order. It is inherent in this definition that dangerousness is not necessarily destructive, although frequently seen as such by specific individuals or social orders threatened by such a quality." Finally, Heller (4) gives us the most complex definition of all: "dangerousness, then, may be viewed as either a transient or lasting state of impairment of certain ego functions . . . secondary to a variety of constitutional, organic, psychologic, developmental or environmental factors, and resulting in a recognizable deterioration of the specific functions of judgment, self-observation and the capacity to defend against anxiety or tension."

These are only three different examples of what some courageous individuals have offered as definitions on the block to be attacked. It is precisely this lack of definition of dangerousness that has concerned a number of legal and medical scholars regarding the use of dangerousness as a valid criterion for involuntary hospitalization.

Another argument is that we do not have any effective treatment for dangerousness. We treat the mentally ill, and sometimes, whatever violent potential may co-exist as part of the mental illness may abate with proper treatment. However, we may ask: What do we do with an individual who was diagnosed both dangerous and mentally ill and committed legally to a hospital for treatment? The treatment happened to be effective and the mental illness remitted. However, the dangerous potential, not an integral part of the mental illness, remained. By rights, this person should be discharged from the hospital since he is no longer mentally ill and since hospital treatment will have no effect on his potential violence or dangerousness. But what doctor, under the current legal rules, will allow himself the luxury of discharging a patient who is not mentally ill but who is likely, in his opinion, to commit a violent act when he leaves the hospital?

There have been instances where physicians have been found responsible for letting loose on an innocent society dangerous people who were not "ready to be discharged." The discharge was designated "premature" and considered to be negligence on the part of the physician. How many of us, however, would blame the warden of a correctional institution for letting a dangerous man out of prison after he has served his maximum sentence? He is not mentally ill, yet he is dangerous; there is no question of keeping him, because he has legally paid his debt to society. When has the mentally ill person who is also dangerous legally paid his debt to society? Should he be discharged when no longer mentally ill, although he is still potentially violent?

What I am driving at is that the concept of "dangerousness," poorly defined, inadequately applied, allowing some degree of comfort for the civil libertarians, has now become the millstone around the neck of the hospital psychiatrist. If we are expected to be able to define dangerousness sufficiently well in a commitment hearing to use it as the criterion for involuntary hospitalization, then surely we will be expected to be able to define and utilize this criterion as accurately when we are considering discharging a patient. To involuntarily commit a person because he is dangerous (let alone mentally ill) is to imply that the incarceration or deprivation of liberty is due primarily to his dangerousness and not to his mental illness. If that is so, then it seems he should remain in the hospital as long as he is considered dangerous, whether or not he is mentally ill. Psychiatrists are not experts on dangerousness; we do not know how to treat this condition. Therefore, I am strongly recommending that now that we have come to the point where psychiatrists are no longer responsible for involuntary commitments, and the criterion for commitment is considered primarily to be dangerousness rather than mental illness, it should be the judge's responsibility to determine when an involuntarily committed patient is no longer dangerous and can be discharged safely to the community. If logic be followed, then standards of nondangerousness should be established so patients may be discharged who are no longer dangerous, though they may continue to be severely mentally ill. Conversely, I would expect those patients to be discharged who are no longer mentally ill, but may continue to be dangerous, under the argument that we do not preventively detain dangerous persons who are not mentally ill. For some reason we detain only those who are mentally ill. In criminal law the judge would have no choice but to discharge dangerous* people who have not committed crimes and who are not mentally ill. It is likely that he will follow the same course in civil law with the mentally ill, who continue to be dangerous but whose mental illness has remitted. Thus all persons who are either mentally ill or dangerous may be discharged, but those who are both may be retained.

Shah (5) notes with some concern, "It is somewhat difficult to discern how this link between mental illness and dangerous behavior came about and why it continues to be maintained with such enduring zeal with regard to the entire group of persons officially defined as mentally ill." He concludes that, in part, the linking of dangerousness with mental illness enables society to utilize preventive detention against certain groups of individuals, namely the mentally ill. Possibly this link has arisen and been maintained out of the generally held myth that all mentally ill persons are not dangerous, but all dangerous ones are considered to be mentally ill.

Pennsylvania's Task Force in 1972, studying the revisions of the mental health laws, concluded: "Since the capacity to

---

* That is, those who are believed likely to cause bodily harm.

predict dangerous conduct is no greater in the case of mentally ill persons than others, preventive detention is no more justified in the case of mental illness than elsewhere" (6).

Peszke (7) argues against dangerousness as a criterion by warning that such commitment procedures utilizing dangerousness as a criterion could be harmful, leading to "an upsurge in belligerent behavior among mentally ill persons who want attention and realize they must appear 'dangerous' to obtain it." Peszke feels that from a medical viewpoint it may be necessary at times to commit nondangerous persons for treatment. If not, he says, this criterion would lead to a "denial of needed treatment for many persons whose mental illness makes them withdraw and are otherwise non-aggressive." Further he states, "It does not strike me as reasonable or responsible that, for the purpose of treatment, individuals who are mentally ill and whose form of illness is expressed in belligerent activity will be treated and those who are withdrawn and catatonic will be neglected."

Monahan (8) argues that to include the criterion of dangerousness for commitment will necessarily lead to a greater number of commitments since psychiatrists making such predictions will err on the side of conservatism and predict people will be dangerous who may not be in order to be certain to include those who are truly dangerous. A number of studies have shown that psychiatrists greatly overpredict dangerousness and tend to isolate a large number of people who may commit a dangerous act.*

Shah (12) asks the two crucial questions regarding

* These studies include the problem of false positives, as in the Baxtrom patients reported by Steadman and Cocozza (9) and Steadman (10). Wenk and Smith (11) found that in over 4,000 California Youth Authority wards there was an eight to one false positive to two positive ratio. The authors concluded: "Concern about violence will inevitably lead to the development of special treatment programs, but the majority of such persons placed in such programs must be false positives—persons who would not commit the act which the program is designed to prevent."

dangerousness: first, "what kinds of behavior are sufficiently threatening to society to be officially defined as dangerous?" and second, "with what degree of certainty can one say that an individual will in the future engage in dangerous behavior and, if so, over what period of time?"

Laves (13), an attorney, responds in her criticism of the current trends in commitment procedures: "The dearth of psychiatric research into the question of dangerousness has led to extreme subjectivity in its definition by professionals and to overprediction of its occurrence." She criticizes generally the research efforts by psychiatrists in arriving at a standard definition of dangerousness and recommends that psychiatrists "abdicate the role of expert in legal proceedings of this nature, since they can by no means aid petitioners for commitment in the production of proof beyond a reasonable doubt or by a preponderance of the evidence."

I submit this standard of proof is beyond psychiatric expertise in many cases, but that should not exclude the psychiatrist from becoming involved in these matters. I am totally against psychiatrists' testifying to philosophical concepts. The psychiatrist is a clinician and the best evidence he has to offer is clinical evidence based on clinical experience, which may not be as valid as scientific evidence, but it is better than speculation, and it is better than philosophical conjecture.

The only valid criterion for prediction of future violent behavior is a history of past violent behavior. Most competent psychiatrists would be able to predict that a patient who has been diagnosed as schizophrenic, paranoid type, with a history of violent behavior while not taking medication and when under the influence of alcohol, would likely become violent again when he is discharged from the hospital if he stops taking his medication and drinks excessively. This is an extreme example, but it is a clear one, based on clinical experience and evidence. Examples of this type are valid for the psychiatrist to present when testifying to potential violent behavior (not necessarily dangerousness).

Peszke (14) reminds us that people tend to confuse the evaluation of a person at the particular time of commitment, with respect to his imminent potential for dangerousness or his violent potential at that particular time, with the predictive element of how dangerous he may be if he is not hospitalized.

Finally, Shah concludes, and I would agree, "In view of the very vague definitions of dangerousness, the very low predictive accuracy and the glaring overpredictions of such behavior and the involuntary and indeterminate loss of liberty that follows civil commitments, the labeling of the mentally ill as dangerous, could in itself be regarded as a rather dangerous activity" (15).

Thus we have heard from the experts that psychiatrists are not able accurately to predict dangerousness and have no standard definition for this concept. But the laws have changed and the trend is toward inclusion of dangerousness as an important criterion in the involuntary commitment of the mentally ill. What then should be the appropriate criteria for involuntary hospitalization, if not mental illness or dangerousness? Peszke says the basic issue in emergency commitment is the patient's welfare, not his potential dangerousness. In his view, commitment should be based on the severity of the mental illness and its treatability as well as the consequences of not treating it; in addition, the impairment of the individual's competence and the availability of less restrictive treatment facilities, such as psychiatric outpatient clinics, should be considered. He feels it would make more "legal, philosophical and medical sense to limit commitment to those whose mental illness is severe enough to affect their welfare in a global sense of the word and who lack the competence to make appropriate and relevant decisions in this regard" (16).

Scott, a lawyer with the Mental Health Law Project, concludes that any involuntary treatment system should include elements of both the treatment and civil liberties approaches (17). He would include the following criteria for commitment: (a) serious mental disorder, (b) available treatment of probable benefit to the individual, (c) inability to make an informed decision about treatment, (d) likelihood of imminent serious physical harm to self or others as evidenced by recent behavior. He feels that only when "all four of these criteria are met and durational limits observed will there be an assurance that the combination of societal and individual interests probably outweigh the potential detriment to the individual."

Finally, we must turn to recent mental health acts for guidelines for commitment. The Mental Health Act of Pennsylvania, Act 143, attempts to define dangerousness as follows (18):

Clear and present danger to others shall be shown by establishing that within the past thirty days the person has inflicted or attempted to inflict serious bodily harm on another and that there is a reasonable probability that such conduct will be repeated. . . . Clear and present danger to himself shall be shown by establishing that in the past thirty days the person has acted in such manner as to evidence that he would be unable without care, supervision and the continued assistance of others to satisfy his need for nourishment, personal and medical care, shelter or self-protection and safety and that there is a reasonable probability that death or serious bodily injury or serious physical debilitation would ensue within thirty days unless adequate treatment were afforded under this Act, or the person has attempted suicide and that there is a reasonable probability of suicide unless adequate treatment is afforded under this Act, or the person has severely mutilated himself or attempted to mutilate himself severely and there is reasonable probability of mutila-

tion unless adequate treatment is afforded under this
Act.

The Act also includes severe mental disability in addition to
posing a clear and present danger as joint criteria for involuntary commitment. Severe mental disability is defined as
follows: "As a result of mental illness, his capacity to exercise
self-control, judgment and discretion in the conduct of his affairs in social relations, or to care for his personal needs, is so
lessened that he poses a clear and present danger of harm to
others or to himself."

We have thus come full circle: the law has concluded that
the only proper reason for involuntary commitment to a hospital is not either mental illness or dangerousness but both.
And it is not just mental illness, but mental illness that is so
disabling as to render a person's judgment faulty, including his
judgment to decide his best interests or his judgment to decide
whether he requires proper treatment; and that because of his
faulty judgment and because of his mental disability, he has
committed, or is reasonably likely to commit, serious harm to
himself or to others. The law specifies not just mental illness,
but mental disability, and not dangerousness, but rather a
history of violent behavior or self-destructive behavior,
including mutilation, suicide, or self-neglect—demonstrable
acts that lead the reasonable person to conclude that the
individual in question is in need of treatment and either
protection or confinement.

It appears that this act of Pennsylvania, which reflects the
concerns of the courts in recent cases, would satisfy the criteria
of Peszke and Scott, as well as the concerns of Shah and Laves.
The law is not asking the psychiatrist to predict dangerousness;
the law is asking the psychiatrist to evaluate a person first for
mental illness; second, to determine whether that mental illness is disabling; and third, whether the mental illness is
disabling to such a degree as to render the individual un-

able to make proper decisions regarding his own interest, and that because of the disabling condition he is likely by neglect or aggressive action to harm himself or others. The law has thus included the nonaggressive mentally ill individual who is so disabled that he was withdrawn to a point that he would be likely to harm himself. These "predictions" are not based solely on mental illness, but on the behavior of the individual with the mental illness.

There is room for accommodation in this highly important issue between the legal and the medical professions. The lawyer and the judge must understand not only the abilities of the psychiatrist but also his limitations. The law must not impose upon the psychiatrist that which he is unable to perform with professional skill. Similarly, the psychiatrist must not extend his expertise beyond his professional limits and must consult with the law regarding individuals in need of treatment in clinical terms, not in philosophical or predictive terms. Psychiatrists must be aware of the implications of their statements as they affect patients and other individuals. They must also be aware of the implications of their statements and/or predictions as they may affect themselves and other psychiatrists in future cases.

Dangerousness may appear to be the current overriding issue in commitment proceedings, but it is the issue only for the law — it should not be the issue for psychiatrists. Psychiatrists should be concerned primarily with the best interests of the patient as a patient. Part of their concern is, of course, the mental illness or disability of the patient. Another part of their concern is the manifestations of that illness in terms of behavior, whether violent, self-destructive, or self-neglecting. The law may interpret the clinical medical statements of psychiatrists in any way it chooses in order to justify its disposition or decision. However, these decisions are not medical or psychiatric; they are legal, judicial decisions based on clinical psychiatric input. The court may choose to deprive an unwilling person of necessary treatment because it deems the individual to be nondangerous. Similarly, the court may order involuntary hospitalization for a nonmentally ill person whom it deems to be dangerous.

Psychiatrists can also function to aid in disposition in these cases by educating the decision-maker regarding the effect of his disposition. All the experts have included in their criteria for involuntary commitment the availability of treatment that will be of probable benefit to the individual for his condition. The psychiatrist may inform the court regarding the availability of such treatment for the particular condition of the person committed.

Finally, I would agree with Scott that the criteria for involuntary commitment should lie somewhere between the polarization offered by the extremist groups. The criterion is not mental illness or dangerousness; it is not even bilateral, but quadrilateral. First, the person should have a serious mental disorder; second, he should be unable to make an informed decision about his treatment; third, there should be available treatment which will probably benefit the individual; and fourth, the illness should be likely to cause imminent serious physical or emotional harm to self or others, as evidenced by recent behavior. On these criteria the mental health acts should be built. As is the case in general in law and psychiatry, we must get away from polarizing issues of mutual concern, and begin to work together toward mutually agreeable solutions that lie somewhere between the poles, are reasonable, and in the best interest of the individual and in the service of society.

REFERENCES

1. Mill, J. S. On liberty. Quoted in: M. A. Peszke. Is dangerousness an issue for physicians in emergency commitment? *Amer. J. Psychiat.*, 132:825-828, 1975.

2. Kozol, H. L., Boucher, R. J., & Garofalo, R. F. The diagnosis and treatment of dangerousness. *Crime & Delinquency,* 18:371-392, 1972.
3. Goldzband, M. G. Dangerousness. *Bull. Amer. Acad. Psychiat. Law,* 1: 238-244, Dec. 1973.
4. Heller, M. S. Dangerousness, diagnosis and disposition. Proceedings of Fourth Judicial Sentencing Institute, Crime Commission of Philadelphia, June 1968.
5. Shah, S. A. Dangerousness and civil commitment of the mentally ill: Some public policy considerations. *Amer. J. Psychiat.,* 132:502-505, 1975.
6. Commonwealth of Pennsylvania. Report of Task Force on Commitment Procedures, MH/MR Act. Dept. Public Welfare, 1972.
7. Peszke, M. A. Dangerousness not the only measure of need. *Frontiers Psychiat.,* 6:3, July 1, 1976.
8. Monahan, J. Dangerousness and civil commitment. Testimony before California Assembly Select Committee on Mentally Disordered Criminal Offenders, Paton, Calif., Dec. 13, 1973.
9. Steadman, H. J., & Cocozza, J. J. *Careers of the Clinically Insane: Excessive Social Control of Deviance.* Lexington, Mass: Lexington Books, 1974.
10. Steadman, H. J. Follow-up on Baxstrom patients' return to hospitals for the clinically insane. *Amer. J. Psychiat.,* 130:317, 1973.
11. Wenk, R., & Smith. Can violence be predicted? *Crime & Delinquency,* 18:393-402, 1972.
12. Shah, pp. 501-502.
13. Laves, R. G. The prediction of "dangerousness" as a criterion for involuntary civil commitment: Constitutional considerations. *J. Psychiat. Law,* 3:291-326, Fall 1975.
14. Peszke, M. A. Is dangerousness an issue for physicians in emergency commitment? *Amer. J. Psychiat.,* 132:825-828, 1975.
15. Shah, p. 505.
16. Peszke, Is dangerousness an issue . . . ?, p. 828.
17. Scott, E. P. Viewpoint: Another look at the crossroads. *Ment. Health Law Project,* 2:9, June 1976.
18. Commonwealth of Pennsylvania. Act 143. The Mental Health and Mental Retardation Act. 1976.

Part VII

Friction at the Interface

> Language is a labyrinth of paths. You
> approach from one side and know
> your way about; you approach from
> another side and no longer know your
> way about.
>
> — *Ludwig Wittgenstein*

Expectations rise when change is underway, anxieties occur, and society manifests a sense of urgency that the benefits from new arrangements will be available to all citizens. The focus of attention then identifies injustices that are redefined as rights.

By the late 1950s and early 1960s, after more than a century of growth and evaluation, during which psychiatry and the mental health professions had freedom to apply new knowledge to patient treatment and develop new organizational arrangements, a series of changes revolutionized care. Administrative decisions fostered open hospitals, work-release programs, informal admissions, and the aftercare concept. New treatments, such as electroconvulsive therapy and chemotherapy, shortened hospital stays making it feasible to treat serious mental illness in a general hospital setting and in local office practice. In the mid-60s the community mental health centers provided early entrance into therapy, crisis intervention, and ambulatory care. Mental (vs. general) hospitals, which had been steadily expanding over the years, began to

311

decrease in resident population. As the census was soon reduced as much as 50 percent, even with an increase in admissions, there was talk of closing mental hospitals.

It was at this point, when treatment was more successful than ever before, when mental hospitals were becoming less populated, and when ambulatory care was becoming the forward mode of patient management, that legal activism and judicial involvement sought to regulate the public practice of psychiatry. A series of decisons reflected the change in judicial attitude. Legal rights of patients were articulated. Personal freedom was viewed as more important than a determined need for treatment. *Suzuki v. Quisenberry* stated persons could not be involuntarily hospitalized solely because they were mentally ill. Procedural safeguards were developed which included notices, hearings, the right to be heard, to cross-examine witnesses, and to prove beyond a reasonable doubt that a mental disorder required confinement. The law's delay and the criminalization of mental illness appalled psychiatrists.

The social principles articulated by the courts were, however, endorsed by the profession as they correctly stated goals. For example, the Supreme Court decision in *O'Connor v. Donaldson* held that a nondangerous patient capable of surviving in freedom by himself, or with the help of a willing and responsible support system, cannot be confined. This was consistent with policy already in the implementation stage to release all mental patients who could be placed in the community — "the least restrictive environment" — and was the beginning of the great deinstitutionalization phase.

The court's order in the St. Elizabeth case was again applauded as it sought to expand community resources for alternate care to that of hospitalization. However, it should be pointed out that the court, in ordering a system be created that did not exist, usurped the powers of the legislative and executive branches of government. Availability of resources and resource deployment and priority among competing interests are not solely determined by the judicial branch in our system of government.

As a concept, consent poses no problem for psychiatry and the mental health professions. Open communication between therapist and patient is the foundation of psychotherapy. It is desirable for the patient to assume increasing responsibility for him or herself and to participate in decisions affecting his or her life. However, the problems in implementation of informed consent are many. Attention span and concentration may be limited, memory and recall impaired. Actions taken in an acute phase of illness may not represent the best judgment of an individual when free of disabling mental symptoms.

Although new methods have been found to be more effective in treating certain illnesses, they often carry with them more side effects and a greater potential for harm. In addition, the public expects miracles from the new wonder drugs. When the miracle doesn't occur, it may be interpreted as lack of interest or of skill of the therapist rather than a variable in response.

Perhaps the most troublesome problem is striking some reasonable balance between alarming the patient and securing his or her cooperation with a therapy that will relieve acute discomfort. The variable response of human beings to different chemical agents is little understood by the public. Even the safe drug aspirin that "everyone" uses to relieve a headache can cause a few to have a bellyache or a more troublesome allergy. The drugs used in psychiatry in identical doses may induce a dramatic remission of symptoms in one person, have no effect on another, make another worse, and, very rarely, induce a fatal blood disorder in another. Informed consent seeks to involve the patient in a choice among alternatives! There is, however, no substitute for a competent physician, a person of integrity who will use his or her best judgment in recommending a selected therapy, and no substitute for the trust of the patient in his or her physician. Whether there is a handshake agreement between two individuals who share mutual trust or an elaborate ritual of written agreements and recitation of package insert information, the result is the same and the underlying principles no different. Trust is the key.

Precise definition of standards for informed consent seems to be a legal exercise in futility. The mental health profession will play the game set by the lawyers, continue to be open with patients, and discuss with them fully the treatment goals to be achieved with their participation to the extent that this is possible.

The malpractice muddle is really a crisis in insurance coverage that followed the withdrawal of many carriers from the liability field as the predictability of risks became difficult and the business unprofitable. Those insurance companies that remained in the field increased premiums to astronomical levels as the number of claims escalated and higher awards by courts favored claims settlements that, too, were inflated. Psychiatrists have attacked the increased premium costs by implementing analyses of all claims to work toward a realistic premium based on the loss experience of *psychiatrists*, rather than contribute to the payment of losses by other specialists at greater risk.

Never before has there been such an outpouring of legislation on a single issue as all states scrambled to find a solution to reduce costs that are passed on to everyone who pays for medical care. Frank discussion of errors with patients and their families, establishment of rapport and trust, waiver of charges for disgruntled patients who believe themselves harmed, and education of the public to understand variable response and the limitation of the state of the art are strategies designed to reduce the number of claims. Unrealistic expectations for cure must be corrected.

Analysis of malpractice claims made against psychiatrists shows allegations of improper commitment to be the leading charge, followed by untoward reaction to drugs, and suicide. There will continue to be disagreements about the need for involuntary hospitalization. However, adherence to state statutes and documentation of the objective signs and symptoms that led to a judgment to confine the individual are essential. Drug reactions do occur and the hazard should be explained carefully before permission is obtained to use chemotherapy. The best prevention of suicide is recognition followed by immediate appropriate treatment.

Because lawyers' liability premiums are also soaring, they may soon become more amenable to a negotiated solution.

The *Tarasoff* decision, dramatic and untenable as it is, actually is not as important as the preservation of confidentiality in the day-to-day encounters that would erode it. It is the rare patient who identifies someone he or she intends to kill. The right of a patient to his or her privacy and the confidential nature of the patient-therapist relationship are fundamental issues in the mental health field since requests are skyrocketing every day for access to data in patient records for purposes other than the direct care of illness. There is an old story current in the black church about a sister who was a notorious gossip and faithful churchgoer. On one Sunday morning the service had gone exceptionally well, the music was moving, the sunlight streamed in through the stained glass windows. The preacher was preaching and the sister was "amening" him right on. "The Lord's gonna get you gamblers, taking the money of your wives and children and betting horses and the numbers." "Amen," the woman said. "The Lord's gonna get you thieves and pickpockets stealing a man's hard-earned cash." "Preach it," the sister said. "The Lord's gonna get you back-sliding church members." "Keep on," she shouted. "The Lord's gonna get you gossipers and scandalmongers." "That'll do! Shame, oh shame!" the sister exclaimed. "*Now* you done quit preaching and commenced meddling!"

The basic problem to be resolved is inculcation of an awareness in all who give direct care and all who are charged with safeguarding the clinical chart that the patient's right of privacy extends to what is recorded. Access to data must establish the right to know for a socially valued purpose. The patient has the right to waive privilege. Because much of what is revealed in the psychotherapeutic process is not in the patient's conscious awareness and because fact and fantasy may be intertwined, we believe what transpires should be protected in the same manner as is the lawyer-client relationship.

The many individuals involved in the extensive new enterprise of quality control through retrospective analysis of clinical records have a particular obligation to preserve the patients' and the therapists' confidences. Even with the use of diagnostic and provider codes, the potential for harm is alarming. As the intended purpose is improvement of performance and better patient care, goal attainment depends on keeping the records of evaluation fail-safe. Computers, when used as repositories of clinical data, cannot be made fail-safe. Confidentiality can be preserved only when all who handle the private records of patients do so with integrity under strict ethical restraints to protect the confidential information revealed in the course of evaluation and treatment.

Competence is a legal concept concerned with the mental capacity of an individual to perform a transaction. One always asks, "Does the person possess the level of judgment required to make a particular decision?" When mental illness is present and as a result there is a defect in judgment, that defect must impair the ability of the individual to act appropriately. Neurotics are nearly always competent, and psychotics may be competent to handle a Social Security check or make a will, but incompetent to stand trial because of an inability to comprehend the object of the proceedings and to conduct a rational defense.

The psychiatrist and mental health professional determining competence should use the administrative tool of decision making. The specific transaction is defined and information about the patient is assessed, often with the aid of procedures that follow the judgmental steps required to carry out the transaction in question, to reach a conclusion as to the person's ability to act rationally. More than opinion or "snap" judgment is required. A ruling of incompetence must be supported by evidence.

For years when *M'Naghten* was the dominant rule, the psychiatrist expert witness complained of lack of ability to present a full account of the mental impairment and the unconscious determinants of behavior. When given the opportunity to do so following the adoption of the *Durham* rule, psychiatrists failed to live up to the expectations of the court and relate illness to its product, the criminal act. Psychiatrists in court are not quasi lawyers but experts invited to state in language a layperson can understand the evidence that impairment of significant or substantial degree exists and to show that an inability to control behavior is present by substantiating facts. The decision that a crime existed, that the individual performed it, and that the evidence presented by the professional witness was substantial is the responsibility of judge and jury.

Probably the issue that causes the greatest friction at the interface between law and the mental health professions is the limitation of involuntary admissions to a mental hospital to those mentally ill persons who are dangerous to self or others. Only a very few of those with serious mental disorders are truly dangerous. The determination cannot be made with accuracy. If an index of violence proneness could be constructed that was accurate enough to identify 50 percent of those who will commit violent actions, its use would also identify eight times as many false positives.

Civil libertarians and legal activists quote John Mill on "Liberty" and press for adoption of statutes that limit admission to the dangerous and create a protective due process. The criminalization of mental illness is regressive.

Many patients who recover from a serious mental disorder which interfered with their judgment to seek help are grateful later that steps were taken to bring them into treatment. A person with manic excitement may speed on the highway, and spend sleepless nights and every day in a frenzy of increasing activity. Another shouts in answer to voices, wanders into restaurants and eats scraps of food left on the dinner plates. Both have a serious mental illness, but are not dangerous; a treatment does exist that will relieve their symptoms, and in medical judgment treatment is required.

Examples abound of fearsome delays with extension of discomfort to patients, family, and society. There is a marked difference of opinion between medicine and law that can be resolved in legal action to revise commitment laws in the model suggested by Dr. Sadoff.

In the late nineteenth century, the focus was on observation, description, and classification. The prevailing view stressed the biological factors in causation. After Freud's seminal contribution, the psychological factors were seen as primary in mental disorders. The focus of interest was on the psychodynamic process in an individual. In the 1960s, the social factors became ascendant. The individual was seen as an integral part of a society, the product of his or her environment, and interacting with it. In this view, some held disturbed behavior was the response to a "sick" society. Today we view mental illness as the consequence of the interaction between biological, psychological, and social factors.

The basis for the collaboration between psychiatry and law is the fact that they are fundamentally similar institutions that deal with the evaluation and control of human behavior.

The interchange of opinion between the professions of law and mental health clarifies perceptions of concepts and of positions each holds dear. In a climate of understanding we should be able to negotiate a position that more closely serves the needs of those who are mentally ill—who we could one day be.

Name Index

321

Subject Index